Henry Irving, Shakespearean

V.W.Bromley.

Henry Irving, Shakespearean

ALAN HUGHES

Associate Professor, Department of Theatre,
University of Victoria, British Columbia

with a Foreword by John Russell Brown

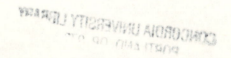

CAMBRIDGE UNIVERSITY PRESS

CAMBRIDGE
LONDON   NEW YORK   NEW ROCHELLE
MELBOURNE   SYDNEY

Published by the Press Syndicate of the University of Cambridge
The Pitt Building, Trumpington Street, Cambridge CB2 1RP
32 East 57th Street, New York, NY 10022, USA
296 Beaconsfield Parade, Middle Park, Melbourne 3206, Australia

First published 1981

Printed in Great Britain
at the Alden Press, Oxford

British Library Cataloguing in Publication Data
Hughes, Alan
Henry Irving, Shakespearean.
1. Shakespeare, William–Stage history–England–1800–
2. Irving, *Sir* Henry
I. Title
792.9 PR3106 79-41608
ISBN 0 521 22192 7

FRONTISPIECE
Irving as Macbeth, 1875 (University of Victoria)

Contents

CONTENTS

CONTENTS

Illustrations

ILLUSTRATIONS

Foreword

John Russell Brown

A bright idea can stop a play in the theatre of our minds: the action freezes as we reconsider everything we know about the text. In this way scholars and critics of Shakespeare set off in pursuit of new theories and new interpretations that may take years before they are elaborated safely and argued trenchantly in a new book about Shakespeare. Each original thesis absorbs and excites the mind of its writer; and so the stock of available knowledge grows annually.

In a real theatre new ideas are quite as plentiful and for the busy, complicated weeks of rehearsal they are tested, developed, exaggerated or discarded in collaborative exploration. Some of these ideas take root and grow strongly as the production plays repeatedly before audiences, each detail finding its appropriate weight and definition. For a number of years, sometimes for centuries, a few discoveries become part of theatrical tradition and so become widely known.

Naturally our own ideas about Shakespeare's plays are irreplaceable, but they are limited by the quality of attention we can give to a text. They also make us eager to learn from others, comparing and augmenting our own notions and discovering new ones which might never have occurred to use. We read books, and we should also go repeatedly to the theatre, sometimes to see a single production several times. Occasionally these two resources can be combined by reading what someone who has spent a lifetime in the production of Shakespeare's plays can tell us about his ideas and how they were shaped by his experience.

If I were to conjure out of the air the 'best' book on Shakespeare that might ever be, I would create a writer of imagination, literary skill, scholarly patience and long theatrical experience, someone who had staged many of Shakespeare's plays and acted leading parts in them, who had worked with the most challenging associates as actors, designers, musicians and technicians and who had played to packed houses of varied audiences. Such wishful thinking will not materialize a book, but it does help to distinguish between demands for attention in each yearly bibliography. A lecture by a theatre director or an interview by a leading actor may prove of equal worth to a painstaking double-volume of literary or historical research. This mode of selection would also direct interest to the publication of Alan Hughes's *Henry Irving, Shakespearean.*

Irving had many of the attributes of my ideal author, but he did not write books. His lectures on acting and articles on Shakespeare have little substance and show signs of the taste of his literary advisers. Irving's originality, practical theatre-sense and continuous self-criticism are not easily appreciated by casual reading in the magazines and newpapers of his time, or in the flattering biographies that followed. But Alan Hughes has conducted long research into all this material, into theatre documents and, most importantly, into the 'study' copies of the plays that Irving and his chief collaborator, Ellen Terry, made for their own use. He has traced the changes made in successive revivals of the more successful productions. He has learnt all he can about Irving's Lyceum Theatre, studied the papers of his business manager, Bram Stoker, that are in the Shakespeare Centre at Stratford-upon-Avon, and weighed conflicting accounts of how the audiences received the plays.

By describing Henry Irving's staging of Shakespeare's plays and the performances of this actor-manager, Ellen Terry and other members of his company, Alan Hughes has come as near as anyone today is likely to do to providing a substitute for the book that Irving himself never did and never could write. Alan Hughes has been a theatre manager, director and playwright, as well as scholar, and so is well qualified to stand in for his hero. That Irving's understanding of Shakespeare has made him the author's hero is unmistakable in the zest with which this book is written and its championship of Shakespearean criticism and production techniques that are founded on a sustained study of 'character' and dramatic structure, and on respect for theatrical vitality.

The value of *Henry Irving, Shakespearean* can be exemplified by its account of the performance of the 'Nunnery Scene', the first meeting of Hamlet and Ophelia. Irving's interpretation did not depend on a particular reading of this line or that, or on the findings of historical or literary research. His prime concern was how to act the scene, to give consistency and strength to his performance, to draw strength from Ellen Terry's Ophelia and to make the play live for his audiences. Shakespeare has given particular emphasis to this meeting, by preparing for it in three earlier scenes and by prefacing it with 'To be or not to be' and a moment of silence. He has given its performers an unmistakable challenge in the charged contradictory words – 'I did love you once' and 'I loved you not' – and in the concluding violence of Hamlet's words contrasted with Ophelia's prayers and silences. In successive productions Irving developed a reading that gave central importance to this short episode that can take only a few minutes to read on the page. Alan Hughes's account of this will challenge many critics and scholars who find the scene of little significance to the play as a whole because it seems to have no direct relevance to the themes of revenge, political order or conscience.

Alan Hughes describes vividly what happened on the Lyceum stage and tells us how this was achieved. If a reader is not aware of the ways in which performance can change the force and relevance of Shakespeare's words, here he can observe the effects of timing, emphasis, stage-grouping, gesture, fully realized and fully demonstrated mental involvement and every aspect of the physical performance of two supremely gifted artists. Irving's reading was at variance with others advanced by previous actors and later critics, and its success depends on some stage business which cannot be justified by textual analysis. His interpretation is hard to sustain in performance if every word is spoken. But Irving's achievement sets the mind to work in fully theatrical terms and relates this scene to crucial issues in the play as a whole. Here, and in many other places in this book, a reader is engaged in Shakespeare's plays as in performance and with ideas that are, at times, in opposition to the orthodoxies of today. Here, too, is a view of Irving that should be set over against that common and easy dismissal of his contribution to theatre which derives from hearsay, fashion and the partisan comments of Bernard Shaw.

Acknowledgements

If I were to acknowledge in full the assistance I have received from innumerable people in Canada, England, Australia and the United States, the reader might be excused for wondering whether I had done anything myself. I owe a particular debt of gratitude for research grants from Macquarie University, the University of Victoria and the Canada Council, and for grants-in-aid from the Folger Shakespeare Library. Thanks are due to the directors and staff of many libraries and museums, including the Shakespeare Birthplace Centre, where my work began, the British Theatre Museum and Enthoven Collection, the Ellen Terry Memorial Museum at Smallhythe, the London Museum, the Garrick Club, the Harvard Theatre Collection, and the Public Record Office. I am personally indebted to Miss Jennifer Aylmer, Mrs Molly Thomas and Mrs Pamela Lumsden, whose friendly help has exceeded adequate thanks as much as it has surpassed mere duty; and to Mr and Mrs John Cavanagh of Motley Books, and Messrs Raymond Mander and Joe Mitchenson, for their kindness and assistance. I am grateful to Karen Moore, who drew the plan of the Lyceum stage on p. 19; to Paul Rice for reading the typescript and for timely ideas; for the indefatigable labour of Warren Lowery, Andrew McDonald and Terry Barber; and the suggestions of Russell Jackson, Dennis Salter, Linda Hardy, Colin Skinner and Eric Low.

Special tribute is due to Laurence Irving's definitive biography and to Charles H. Shattuck: without his book, *The Shakespeare Promptbooks*, this work simply could not have been undertaken.

To John Russell Brown I owe far more than his generous Foreword. Our ideas have always marched together: his in front, mine behind. It was he who suggested that I investigate Irving; my labours in the decade since then have been sustained by his unflagging help and encouragement.

Finally, I know I can never repay my wife and children for their forbearance: they have put up with Irving and Shakespeare ever since they have known me.

Note on texts

In descriptions of Irving's productions I have quoted his acting versions, which sometimes vary from the received text. Whenever the plays themselves are the topic, I have quoted and referred to Shakespeare's text in the New Arden edition wherever it has been available: *Macbeth* and *King Lear*, ed. Kenneth Muir (1966 and 1964), *Othello*, ed. M. R. Ridley (1965), *Twelfth Night*, ed. J. M. Lothian and T. W. Craik (1975), *Cymbeline*, ed. James Nosworthy (1969) and *The Merchant of Venice*, ed. John Russell Brown (1967). The Signet edition has been used for the remaining plays: *Hamlet*, ed. Edward Hubler (1963), *Romeo and Juliet*, ed. J. A. Bryant Jr (1964), *Richard III*, ed. Mark Eccles (1964), *Coriolanus*, ed. Reuben Brower (1966), and *Much Ado about Nothing*, ed. David L. Stevenson (1964).

The dates that follow my chapter headings indicate opening nights of Irving's productions. When a play was given two full productions at the Lyceum, I have given both dates.

Introduction

If history proves anything, it is that the man and the moment create one another. Success in the theatre is usually a collaboration between talent and opportunity. Like most great men, Henry Irving prefigured the future; but he was also the product of a unique time and place, outside which he could not have flourished, and which would have been less itself without him. He arose in an auspicious hour. On 25 November 1871, while he waited in the wings to step into the limelight and history as Mathias in *The Bells*, London and its theatres stood on the threshold of unprecedented prosperity.

The prerequisite to theatrical success is a large potential audience which can afford to pay. Between 1801 and 1901 the population of Greater London increased nearly sixfold, but the 1870s saw the most rapid growth in the century.[1] This population was transformed into an audience by new developments in public transport. The intricate railway system, which was virtually complete by the 1860s, provided cheap and easy access from the suburbs to the city centre, where the theatres were. It also brought a vast concourse of provincial visitors. After 1863 the commuter could take the world's first underground railway from station to theatre. Most, however, preferred the ubiquitous horse-drawn omnibus, a conveyance that had become very comfortable and cheap by the 1880s, particularly in the Strand where Irving's Lyceum Theatre stood: a price war reduced fares between Liverpool Street or Victoria Station and Charing Cross to a penny.[2] At the same time, the heart of the city became more attractive to visitors. Once, most of those who entered the tenebrous, slum-fringed neighbourhood of the theatres at night were either folk who could afford cabs and carriages, or those with nothing to lose. But from the mid-century onwards, prosperous business premises steadily displaced overcrowded and noisome slums; the Metropolitan police, founded in 1829, grew in power and prestige; and gas lighting made the streets brighter and safer.

The reduction in omnibus fares was only a symptom of economic conditions which were becoming very favourable to theatrical enterprise. After 1873, prices began to fall while wages remained stable; real incomes rose at a rate of approximately 25 per cent per decade in the 1880s and 1890s.[3] Managers responded by increasing prices and replacing cheap Pit seats with expensive Stalls.[4] Since there was no corresponding improvement in the wages of theatre staff, the margin of profit became enormous; many theatres could break even when considerably less than half full.[5] Profits were further enhanced by long runs. Irving played *Faust* more than five hundred times, and while it had been proverbial a generation before that 'Shakespeare spells ruin', his two productions of *Hamlet* ran for a total of 308 performances.[6] When success was so handsomely rewarded, managers were prepared to take risks to win it. They could afford to gamble on a new play, or on Shakespeare; and they could improve production standards. There were longer rehearsal periods, better designs, elaborate mounting and important technical innovations.

Everyone could afford to attend the theatre, and there were theatres for everyone. Suburbs of all classes enjoyed their own places of amusement. A newspaper reported in 1882 that Greater London had 57 licensed theatres and 415 music halls with a total nightly capacity of 302,000.[7] South of the Thames and in the East End there were large working-class theatres like Hoxton's Britannia, the predominantly Jewish Pavilion in Whitechapel Road, the Surrey and the Royal Victoria (nicknamed 'the blood tub'), where crude melodrama flourished; even in West End theatres like the Lyceum, a lower-class element in the shilling Gallery and scattered through the Pit was numerically, if not financially, significant. But newspapers were interested only in the major West End playhouses, and represented the point of view of the middle-class sections of the house. When an occasional critic ventured across the river or sat in the Pit, he described his adventure as though it were a sojourn amongst the Hottentots. Indeed, as Michael R. Booth has shown, 'The most significant fact of English theatrical history in the second half of the nineteenth century is the slow but sure upper-middle-class takeover of both the theatre and the drama, and the steady rise of theatre into that middle-class respectability it is even now trying so hard to shake off.'[8]

In the early decades of the century the theatre had dropped out of the mainstream of London's life. It was condemned by the clergy and shunned by the middle class, who declined to bring their wives amongst disreputable audiences in order to hear scandalously bohemian actors. Early in the reign of Queen Victoria, however, theatres began to pass into the hands of actor-managers who yearned for respectability, not merely for the commercial success it would bring, but for their own dignity and the honour of their art. William Charles Macready's management of the Covent Garden and Drury Lane theatres (1837–9 and 1841–3) began a long campaign to improve the quality of the repertory, and of professional and artistic standards. Charles Kean followed his example at the Princess's (1850–9), establishing a solid repertory of 'gentlemanly melodrama' and scholarly productions of Shakespeare, a policy which was enormously assisted by the Queen's patronage. Samuel Phelps's admirable Sadler's Wells company (1844–62) firmly re-established Shakespeare on the popular stage; Marie and Squire Bancroft introduced the intelligent social dramas of T. W. Robertson in a series of conscientious productions at the Prince of Wales's (1865–79). In the 1880s at least a dozen really well-conducted playhouses in the West End offered a variety of entertainment from burlesque to poetic drama under such eminently respectable managers as the Bancrofts, J. L. Toole, Augustus 'Druriolanus' Harris, John Hare, George Edwardes and Richard D'Oyly Carte.

Their acknowledged leader and spokesman was Henry Irving. His artistic eminence and personal distinction broke down old prejudices. Campaigning aggressively for official recognition that acting is an art as legitimate as painting or music, he addressed innumerable learned and professional institutions, wooed the clergy, entertained the influential in his private dining room at the Lyceum, unveiled statues of actors, and supported charities.[9] Recognition followed. At a Church Congress in 1878, the Bishop of Manchester led a well-publicized revolt against Church opposition to the stage, and in 1885 the popular American evangelist Henry Ward Beecher told the *New York Herald*, 'I have heard Mr. Irving with delight thirteen times . . . and if all theatres were such and all actors such I would recommend them to my people as means of Grace.'[10] Irving received honorary degrees from the Universities of Dublin, Cambridge and Glasgow; and he was elected not only to bohemian clubs like the Garrick and the Savage, but also to the Athenaeum, the Reform and the august Marlborough, where his sponsor was the Prince of Wales. Leaders of the recognized arts were knighted as a matter of course. In February 1895, Irving bluntly told the Royal Institution, 'The great bulk of thinking – and unthinking – people accept Acting as one of the Arts; it is merely for a formal and official recognition that I ask.'[11] He did not have to ask twice. His campaign on behalf of the stage had been so successful that his name promptly appeared on the Queen's birthday honours list, and in July he became the first theatre knight.

Irving helped to bring about an overwhelming change in popular attitudes. 'He has drawn to the theatre numbers who formerly held aloof from it,' said a London paper in 1878. 'The elevation of public taste in theatrical matters during the past few years is mainly to be attributed to his efforts.'[12] Another said that Irving's company 'have gone far towards redeeming the stage for the Anglo–Saxon race as a popular educator. Until a few years since the drama had ceased to be a topic of thought or conversation among the educated classes, at any rate in this country. Now it may be fair matter of complaint that controversies on the merits of theatrical interpretations occupy too much space rather than too little.'[13] The bohemian playhouse where a respectable woman hardly dared to go was not only purged, but quite forgotten. 'It is one thing to be famous – it is quite another to be the fashion. Henry Irving has the bewildering fortune to be both. One dresses in state when one goes to hear Irving, just as one does for Italian opera. It has become a matter of course.'[14]

4

I

An actor's commentary

Edward Dowden was speaking of Henry Irving when he said, 'After all an actor's commentary is his acting.'[1] With these words, the scholar recognized the actor as a colleague. Irving had a thorough knowledge of textual issues and he was an earnest student of contemporary Shakespeare criticism, but his own published criticism does him little credit; no doubt he would acquit himself poorly if his shade were summoned before a postgraduate seminar. The same is true, however, of Shakespeare. They were both artists, and the actor understood the dramatist as one artist understands another, putting his perceptions into practice instead of words. 'If I wanted to read a book about Hamlet,' said Ellen Terry, 'I would not go to a book written by an actor, but I doubt if in all the books to which I should go . . . I should find any criticism equal to that given by Henry Irving in his acting of the part.'[2] This is the sense in which I offer him as a 'new' commentator of what Traversi calls 'the great tradition of the nineteenth century', with all the assumptions and goals, the methods and limitations, all the vision and weakness of that tradition. At times we must acknowledge that he was wrong, if we believe that we have learned anything from the criticism of the last seventy-five years. Coleridge, Schlegel, Gervinus, Dowden, Bradley and Granville-Barker were all sometimes wrong in the light of what we have learned. But there is still much they can teach us, and Irving deserves a place in their illustrious company.

Most Victorian critics were all but oblivious of the issues which, until recently, have preoccupied modern scholars: image, convention, structure, symbol and archetype were more or less outside their competence, and their knowledge of Renaissance life, thought and theatre was rudimentary. But while an actor's critical apparatus may be so

5

defective that he cannot distinguish between an image and the archetypal ogre, he must *play* them if they are truly in the text. There was imagery before Spurgeon; Newton described gravity, he did not invent it. And in choosing *how* to play, the actor makes an artistic commentary which we may translate, if we wish, into modern critical terms.

Victorian critics and actors communicated with enviable equality because they looked at Shakespeare from the same point of view. An actor cannot regard a play as 'so many lines of verse on a printed page which we read as we should read any other poem', and no commentator would have suggested that he should. 'Shakespeare's works should properly be explained only by representation,' said Gervinus. 'For that, and for that alone, were they written.' A commentator's job is to write for the actor.[3]

Irving called the drama 'the art of human nature in picturesque and characteristic action'.[4] In other words, a play is an action which springs from character. The assumption that character is the cornerstone of drama is essentially romantic. Reacting against the neo-classical view of dramatic characters as ideal types, romantic critics saw Shakespeare as the dramatist of the individual, the supreme observer of human nature, whose creations were as complex as they were true to life. 'Shakespeare knew the human mind, and its most minute and intimate workings,' Coleridge said, 'and he never introduces a word, or a thought, in vain or out of place: if we do not understand him, it is our own fault . . . and the smallest fragment of his mind not unfrequently gives a clue to a most perfect, regular, and consistent whole.'[5] Since each character is true in the dramatist's conception, it follows that any other interpretation is false. The business of criticism is to discover his meaning: to follow the clues in the text to the *right* interpretation of character and motive. This assumption ensured that critics and actors would pursue similar lines of investigation. The vital link between the two estates was the ruling principle of illusion.

Every actor understands that when he assumes a role he must know who he is: that is the only way he can say what is set down for him and do as the script directs him. If he does not understand his character and motives, neither will the audience. If he truly imagines his character into life, he will know why he says every word; then he will seem natural, which is to say that he will project the illusion that he is the character. But lifelike characters, like real men and women, are the

6

sum of all their experience. Their motives must sometimes be sought in the past, and the actor should imagine a 'pre-life', before the play. Romantic critics also assumed that since Shakespeare's characters gave the illusion of life, a legitimate technique of comprehending their true nature was to adopt the fiction that characters and events had an objective historical reality: that is why we often find them writing about Juliet or Falstaff in the past tense.

This is an honest approach so long as the text and the subtext alone are used as evidence. If it is reasonable to study Iago's soliloquies to determine his present motives for hating Othello, it is equally reasonable to search Macbeth's conversations with his wife for clues which may tell us whether they have talked about killing Duncan before the play. This is something the actors must know. But only those bits of the past which are documented or implied by the text may legitimately be used. One weakness of this method is that it can turn into fiction.[6] Another is that the convention of historical objectivity may be mistaken for reality, and the real facts about Richard Plantagenet brought in to muddle *Richard III*: this was a danger in the theatre of illusion, where archaeological accuracy sometimes conflicted with the spirit of a play.[7] These are not faults of the critical method as such, however, but of its abuse. The intrinsic flaw is its inflexibility. If a critic assumes that there is one right answer to even such a simple question as Hamlet's age, he overlooks the supremacy of dramatic effect over prosaic facts. And when the same assumptions are applied to complex problems like Iago's motives or the state of Hamlet's mind, the dramatist's rich ambiguities are lost. One of the most valuable functions of criticism is to show how many 'right answers' there are.

Here at last the actor must part company with the critic. Lady Macbeth's faint in the 'discovery scene' (II.iii) is ambiguous: is it real, or feigned? A critic is doing his job when he says, 'The solution, perhaps, is to admit the validity of *each* case, to move into the zone of negative capability and recognize that this moment defines *two* Lady Macbeths.'[8] But an actress can only play one of them at a time, and even if the audience is left in doubt, *she* must know what she means. An actor's commentary, then, has this limitation: while he should recognize the full range of choices which a complex text offers him, he must choose one and reject the others. In the end his originality will lie in his ability to add one more defensible choice to that rich texture.

7

The theatre of illusion

Irving had to defend his art against those who questioned its material and moral value. Matthew Arnold called these people Philistines. Ever since Aristotle – a card-carrying Philistine – justified tragedy by assigning it a therapeutic function, apologists for the theatre have played into Philistine hands. Jeremy Collier said the theatre corrupts morals, and Restoration dramatists replied with epilogues paraphrasing Horace: the drama pleases in order to instruct. This argument is feeble because it accepts the enemy's assumptions; in debate, the best defence is to attack the other fellow's premises. It also happens to be a false argument. While the theatre may sometimes acquire an extrinsic purpose, its natural value is intrinsic. Few people devote their lives to the pursuit of perfection in an art, as Irving did, from a pious desire to educate, purify, or even entertain their fellow-men. The art and its excellence are good in themselves: that is what Philistines cannot understand.

Irving gave the Philistines his version of the old Horatian oil: the theatre lends 'great aid to taste and thought and culture . . . *in the guise of amusement*' and it has an elevating influence on national morality. At worst, he says, it is a more wholesome place of entertainment than a gin palace and an escape from 'the intellectual mists of sordid reality'. Of course the theatre is 'an educational medium of no mean order', where the masses can learn about 'the costumes, habits, manners and customs of countries and ages other than their own', but Irving prudently avoids referring to the standard of historical truth in plays like *Richard III* or W. G. Wills's *Charles I*. He claims, moreover, that the theatre acquaints the public with great ideas and great literature: 'Without it Shakespeare might have been for many of them a sealed book.'[9]

Perhaps Irving believed these pieties, but he seems more sincere when he praises the theatre as a bearer of sweetness and light. It combats dullness and coarseness, stimulates imagination and fosters 'thought and grace and sweetness'. Direct teaching is secondary to its 'transcendental' value: theatre is an experience of passion and beauty which enlarges the mind and sympathies, 'raises in the scale of creation all who are subject to its sweetening influences'. In fact, men are made better by contemplation of the good, which is equated with the beautiful: 'Finally, in the consideration of the Art of Acting, it must never be forgotten that its ultimate aim is beauty.'[10]

Irving continues, 'Truth itself is only an element of beauty, and to merely reproduce things vile and squalid and mean is a debasement of Art.' Here we confront the philosophical difference between a romantic artist and the school of Ibsen and Shaw whose realism still dominates our thinking. When deciding whether a phenomenon should be represented on the stage, we accept as decisive the argument, 'That is what it is like in *real life*.' It is important to understand that this cut no ice at all with Irving; in his kind of romanticism, it was the 'ideal' that was 'true'. The artist selects from nature only 'what is pleasing and harmonious', never what is sordid. 'There can be no higher aim than to reproduce nature – nature shorn of such external accidents as would distract the mind of the spectator – nature epitomized and yielding her sweet meaning.' This is 'naturalism'; the 'realism' of Zola and Ibsen is inartistic because it is mere photography, and false because it is pessimistic. Truth is the optimistic art that 'harmonizes the seeming divergences in the great scheme of creation'.[11]

Irving believed that true art heightens nature in order to seem real. 'To appear to be natural, you must in reality be much broader than nature. To act on the stage as one really would in a room, would be ineffective and colourless.' The theatre is above all the art of *illusion*. 'It must never be forgotten that all Art has the aim or object of seeming and not of being; and to understate is as bad as to overstate the modesty or the efflorescence of nature.'[12]

In the nineteenth century the assumption that the theatre must strive to create a perfect illusion was universal and indisputable. The development of acting style, the emergence of the director, changes in scene design, costume and lighting were all guided by an unremitting search for perfection within this convention, which is best called the 'theatre of illusion'. Scenic illusion could be assessed objectively. Everyone could judge whether sets looked real and were illuminated naturally, or whether costumes were historically correct; romantics and realists merely debated whether beautiful or ugly aspects of nature ought to be selected for accurate representation. Acting style was a different matter.

9

Acting style

Audiences in every age find their favourite actors more natural than those of the last generation, because our way of perceiving nature is constantly changing. 'Nature' in acting is whatever creates illusion *for us*. In France a neo-classical style was still dominant. Constant Coquelin complained that English actors in general and Irving in particular created individuals instead of 'ideal types'; they 'carry their taste for originality so far as to love even eccentricity. We in France are generalizers; the English . . . concern themselves chiefly with the individual; I will even say with exceptional individuals.'[13] The neo-classical actor submerged his personality in the generalized type he portrayed, using standardized gestures, attitudes and declamation. His ideal of beauty was graceful, statuesque and melodious. But a romantic actor sought the 'picturesque', a term that implied singularity, irregularity and asymmetry rather than balance and proportion. Irving cultivated his own personality as a basis for detailed characterizations of unique and fascinating individuals. Thus while Coquelin played Mathias in *The Bells* as a typical Alsatian burgomaster, Irving made him an exceptional and curious person who happened to be a burgomaster. In melodrama his romanticism often became Gothic; in supernatural figures like Mephistopheles and criminals like Mathias, individuality easily became eccentricity and the picturesque merged with the grotesque. When this happened, Irving's unique manner could turn into mannerism.

The peculiarities which would have hampered Irving if he had aspired to a generalizing style were developed until they became assets. With maturity his bony, strong-featured face became distinguished: 'No one was ever as great as Irving looked.'[14] He could look greatly ascetic, greatly satanic, greatly sardonic or melancholy; he was never ordinary. His eyes were large and dark, like Garrick's and Kean's; his eyebrows were heavy and mobile, his mouth wide and thin. When prolonged study and labour at length gave him perfect control of these features, Irving's face became a superlatively flexible instrument. Like Garrick, he could show an audience a rapid succession of emotions with absolute clarity, using only his face; and in *The Lyons Mail* he played two utterly different characters without altering his makeup.[15]

Irving developed the same sort of control over a body that was anything but the neo-classical ideal. A tailor's bill gives his measurements at the age of sixty: 'Chest 40, waist 37, sleeve 33, height over six feet.'[16] His legs were proverbially thin, and while some critics thought it unfair 'to throw Mr. Irving's legs in his teeth', many censured the use he made of them. One compared his gait to that of a 'a fretful man trying to get very quickly over a ploughed field', and others declared that he simply could not walk at all: at moments of high excitement he

1 Irving's peculiar gait: *Hamlet* I.iv, 1874 (State Library of New South Wales)

lowered his head, thrust his shoulders forward, planted one foot on the stage, and dragged the other after it.[17] Plate 1 shows that this description is substantially accurate. His angular gestures and attitudes were exactly what neo-classical actors were taught to avoid: he often raised his arms above his head (see frontispiece), gestured with his left hand alone (plate 1), held his fingers stiff and straight (plate 33) or as crookedly as claws (plate 2). Even the friendly eye of the artist seldom found him graceful, while the rare photographs show that his attitudes were more frequently calculated to focus attention upon hands or face than to create a unified composition of balanced constrasts.[18]

Henry James, who admired French acting, believed that 'the basis, the prime condition of acting is the art of finished and beautiful utterance'. Irving, he protested, 'does not pretend to declaim or dream of declaiming'.[19] But if we may judge by the extant recordings, he emphasized Shakespeare's verse rhythms and end-stopped lines more than any modern actor. A word was often stressed by sustaining the vowel sound longer than we expect today, or by a stylized quaver. It is only when we listen again, or compare Irving's speech with that of Edwin Booth or Ellen Terry, that we come to see why H. A. Saintsbury said, 'He would have made mincemeat of Racine's Alexandrines.'[20] His speech was full of little pauses and cross-rhythms that subordinated form to content, rhythm to sense. To his contemporaries, however, the most striking feature of Irving's speech was his pronunciation. William Archer claims that as Hamlet he said, 'I'll mek a gost of him that lats me', and that many of his vowels were flattened.[21] The recordings show that there is some truth in this. Several vowels have affinities with the West Country where Irving was raised, and he pronounces the 'r' in words like 'heart' and 'charge.' Nevertheless, an eminent elocution teacher wrote a whole volume to show that Irving was 'a stage elocutionist of singular versatility, . . . a ripeness simply beautiful, comprehensive, powerful and majestic'.[22] He could hardly have said this of an actor with a provincial accent. Irving's dialect was carefully constructed for use in the theatre. 'Pronunciation on the stage,' he said, 'should be simple and unaffected, but not always fashioned according to a dictionary standard.'

2   Wolsey in *Henry VIII*, 1892 (Crown Copyright, Victoria and Albert Museum)

He found 'received English' undramatic and flat, and consequently fashioned a manner of speech that was 'expressive rather than refined'. Archaic sounds stressed the colour of Shakespeare's language, and final syllables were given phonetic values for the sake of clarity: 'His *eds* are *eds*, not *ids*,' wrote the elocutionist, and he said 'trammel' instead of 'tramm*ul*'. This language could be intrinsically dramatic: bent on murder, Mathias remarked how the dogs on neighbouring farms 'how–ow–owl–l–l–l–l', and when he said he would be rich – 'ritz–ritz–ritz' – the audience was 'horribly thrilled' by the sound alone.[23]

Edward Gordon Craig, whose conception of acting and the art of the theatre was years ahead of his time, saw Irving as the prototype of the actor of the future, 'the nearest thing ever known to what I have called the Ubermarionette'. By this he meant an actor who has every detail of his physical equipment under absolute control. Irving's face was a mobile mask, his speech was really song, his gait seemed strange because he did not really walk, he danced:

Irving positively designed . . . dances which fitted perfectly to the speeches given him by Shakespeare.

When he came to melodrama . . . he realized that a great deal more dance would be needed to hold up these pieces – and then it was that, putting out all his skill, he wiped the floor with the role and danced it like the devil. When it was Shakespeare he was dealing with, he had merely to wipe the beautiful glass window-panes.[24]

Irving studied his parts sympathetically, identifying so thoroughly that when he played Mathias his heart throbbed painfully at the sound of the fatal bells and his face turned pale. But he retained control because he developed what the French actor François Joseph Talma called 'dual consciousness': while the 'inspiring and directing self' identified and felt, the 'executive self' remained detached and observant, controlling and selecting the most effective gestures and intonations.[25]

No actor can achieve real success through technique alone. If a robot double of an Irving or an Oliver could be programmed to reproduce every movement and inflection, the result would be ludicrous. Great acting is only possibly when performer and audience share *belief*. If we believe, no acting technique or convention seems unnatural: illusion is perfect. Irving had a greater power of compelling belief than any actor after Garrick, and he achieved it through the exceptional concentration his contemporaries called intensity. 'I have never seen an actor whose absorption in his work was so nearly complete as his,' wrote an American critic. 'He never trifles, never forgets himself, never wearies, never relaxes the grip which he at once takes upon his part. . . . The dramatic consequence of such a high intensity is obviously great, but the value of the quality in holding the attention of audiences is inestimable.'[26] There were a few, however, who resisted Irving's magic and saw him as we might see the automaton. To these, his acting seemed a bundle of tricks and attitudes. Chief amongst them was George Bernard Shaw, and it is a great pity that many people today have learned to see Irving through his uncomprehending eyes.

The 'stage manager'

Few modern directors act, and fewer still direct productions in which they also take leading roles. I have called Irving a 'stage manager' because that is how he would have described himself, and because if we think of him as a director in the modern sense we shall see him as a very faulty one, hampered by the necessity of acting in the plays he directed. This would be a serious blunder. A modern director is like a general in a modern army: he commands from the rear. But an old-fashioned stage manager was like an old-fashioned general: he *led* his troops, and if things went wrong, he was the first to fall. The essence of the job was that he was the *leading* actor.

All contemporary accounts of Irving's rehearsals describe his 'despotic' attention to detail, but witnesses who were accustomed to the casual methods which survived in most other theatres were more impressed than we should probably be. We are frequently told how he rehearsed some Walking Gentleman over and over again until the man got his business as nearly right as it lay in him to do; we hear how he drilled the 'supers', chivvied the gas-men, bossed the scenic artists and harassed the musicians. But we never hear of him instructing another 'principal' in his stage business or interpretation.[27] Experienced Victorian actors seldom needed this kind of direction because they were not used to getting it. They were accustomed to being led. The actor-manager established his interpretation of the play, which he expressed in his performance of his own part, and his colleagues followed his lead. The secret lay in hiring, and keeping, actors who knew their business. Of course, in a theatrical style that emphasized the picturesque, one person had to control the blocking, and his prompt-books yield ample evidence that Irving was responsible for groupings and movement. Some early arrangements were stiff and unimaginative (see plate 4), but he later achieved a mastery of kinetic crowds and natural, beautiful tableaux which greatly enhanced illusion.

A modern director who handles a cast of thirty soon begins to feel like a one-armed juggler, and all such will understand why Irving delegated a good deal of his authority. Lyceum productions were operatic in scale. More than a hundred supernumeraries were frequently used, and in *Robespierre* (1899) there were 235, as well as 69 speaking parts. To assist him, Irving had H. J. Loveday, a stage manager in the modern sense of the term, with two assistants, a prompter who often showed new actors their business, a choreographer, and a 'super master'. Ellen Terry often helped to direct the women. The Lyceum had a chorus, a ballet, and a thirty-piece orchestra, all under their own leaders. The support-staff backstage and front-of-house was enormous: at various periods there were as many as 90 'carpenters' (stage hands), 32 props men, 19 gas and 20 limelight men. There were box-office and publicity staffs, wardrobe and dressing crews. Irving also employed his own ushers, pages, commissionaires, cleaners, firemen, baggage crews, hairdressers, an armourer and a perruquier.[28] Loveday told reporters that six hundred people worked regularly at the Lyceum, a figure which can be confirmed from independent sources.[29]

Irving's quest for beauty and illusion led to scenic innovation. The advances in control and colouring of gas, lime and electric light which were made by Lyceum technicians at his instigation transformed stage lighting from a blunt instrument for simple illumination or crude effect, into an art which was capable for making subtle thematic statements as well as emphasizing mood or beauty. At the Lyceum, light and shadow had mass and movement. Irving darkened the auditorium during performance, which allowed him to use a lower intensity on stage; thus his sets were not exposed in their naked artificiality, and his scenic artists could use subtler colours which he complemented by augmenting and mixing the hitherto extremely limited range of colour media.[30] Ramps and platforms were used

16

extensively to give the stage plasticity for outdoor scenes like the Brocken in *Faust* or in the first act of *The Cup*, where action took place on three levels. Indoor scenes, like the famous Temple of Artemis in the latter play, or the courtyard in *Macbeth* (see plate 13), were massively 'built-up' of three-dimensional pieces with textured surfaces and decorations in relief.[31] Elaborate sets usually alternated with 'carpenter's scenes', painted drops hanging close behind the proscenium arch. No curtain was used for scene changes during an act; the stage was darkened, the drop was 'flown' while furniture slid off into the wings, and the lights revealed the built-up scene which had been erected behind the drop. In this way the scenes 'seemed to melt into each other' and Shakespeare's rapid pace was maintained except where it was interrupted by the short intervals.[32]

In the theatre of illusion, the action of each play was tied to a specific place and historical period. Costume and scenery could become a vehicle for archaeological pedantry. For a decade, beginning with *Romeo and Juliet* (1882), Irving's productions became increasingly 'correct' and spectacular, under the influence of the scholarly painters he sometimes engaged to design sets and costumes. For *Macbeth* (1888) Charles Cattermole searched the museums for 'authority for every article of costume, weapon, furniture, and domestic utensil down to every nail and button and blade'. The climax came with *Henry VIII* (1892), with costumes designed by Seymour Lucas; the pageantry and spectacle swamped the play and cost a staggering £16,500.[33] Irving had always insisted that drama was more important than accuracy or spectacle, and his revulsion was swift. In his next production, *King Lear* (1892) archaeology played a minor part and sets were mostly constructed in the simpler, traditional way, using drops and wings.[34] *Coriolanus* (1901) was mounted in the same fashion, despite the authenticity of the canvas pictures.

Music played an important part in Lyceum productions. Besides the songs and dances required by the plays, the orchestra provided overtures and *entr'actes* selected or composed by the resident musical director and guest composers.[35] But there was also unmotivated incidental music which prepared moods and underlined emotions very much as it still does, unnoticed, in films. Special 'ghost music' was used in *The Corsican Brothers* and *Hamlet*, and 'hurry music' anticipated Irving's entrance in *The Bells*; in *The Dead Heart* the accompaniment was 'almost uninterrupted from beginning to end'.[36] Sometimes characteristic themes were identified with the major figures, and these were usually introduced in the overture. A dramatic statement could be made by recapitulating one of these themes at an unexpected time.[37] Incidental music was used less freely in Shakespeare than in melodrama, but Queen Katherine's dying speech was accompanied, and 'casket music' played while Morocco wondered which choice would win Portia.

The Lyceum

The columned portico in Wellington Street is all that remains of Irving's Lyceum, which was demolished in 1904. It was never a really large theatre. Between 1871 and 1881 it seated perhaps 1,250 people; then Irving began a series of modifications which gradually increased the capacity to 1,700 in 1903.[38] It was about the same size as the Adelphi, larger than the Haymarket or Her Majesty's, but dwarfed by the old patent houses and suburban giants like the Grand, Islington.[39] Victorian theatres were crowded, and the auditorium was not so large as the figures may seem to suggest; the remotest spot in the gallery was never more than 85 feet from the stage, and all but a handful of the audience were always within 70 feet. There was plenty of room on the big stage for broad, firm movement, fluid crowds and massive sets: the proscenium opening was $33\frac{1}{2}$ feet wide and perspectives could be 68 feet deep.[40]

Like other Victorian theatres, the Lyceum was equipped with the traditional 'grooves' used for changing 'wings'. This obsolescent system was seldom used because Irving usually preferred built-up scenery, but it served as a conventional reference in stage geography. There were five sets of grooves parallel to the footlights and about 6 feet apart. These were numbered upstage from the proscenium arch. Thus when a set-piece was to be erected in the 'third grooves' the carpenters knew just how far upstage to place it. The spaces between the wings were 'entries', and were similarly numbered; the fourth, and farthest upstage, was usually called the 'upper entry'. These terms were commonly abbreviated, the second entry at stage left, for instance, as L2E and the fourth at right as R4E or RUE. Stage left was also frequently known as 'prompt' and right as 'opposite prompt', or

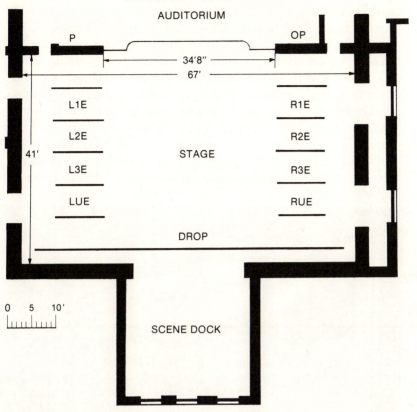

OP (see plate 4 and pp. 229 and 231–2 below). The diagram above shows the approximate positions of these points on the Lyceum stage.

The Lyceum was built in 1834, and by 1878 it was an old-fashioned theatre. The three tiers – Dress Circle, Upper Circle and Gallery – were shallow and supported by iron columns which obstructed some sightlines. The tiers described a deep horseshoe around a raked floor where expensive, fashionable Stalls gradually expanded and thrust the proletarian Pit away from the stage.[41] Irving cultivated a dignified atmosphere. Broad stairways led from an imposing foyer to the ornate, 'bastard Pompeian' auditorium where the dominant tones were blue, amber and gold (see plate 3).[42]

The Stalls and Dress Circle sat at ease, resplendent in evening dress and flattered by luxury. Their polite *sang froid* tended to restrain the

19

traditionally demonstrative Pit behind them, whose quick response to claptrap had helped to give melodramatic acting its character. The attentive hush of the Stalls helped to create the Lyceum acting style by discouraging showy effects and appreciating subtlety; at the same time, the size of the house ensured that acting would not be scaled down to realistic measure. The Stalls seldom applauded during a scene, particularly after Irving began to black-out the auditorium. This practice also had the effect of heightening illusion. An audience that sits in the dark becomes less conscious of itself. All eyes are drawn to the stage, which becomes more vivid and, simultaneously, remote.

3   Interior of the Lyceum Theatre after 1885 (Crown Copyright, Victoria and Albert Museum)

The framed world is set apart by a barrier of light, strongly marked by the glare of gas footlights.

The plays

During his artistic control of the Lyceum, Irving produced some thirty-seven plays of which only twelve were by Shakespeare.[43] Almost all of the remainder were melodramas. It has been justly said that melodramas were almost the only Victorian plays that dealt with contemporary social issues.[44] Irving's taste, however, ran to melodrama of an entirely different order; not for him the proletarian themes of urban alienation, poverty, drink and gambling. Plays that suited the romantic Lyceum style were mixtures, in various proportions, of flamboyant ingredients: picturesque historical and exotic settings, spectacle, the supernatural, pathos, crime and the psychology of guilt. *Charles I* (W. G. Wills, 1872 and 1879) and *Robespierre* (Victorien Sardou, 1899) derived their interest primarily from history, but the former was intensely pathetic and the latter had a spectacular ghost scene. *The Bells* (Leopold Lewis, 1871) probed the conscience of a murderer, whose nightmare of exposure at the hands of a Mesmerist was in the best terror-Gothic tradition; but *Louis XI* (Dion Boucicault, 1878) studied a senile criminal in a far more romantic and colourful setting. *Faust* (Wills, 1885) was simultaneously supernatural, spectacular, historical and exotic. *The Medicine Man* (H. D. Traill and Robert Hichens, 1898) was Irving's only 'coat and trousers' melodrama, and a dreadful, unsuccessful play. It revolved around a romantic figure, the mad hypnotist of uncanny power who 'worships nothing in the world but knowledge – nothing, nothing in the world. Ha! ha! ha!' Many of these pieces had literary pretensions, and most were splendid plays for the theatre by men who knew how to give an actor an opportunity. Wills, the author of five of them,[45] was considered an important modern verse dramatist; Sardou was the leading French playwright; Tennyson (*Queen Mary*, 1876; *The Cup*, 1881; *Becket*, 1893) was Laureate and had great prestige.

Six melodramas, all adapted from the French, were old favourites in which great actors of the past had won fame. Guilty Sir Edward Mortimer in *The Iron Chest* (George Colman, 1879) had been one of Edmund Kean's great parts; Bulwer Lytton's *Richelieu* (1873 and

1879) and *The Lady of Lyons* (1879) were originally successes of Macready's, but were part of the repertory of most later stars; Boucicault's *Louis XI* (1879) and *The Corsican Brothers* (1880 and 1891), and *The Lyons Mail* by Charles Reade (1877), were all produced at the Princess's by Charles Kean. These pieces had become theatrical classics, in which actors showed what they could do and challenged comparison with their predecessors.

Shakespeare was used for the same purpose, with the result that plays without a stage tradition to challenge were seldom produced. Victorians often said that 'Shakespeare did not write good plays for the modern stage.' He required too many scene changes, the histories and some of the tragedies lacked 'love interest', the comedies used strange conventions and were encumbered by 'low' clowns and coarse jokes. Thus despite the efforts of Phelps and the younger Kean to introduce the less well-known plays, the Shakespearean repertory in Irving's time remained small. *Hamlet, Macbeth, Othello, Romeo and Juliet, Richard III, Henry V, Henry VIII, King John, As You Like It, Much Ado about Nothing* and *The Merchant of Venice*: these were the only plays that were to be seen at all frequently.

When the new manager of the Lyceum, H. L. Bateman, hired Henry Irving in 1871, the London stage was ready for a new leader. The old stars had set: Phelps was growing old, and had long since relinquished the management of Sadler's Wells; Charles Fechter, whose romantic interpretations of Shakespeare enjoyed a considerable vogue in the 1860s, had emigrated to America in 1870; the Bancrofts' line was contemporary drama. After two months of disappointing business, Bateman yielded to Irving's suggestion that they try *The Bells*. Nothing like the resulting triumph had been seen since Edmund Kean's debut as Shylock, and the manager exploited it for three seasons with a series of melodramatic vehicles for his star. He was reluctant to risk Irving's reputation by attempting Shakespeare, but *Hamlet* in 1874 was *The Bells* all over again. Bateman died in the course of its record-breaking run, leaving the management to his wife, but effective artistic direction fell to the actor.

Irving raised artistic standards as far as the widow's parsimony allowed. From the provincial stock-companies where he had served a long apprenticeship, he recruited old professionals like Sam Johnson, Tom Mead and John Archer, who would form the reliable nucleus of his own company; some stayed for thirty years.[46] Arthur Wing Pinero joined in 1876; Irving staged his first curtain-raisers, and Pinero acted at the Lyceum until he turned full-time dramatist.[47] H. J. Loveday was summoned from Liverpool to begin twenty-nine years of service as stage manager.

Irving set out to work his way through the standard Shakespearean repertory: *Hamlet* was followed by *Macbeth* (1875), *Othello* (1876) and *Richard III* (1877). At the same time he began to vary the bill with revivals of the old melodramas in which the great actors with whom he meant to take his place had made their reputations, such as *The Lyons Mail* and *Louis XI*. Indeed, Irving 'created' only three new roles between 1875 and 1889.[48] Each production generated more excitement and controversy than the last, and by 1878 his place at the head of his profession was secure.

Irving took over the management at the end of August in an atmosphere of thinly veiled acrimony. He was rumoured to have told Mrs Bateman that he needed actors to work with, not dolls, an unkind cut at the daughters she had resolutely starred.[49] Some of the company followed the widow to Sadler's Wells, but many stayed with Irving. It was a fateful decision for Hawes Craven, the young scenic artist: he stayed to become leader of his own profession. When the Acting Manager left, Irving sent to Dublin for Bram Stoker, who served his business interests until 1905. Most important of all, he engaged Ellen Terry to play Ophelia in the revival of *Hamlet* which would inaugurate his management in December.

The first two seasons were mostly spent in reviving the melodramatic successes of the Bateman years and in making money, six of the former and £20,000 of the latter. With a solid repertory and bank account to fall back on, Irving announced that he would present *Coriolanus* in the autumn. This was a most unusual choice; however, authentically detailed paintings of life in the ancient world were the fashion, and Lawrence Alma-Tadema, the leader in the genre, had agreed to design.[50]

During the summer Irving changed his mind. *Coriolanus* had been a good vehicle for classical actors like Kemble, but the romantic school neglected it; besides it had no 'love interest', which meant that there was no part for Ellen Terry. It was probably the memory of her exquisite Portia at the Prince of Wales's in 1875 as much as the local colour he absorbed on vacation in the Mediterranean that persuaded Irving to substitute *The Merchant of Venice*, which was hurried into production in November to atone for the failure of that leaky old melodrama, *The Iron Chest*. Perhaps it was a sense of obligation to Alma-Tadema and the public which made him announce *Coriolanus* again at the end of the season (1879–80). This time his plans were changed by his only serious rival, Edwin Booth.

The American tragedian had originally hoped to act at the Lyceum while Irving toured, but late in 1880 he appeared at the Princess's in his major roles. A pusillanimous management and Booth's old-fashioned indifference to the details of rehearsal and production weakened the impression his acting ought to have made. With characteristic generosity, Irving offered to mount any play Booth wished and to share the profits. Irving suggested *Venice Preserv'd* but his guest preferred *Othello*, with the two stars alternating weekly as Iago and the Moor. Booth went home solvent but, Ellen Terry shrewdly suspected, secretly humiliated by his rival's magnanimity.[51]

At the end of the season, Irving announced somewhat doggedly that he would present *Coriolanus* in 1881–2, preceded by *Romeo and Juliet*. Shakespeare's lovers were as popular then as they are now; and the premature death of Adelaide Neilson, the reigning Juliet, had given the signal for a polite rush to claim the role.[52] Irving meant to make use of Ellen Terry's youth while she had it, but Romeo was outside his range and reviews were hostile. Nevertheless, the piece ran to the end of the season, which left no time for the star-crossed *Coriolanus*.

Irving continued to choose plays with juicy parts for Ellen Terry. He was planning a North American tour, and he badly needed to extend the Shakespearean part of his repertory, which consisted of only two reliable crowd-pleasers, *Hamlet* and *The Merchant of Venice*. Terry's success in *The Belle's Stratagem* in 1881 pointed towards comedy, and *Much Ado about Nothing* was selected.[53] While all three of Shakespeare's mature comedies feature charming young women, only Benedick offered Irving an opportunity. He made the most of it, Terry became the definitive Beatrice, and the Lyceum enjoyed the most prosperous season of Irving's reign.[54] This triumph suggested another comedy, and rumour had it that *As You Like It* was planned.[55] Victorians admired Rosalind more than she deserves and every *ingénue* under fifty played her with the leggy impudence of a

24

'principal boy' in pantomime. But there was nothing in it for Irving save Jaques, the usual choice of middle-aged managers, and Touchstone, which he preferred because the clown 'is in the vital part of the play'.[56] *Twelfth Night*, however, offered Malvolio, which was much more in his line. It was rarely seen on the stage, and the production in July 1884 was received with an indifference which damped Irving's enthusiasm for comedy.

With *Twelfth Night* Irving's Shakespearean impetus spent itself. From now on the plays would have to be carefully chosen, the manifest disadvantages of each weighed against dubious opportunities. He considered *The Tempest*, *Julius Caesar* and *Henry IV*, *Part 1*. Caliban appealed to him but, as he said, 'the young lovers are everything, and where are we going to find them?' Brutus was an actor's part: 'But the actor-manager's part is Antony – Antony scores all along the line. Now when the actor and the actor-manager fight in a play, and when there is no part for you,' he told Terry, 'I think it wiser to leave it alone.' At length he decided to play Falstaff, only to be forestalled by Tree's success in *The Merry Wives of Windsor*.[57] So seven of Irving's best years were filled with melodramas like *Faust*, which ran for two full seasons, and the only Shakespeare production was his 'grudge match' with *Macbeth* at the end of 1888, in which his matured powers vindicated the controversial Irving interpretation.

When he returned to Shakespeare in 1892 the Lyceum had passed its meridian. *Henry VIII* held the stage throughout the century as a spectacle, and Irving's production was 'a great deal more of picture than of Shakespeare'.[58] The public loved it, but running costs outstripped the receipts from full houses and the season ended in the red. Henceforth the Lyceum lost money consistently, but Irving maintained it as a base where he could build the repertory which made his tours pay. He searched for a Shakespearean play with the enduring popularity which his repertory demanded, but *King Lear* (1892) was almost unknown on the Victorian stage and Irving's production confirmed the prejudice against it. *Cymbeline* (1896) gave Terry a Rosalind part, and it might have done well on the road but for the first of a series of disasters. In December 1896 Irving revived *Richard III*, which seemed certain to become a reliable money-spinner; had it contained a part for Ellen Terry he would probably have turned to it earlier. But after the first performance, an injury took Irving out of the bill for weeks; losses mounted to £10,000 for the season and Richard, his freshness lost, was consigned to oblivion.

By now Irving had produced all of the old, stock melodramas, like *The Corsican Brothers*, which suited his style, and three contemporary plays in succession failed. A fire in February 1898 destroyed the sets for almost his entire repertory; of the Shakespeare productions, only *The Merchant of Venice* was saved. For some time he had contemplated *Richard II* – an unusual choice in the nineteenth century – and now construction began for a production in 1899; a revival of *Othello* was already in preparation. Then Irving fell seriously ill. This was the last straw. He abandoned his plans and handed over the management to a Limited Liability Corporation which disrupted his staff, kept him almost continually on tour, and collapsed in 1902 when it failed to meet the costs of renovating the Lyceum to comply with new fire regulations. Only two productions were mounted in this period, *Robespierre* and the long-delayed *Coriolanus*, which failed. Irving produced no more Shakespeare, and when Ellen Terry reluctantly left him, only *The Merchant of Venice* remained in his repertory: he was scheduled to play Shylock in Bradford on the night after his death on 13 October 1905.

2

Hamlet

31 October 1874
30 December 1878

Theatrical context

There is room for only one Hamlet in a generation. No other part matters so much as a test of star quality, and none carries such a burden of tradition. When Irving was first announced to play it, the public understood that he was claiming a place amongst the greatest reputations of the past, with Garrick, Kemble, Kean, Macready and Phelps. In 1874 London lacked a reigning Hamlet. Charles Fechter had achieved a sensational run of 115 performances at the Princess's in 1861, a record which Irving deliberately set out to break. Fechter's greatest rival was Edwin Booth, who also appeared in London in 1861. America was Booth's domain; his *Hamlet* played New York's Winter Garden for a hundred nights in 1864. In London, however, Fechter's reputation stood unshaken even after he left England in 1870, until he made the mistake of returning for a brief engagement in 1872. His comparative failure declared an open season on *Hamlet*. Irving was simply the most successful of the five actors who came forward to claim the part in the next three seasons.

Daniel Bandmann was too robust and old-fashioned; besides, he spoke with a German accent. At sixty-one, William Creswick was too old; his opening shortly after Irving's was evidently intended as a direct challenge, but it misfired: 'In the fencing scene,' said a review, 'the Queen's remark that Hamlet is fat and scant of breath is only too true.'[1] Tomaso Salvini appeared at Drury Lane in May 1875 in a performance that paid Irving the compliment of adopting some of his stage business. A lesser Italian, Ernesto Rossi, could not escape his countryman's shadow.

By the time Booth revisited England in 1880, Irving was unshakeably established. In 1884 Wilson Barrett's production at the Princess's, designed with archaeological accuracy by E. W. Godwin, was regarded as a substantial challenge to the Lyceum staging; but as to Barrett's acting, *Punch* told Irving, who was touring America: 'Don't you be afraid; it's all right, your position is secure. Hamlet Junior has not caught you up, or come anywhere near you.'[2] Nor did anyone else while the play remained in Irving's repertoire. Unlike Phelps, who played Hamlet until he retired, Irving dropped the part before he became too old: his last performance took place on 8 May 1885. No Hamlet of real stature was seen in London again until Forbes-Robertson opened at the Lyceum in 1897.

It is difficult to estimate the degree to which Irving was influenced by other Hamlets. Like most Victorian actors he was familiar with numerous traditions, some of them as old as Betterton. His biographer describes how he sought out Edmund Kean's Polonius, to enquire how the great tragedian had played the closet scene.[3] Irving had supported Booth and Fechter, in each case as Laertes, when their tours brought them to the provincial theatres where he was a member of the local stock-company – Manchester in 1861, Birmingham in 1865. No doubt he watched them closely; he owed something certainly to Phelps, whom he had first seen at the age of twelve. A man's first Hamlet often sticks in his mind. One definite influence was an experimental production presented by Tom Taylor at the Crystal Palace on 3 May 1873. The Hamlet was James Steele Mackaye, an American pupil of François Delsarte who subsequently earned a great reputation in his homeland as a teacher, playwright and theatrical innovator. Irving was sufficiently impressed to adopt some of the stage arrangements in 1878, and in 1874 he engaged Taylor's Laertes, Edmund Leathes, for the same part at the Lyceum.

A performance of *Hamlet* had become more ritual than play. First-night audiences were familiar with the usual acting text and the traditional business. Above all, they knew the 'points'. These were moments when the actor was supposed to make a sensation by revealing, with a single vivid strike, the meaning of a scene, speech or action. Kean was a master of this technique, which is why Coleridge said that seeing him act was like reading Shakespeare by flashes of lightning. The Pit anticipated the points attentively, swiftly and expertly judging whether they were fumbled or well played. One of the most famous was the 'tag' to Act II where Hamlet ends his soliloquy:

The play's the thing
Wherein I'll catch the conscience of the king.[4]

The point lay in executing a sudden transition of mood, as though the stratagem of the Mousetrap had suddenly sprung to mind. This might be illustrated by a gesture like Kemble's 'double sweep' of the arm, but the essence of the point is verbal. Well played it is a thrilling moment, but inherently melodramatic. It is arresting as a display of declamatory virtuosity; its single, obvious meaning, however, may be inconsistent with Hamlet's character or a coherent interpretation of the play. The soliloquies were full of such points and hence tended to become detached recitations, like familiar operatic arias filled with difficult trills and high notes that test the technical skill of the singer but have little to do with the meaning of the *libretti*. A new actor was always at liberty to discover new points, but woe betide him if he missed too many of the old ones.

Traditional stage business was so well known that anything new, however minute, caused a sensation. Innovation for its own sake was discouraged, but a new idea which pleased the audience was hailed as a stroke of genius. Thus Macready was acclaimed for illustrating Hamlet's 'I must be idle' (III.ii.92) with a 'quick and salient walk up and down the front of the stage, waving a handkerchief as if in idle and gay indifference, but ill concealing ... the sense of approaching triumph'.[5]

The only significant variable in the ritual of *Hamlet* was the star actor, who sometimes reduced his part to a mere bag of points. Irving challenged this practice. He was hampered in both of his productions by limited resources, and in the first (1874) by the fact that he was not his own master. Even in 1878 he had not yet gathered the skilled ensemble which supported him in his later productions. Nevertheless, he set out to present the most truthful interpretation possible. He took a fresh look at the text, discarded traditional points, invented new business and gradually developed a conception of the play as a whole. No doubt he undervalued language, which he entirely subordinated to character. He was determined to show what every word meant rather than to recite beautiful sounds. Inevitably his own part was overemphasized by omissions, simplifications and the sheer focusing power of his genius, but the production was probably not as oversimplified as most we see today, and Irving's Hamlet was a complex, mysterious but

29

believable human being. Indeed, his characterization was so free of theatrical tricks, so naturalistic by prevailing standards, that the first audience in 1874 was baffled and failed to applaud until the third act.

Text

Henry Irving took great pains with his acting versions. An examination of his study-book, prompt-books and printed texts shows that he repeatedly revised *Hamlet* in a conscientious effort to give his audience the soundest possible text consistent with contemporary stage conventions. Four successive states of the text can be identified, each reflecting significant changes in the emphasis of his interpretation. The most remarkable fact which emerges is that Irving's conception developed, at least in part, in response to his growing awareness of the textual issues as they were then understood. The two earlier texts represent a preliminary draft and a final acting version for the 1874 production. The third was used in the revival with which his management of the Lyceum commenced in 1878. The fourth was prepared when it became clear that the third was too long.[6] Each is based upon the current received text. This contains a number of readings which would be unfamiliar to a modern audience, because editors then believed that F1 was the most reliable text, whereas Dover Wilson has established the relative authority of Q2.[7] Thus where many modern editions emend Hamlet's 'too too sallied flesh' (Q2) to read 'sullied', Irving read 'solid' as in the Folio, forfeiting thereby the key to a whole series of images with which Hamlet expresses the corruption he perceives in his mother's remarriage.

The first draft of Irving's acting version cuts some 1,216 lines. His omissions were largely traditional, but a variety of motives underlie the deletion of various passages. The greater part reflect the actor's perennial need to shorten the play; Irving followed a theatrical tradition as old as Davenant in omitting all of the matter relating to Fortinbras and the mechanism by means of which Hamlet returns from the sea. The broad effect is to domesticate the action by expunging all reference to a world outside Denmark, and to lose the sense that Providence had brought Hamlet safely home. Perhaps as a partial counterweight, Irving rescued from the wrack Hamlet's lines,

There's a divinity that shapes our ends,
Rough-hew them how we will

(V.ii.10–11)

and substituted them for the difficult sentence which follows 'The readiness is all' (V.ii.224–5). Particular sacrifices included the soliloquy in IV.i and everything after 'The rest is silence', which became the last line in the play.

Some passages were cut for thoroughly illegitimate reasons. Speeches which seem to contradict the prevailing romantic notion of a 'lovable' Hamlet were omitted.[8] Hamlet is anything but lovable when he tells how he has sent Rosencrantz and Guildenstern to their deaths; even Horatio seems shaken (V.i.38ff). If his 'antic disposition' is largely or entirely feigned, as it was in Irving's interpretation, his apology to Laertes before the duel is apparently founded upon a brazen lie:

What I have done
That might your nature, honour, and exception
Roughly awake, I here proclaim my madness.

(V.ii.231–3)

And the speech in which he debates whether to kill the praying King (III.iii.73–96) reveals such ferociously unchristian sentiments that Dr Johnson thought it 'too horrible to be read or uttered'.[9] Irving's restoration of this last passage in both prompt-books, however, suggests that he was coming to see that if his conception of Hamlet did not agree with Hamlet's lines, his conception must be wrong. For similar reasons he restored in 1878 the passage in which Hamlet calls the ghost beneath the stage 'this fellow in the cellarage' and 'old mole' (I.v.145–63).

Irving's first draft omits some passages apparently for no better reason than that he could see no effective way of playing them. Amongst these was Hamlet's exclamation after the Ghost has left him,

O all you host of heaven! O earth! What else?
And shall I couple hell?

(I.v.92–3)

He also cut the last seven lines of the same speech, perhaps because he had not yet devised his famous business with the tablets (see below,

31

p. 54). Both of these passages were restored in the 1874 acting version. The dumbshow was cut in all texts.[10] In the draft, the first of Hamlet's doggerels after the King's flight was retained and the second cut; in performance, the second was restored and the first cut, in order to permit Irving to introduce his celebrated business with Ophelia's peacock-feather fan (see below, pp. 59–60).

Victorian propriety took its inevitable toll. Irving's first draft was based upon a slightly expurgated edition of the received text which omitted Hamlet's banter with Rosencrantz and Guildenstern about Fortune's 'privates' (II.ii.237–9), the obscenities directed at Ophelia in the play scene (III.ii.115–24, 149–53) and some of her spicier songs (IV.v.52–66).[11] These deletions are common to all versions, but to his credit, he restored after the draft the lines in the closet scene,

> Nay, but to live
> In the rank sweat of an enseamèd bed.

(III.iv.92–3)

Delicate sensibilities were spared the rest of the speech, however.[12]

Some alterations may have been based upon textual study. Not unreasonably, Irving seems to have thought that any passage omitted in either F or Q2 could be dispensed with. Some of these are embedded in longer omissions, but several were cut exactly as in Folio or Quarto; for example, the only lines expunged from the entire gravedigger sequence are those which do not appear in Q2, the Clown's explanation of his wisecrack about Adam (V.i.35–7). The actor's interest in textual issues extended to the 'bad' quarto, which was then the subject of much controversy; William Poel went so far as to stage it in 1881. The general feeling was that it must be either an early revision by Shakespeare of the *Ur-Hamlet*, or a faulty and probably surreptitious copy of Shakespeare's complete play, or perhaps some combination of the two. Irving evidently believed that parts of Q1 carried some authority, for he followed its text in one respect. In all versions save the first draft he transposed thirteen lines from IV.ii, a scene he had originally meant to omit, to III.ii. Thus Hamlet, rebuking Rosencrantz and Guildenstern, says, 'Call me what instrument you will, though you can fret me, you cannot play upon me' (III.ii.379–80) and continues, 'Besides, to be demanded of a sponge . . .' (Iv.ii.12). He concludes, 'a knavish speech sleeps in a foolish ear' (IV.ii.23–4), Polonius enters and III.ii continues.

The first draft reveals a cautious tendency to abbreviate without altogether cutting out anything beyond traditional omissions such as Fortinbras. But the 1874 prompt-book shows more decision; here Irving cut a further 383 lines, evidently following a clearly conceived policy. The attempt upon Hamlet's life which underlies the ostensibly therapeutic voyage to England was entirely omitted. Indeed, he all but cut the voyage itself; this acting version refers to it only twice. Before the Mousetrap scene, Claudius seems innocent of ulterior purpose when he tells Polonius,

> he shall with speed to England
> For the demand of our neglected tribute
>
> (III.i.172–3)

and Hamlet's letter in Act IV merely informs the King that 'I am set naked on your kingdom' (IV.vii. 43–4). Thus Rosencrantz and Guildenstern's part in the scheme disappears with the scheme itself; they are neither seen nor mentioned after the transposed passage in III.ii. Irving also cut to the bone those passages in which Claudius soothes the angry Laertes, persuades him that Hamlet is his real enemy, and plans with him the intricate stratagems of the duel scene. Act IV suffered most; 444 of its 655 lines were cut, 145 more than in the draft. The first four scenes were entirely omitted, so that the closet scene was immediately followed (after the interval) by Ophelia's mad scene and the return of Laertes. The events of the play as a whole were greatly simplified, of course, and widespread economies were effected in passages which Irving probably considered mere story-telling.

The first state of the 1878 prompt-book is some $98\frac{1}{2}$ lines longer than the previous acting versions; while almost 80 lines are newly omitted, more than twice that number are restored. In the final revision, some of these restorations are cancelled and many new cuts made. The latter is Irving's shortest text, $1,643\frac{1}{2}$ lines or $42\frac{1}{2}$ per cent being omitted. Nevertheless, his approach to the text was more responsible than it had been in 1874. Some passages, deleted in the earlier production merely because they were difficult to play or presented Hamlet in an unlovable light, were restored in 1878. Amongst these were the startled exclamations of the sentinels as the Ghost vanishes: ''Tis here. 'Tis here./'Tis gone', parts of the soliloquy that follows (I.v.92–3, 105–11), the 'old mole' flippancies and the suggestive 'Lady, shall I lie in your lap' in the Mousetrap scene.[13] The remaining restorations were passages Irving apparently preferred to retain, but believed to be inessential, since he cut them again in the last revision: Hamlet's philosophizing with his schoolfellows (II.ii.261–70), Ophelia's description of his distracted visit to her closet, a few details of the sea voyage (III.i.172–81; III.iii.24–6). In the last version all traces of the voyage were cut, together with portions of the remaining Rosencrantz and Guildenstern scenes (e.g. IV.vii.36–7, 41–9).

The fourth version shows no restorations, and some 110 lines are omitted which were retained in all previous texts. Earlier abbreviations in the parts of Polonius, the schoolfellows, the Player, the Player Queen and the Clowns are simply extended. A few lines are cut from the King's soliloquy, the Queen no longer refuses to see mad Ophelia, and Claudius takes fewer lines to calm Laertes.

In order to minimize set changes, Irving reduced the original twenty scenes to thirteen in 1874 and fourteen in 1878 by cutting and amalgamating. The last scene, however, was always divided in two. In similar fashion he tried to eliminate superfluous characters. Like the Folio, the 1874 text assigns to Horatio the lines of the anonymous Gentleman (Q2) in Ophelia's mad scene. Horatio was also sent to 'Follow her close' (IV.v.74). The Messenger who warns Claudius of his danger from Laertes and the mob was replaced by Marcellus. In 1878 Marcellus assumed all of these functions.

Contemporary criticism

Like the critics who influenced him, Irving was more concerned with the Prince than the 'poem'. In fact, it is unlikely that he would have appreciated the distinction. To him the interpretation of *Hamlet* was mainly a matter of determining the character and motives of the hero, whom he treated as a real person with a past as well as a present. This was the approach taken by Goethe's Wilhelm Meister in his attempt to solve the 'riddle' of *Hamlet*. 'I set about investigating every trace of Hamlet's character, as it had showed itself before his father's death,' says Meister, ignoring the fact that an audience is shown nothing of the kind. He invents for Hamlet a complete character as he might have been before personal distress overwhelmed him. 'This delineation was received with warm approval,' he concludes; 'the company imagined they foresaw that Hamlet's manner of proceeding might now be very satisfactorily explained.'[14] The explanation which was sought, of course, was the true reason for his delay in carrying out the Ghost's demand for vengeance: henceforth this delay, and psychological reasons for it, became the central issues of *Hamlet* criticism.

Goethe saw Hamlet as a weak and sensitive creature, full of the daintier virtues but 'without the strength of nerve which forms a hero'. Excluded from the succession and saddened by his father's death, he is wounded by his mother's marriage and becomes a prey to melancholy. The Ghost's command is the last straw. 'To me it is clear,' says Meister, 'that Shakespeare meant, in the present case, to represent the effects of a great action laid upon a soul unfit for the performance of it . . . There is an oak-tree planted in a costly jar, which should have borne only pleasant flowers in its bosom: the roots expand, the jar is shivered.'[15] This metaphor became a cliché; in Irving's time any newspaper critic could quote it from memory, and dozens did. It raised the final component of the 'riddle' of *Hamlet*: how much of the 'antic disposition' is feigned, and how much is real mental disorder?

Schlegel and Coleridge both reject madness as an explanation. Basing their interpretations upon the assumption that thought and action are antithetical, they seek the cause of Hamlet's delay in his habit of 'thinking too precisely upon th'event'. Shakespeare's purpose, indeed, is to illustrate the moral 'that action is the chief end of existence, – that no faculties of intellect, however brilliant, can be considered valuable . . . if they withdraw us from . . . action'. They differ only in emphasis; whereas Schlegel roundly condemns Hamlet as a self-deceiving hypocrite, who feigns madness to hide a lack of resolution rooted in fear of the consequences revealed by excessive thought, Coleridge finds him a brave man whose 'almost enormous' mental activity leads him to prefer 'his thoughts and the images of his fancy' to the real world. 'Hamlet's character is the prevalence of the abstracting and generalizing habit over the practical.'[16]

These three early commentators – Goethe, Schlegel and Coleridge – defined the issues and presented the major viewpoints. Subsequent writers refined or exaggerated their views, synthesized them in various ways, or coined a memorable phrase. Hazlitt, for example, follows Schlegel: Hamlet's 'ruling passion is to think, not to act' and 'He is full of weakness and melancholy.' His contribution to the main debate is confined to the rather acute observation that Hamlet can act 'only on the spur of the occasion, when he has no time to reflect'. Gervinus develops this idea. It is imagination rather than excessive thought which weakens Hamlet's will by exaggerating the dangers and difficulties around him. But under the stress of occasions like the encounter with the Ghost, the play, the closet scene or Laertes' 'ostentatious lamentation' at the graveside, this superabundant imagination becomes heated to a state of 'sensitive excitability'. In this state Hamlet is able to act, but his resolution cannot be sustained when the excitement subsides.[17]

While the major critics busied themselves with the psychological causes of Hamlet's delay, lesser figures did battle over the question of his madness. There is a potential simplification here. If it can be shown that Hamlet is really mad, there is no need to account further for his behaviour. Here rests the fundamental absurdity of the question: a crazy Hamlet is without significance, and his story not worth the telling. Nevertheless, this was the burning question in Irving's time. It is the only interpretative issue given a section entirely to itself in the Variorum edition of 1877, where the debate covers forty-one closely printed pages. By that time the 'crazies' had carried the day. The editors of the text which Irving used for a study-book endorse Goethe's interpretation of the play, but they conclude: 'Goethe does not recognize the reality of Hamlet's madness, which has formed the subject of special investigation by several writers.'[18] There was debate about the nature of the disorder; and whether it is incipient before the play opens, precipitated by the Ghost, a by-product of the 'antic disposition', or a condition which that charade is intended to hide. But the consensus certainly held that 'in plain terms, Hamlet is mad'.[19]

Irving disagreed with the consensus. Like Gervinus, he believed that Hamlet is a fundamentally sane man whose sensitive imagination excites a kind of hysteria at moments of stress. Like Goethe, the actor seems to have arrived at his interpretation by reconstructing Hamlet's life before the play: a questionable proceeding from the critical stand-point, perhaps, but useful to a player intent upon building a charac-ter.[20] Irving's emphasis on the role of love in Hamlet's early life is original. His relationships with his parents, Ophelia, his schoolfellows, Laertes and perhaps even his uncle have been ruled by an ingenuous affection based on trust in the essential identity of appearance and reality. But events prove that the idyll was an illusion. Hamlet, already shaken by his father's death, is outraged by his mother's o'erhasty marriage, which suggests that her apparent devotion to her first husband was a mask for adultery. The Ghost confirms his worst suspicions of Claudius. Next, he learns that his friends Rosencrantz and Guildenstern are in league with his enemies; and, finally, it seems that Ophelia, whom he has loved most of all, is his enemy too. Ironically, the surface of things has changed little: the court retains its air of domesticity, Claudius is plausibly avuncular and love is on everybody's lips. But nothing is as it seems, and the harmonious love of the past has been transformed by events beyond Hamlet's control into a force whose conflicting demands drive him to the brink of madness. His love for his father demands revenge; but this duty requires that he treat brutally the people whom, despite their treachery, he loves best. The hysteria which resembles madness is his response to this tragic dilemma: 'Hamlet . . . has a trick of fostering and aggravating his own excitements.'[21] He has too much imagination for his circumstances, and reacts to stress by working himself up to the point of instability. The 'wild and whirling words' in the Ghost scene are typical of this state of mind.

Irving gradually clarified his design. In 1874 the critics were confused and contradictory, some claiming him for the Goethe school and others for Schlegel and Coleridge. However, with the substitution of Ellen Terry for the comparatively ineffective Isabel Bateman in 1878, he was able to make a great deal more of Hamlet's love for Ophelia, and Georgina Pauncefort (Gertrude) rose to the occasion by giving a stronger sense of love between Hamlet and the Queen. Thus the internal conflict which caused his hysteria was clarified. At the same time, the audience seems to have found it easier to grasp Irving's conception of Hamlet's mental state. The instability was more marked, particularly in the Ghost scene, where significant textual restorations had been made. Moreover, one critic noted that 'a simulated insanity keeps pace with, and yet is distinct from a mental excitement near akin to absolute disease of the brain'.[22] Evidently Irving had found a way of getting across to some spectators the distinction between the 'antic disposition' and real hysteria. By 1884 this distinction was clearly marked; genuine disturbance was exhibited upon precisely those four occasions indicated by Gervinus: after the visitation of the Ghost, with Ophelia in the nunnery scene, in the Queen's closet, and at the grave.[23]

Performance

At Elsinore during the brief reign of Claudius everything is 'business as usual'. The spectator in a theatre is better able than a reader to appreciate this fact. The King does everything in his power to preserve appearances with stately ceremonies and gracious shows. Only Hamlet disturbs the smooth surface of court life, but after the death of Polonius Claudius strives desperately to make peace. Laertes's rebellion and Hamlet's return from the sea are serious setbacks, but the King soothes them both and channels their enmity into the ceremonious form of a duel. Beneath this fair seeming, however, lies a web of intrigue with Claudius at the centre pulling the strings. Irving took exceptional pains to emphasize this contrast.[24] The behaviour of the knot of watchers in the first scene served to undercut the meretricious pageantry of the throne-room scene which followed. Horatio, Marcellus and Barnardo met like conspirators. Francisco was discovered at centre on solitary sentry duty. Barnardo's 'Who's there?' came from the darkness offstage left. Francisco started, and challenged. Barnardo entered, saying 'Long live the King', and the sentry shaded his eyes as he enquired, 'Barnardo?' He sighed with relief on 'You come most carefully upon your hour', handed over his halberd and whispered the password of the day; now the guard had been formally changed and Barnardo set off on his beat at 'Get thee to bed, Francisco.' Crossing left, Francisco paused pensively and remarked that he was 'sick at heart'. Barnardo hesitated: had the other man seen the Ghost? He must not be allowed to talk. 'Have you had quiet guard?' he hinted. Reassured by the reply, he said goodnight, going off right. Before Francisco could exit, he heard Marcellus and Horatio, and challenged them. Horatio answered from the wings, and Marcellus completed the formula as he entered. Horatio kept out of sight, unwilling to be seen by one who was not in the conspiracy.[25] Marcellus waited for Francisco to go before he called Barnardo, who seemed surpised not to see Horatio: 'What, is Horatio here?' Horatio entered and the three men began to disuss the Ghost.

The theatre today is shy of ghosts. In modern productions 'the majesty of buried Denmark' is often represented by some technical contrivance – a shadow, a blinding light, Hamlet's reflection in a mirror. An audience is uncertain how to take the Ghost: is it real or imaginary? If it is the latter, Hamlet is perhaps already close to madness, but we may wonder why his friends share his hallucinations. Victorians had no such problem. In their theatres the spectre was always visible, played by an actor of dignified mien, costumed and made up as described in the text: in armour (I.i.60; I.ii.200), bearing a truncheon (I.ii.204), his visor open (230) to reveal a pallid (234) bearded countenance (240). Irving did not overturn this tradition because to him the objectivity of the Ghost was fundamental. It was the true spirit of Hamlet's beloved father, sent perhaps by a divine Providence intent upon purging Denmark of Claudius and his guilt, and endowed with supernatural power in addition to paternal authority.

Irving's staging was calculated to establish this interpretation. Salvini was impressed by the 'perfect' moonlight achieved by blending dim green light from the 'floats' (footlights) with dimmer blue from border battens (rows of overhead gas jets behind the proscenium arch).[26] Throughout the play, each time the Ghost appeared the floats were dimmed, distant 'Ghost music' was played, and a limelight illuminated the spectre. When Barnardo recalled that the first manifestation had occurred, 'The bell then beating one – ' (I.i.36), a large bell tolled. Hamlet likewise would encounter the spirit on the stroke of one (I.iv.38), and its appearance in Gertrude's closet, heralded by the bell and spooky music, must have had a spine-chilling effect.[27]

Casting reinforced the sense of the supernatural. Marcellus was a young soldier but Barnardo was a grizzled veteran who looked too reliable to go about imagining ghosts. Horatio's scepticism was impressive in the 1878 production, where he was played by Thomas Swinbourne, aged fifty-five, the Claudius of 1874. Some critics thought him a trifle old for a student, but one helpful soul suggested that he might have been a professor at the university.[28] The collapse of his disbelief was emphasized by Swinbourne's 'very solemn' delivery of the oath,

> Before my God, I might not this believe
> Without the sensible and true avouch
> Of mine own eyes.

(I.iv.58–9)

The Ghost was Tom Mead, noted for his saturnine face, sepulchral voice and dignified carriage. He wore the traditional armour, but his helmet, like those of the living soldiers, lacked the 'beaver' or visor mentioned by Horatio (I.ii.230): so, rather absurdly, he wore his ear-flaps up (see plate 1). In 1874 he had to cross near the footlights, because I.i. and I.iv were 'front scenes'. The castle was a drop in the 'second grooves', about twelve feet behind the proscenium. This was a convenient arrangement because the drop had only to be raised to reveal the full stage sets for scenes ii and iv; but unfavourable comparison with Tom Taylor's battlement set at the Crystal Palace persuaded Irving to hang the castle drop far upstage in the fifth grooves in 1878. About six feet downstage at left, a flat stood at an angle to the drop. It probably represented a tower; 'reveals' (thickness-pieces) behind its edges made it seem solid and three-dimensional. Light glowed in the windows and the star mentioned by Barnardo (I.i.35) shone in the sky. With the full depth of the stage available, Mead was able to enter from behind the tower and cross upstage, which prevented the audience from noticing his too too solid flesh. Irving rejected an innovation of Fechter's, whereby Horatio made the sign of the cross on 'I'll cross it, though it blast me' (127): this would have suggested that the Ghost might be evil. Swinbourne simply crossed in front of the spirit, which raised its truncheon as though to speak (139). Then a cock crowed. Here Irving introduced an innovation of his own. The Ghost retreated behind the tower. The 1874 text followed traditional theatrical economy by cutting to ''tis gone' (142), but in 1878 an actor doubling for Mead appeared near Barnardo, who cried ''Tis here'. Mead re-entered for an instant, Horatio too cried ''Tis here', and both spirits vanished. There could be no doubt that it was a real phantom.

Irving's handling of the next scene was indecisive. His interpretation of the play called for a rather domestic atmosphere, which would recall Hamlet's lost family idyll. Claudius, for example, was more uncle than king. But Irving fell between two stools by attempting to compromise between domesticity and formal ceremony. A march played on 'melodious but primitive harps'[29] ushered in a procession; lords and attendants preceding the royal family bowed and walked backwards. The occasion was made even more formal by Irving's

4 *Hamlet* I.ii, from the 1874 prompt-book (Harvard Theatre Collection)

6 Men in Chain mail discovered at back C.
       Order of Entrance all from R. U. E.
Ladies and 5 Courtiers bowing (backwards) down to R. 1. E.
4 other Pages backwards (bowing) to behind chairs L
Polonius to R C. up stage
King and Queen to Chairs L.
Hamlet to stool up L of Chairs
5 Ladies who fill up R. U. E.
Other courtiers who fill up R. 2 & 3 E.

inexpert management of the crowd, which was ranged opposite the dais with artificial symmetry (see plate 4). The ground plan was as symmetrical as the blocking, with the result that a vast and useless wedge of empty space divided the court: the courtiers were simply parked at an improbable angle and left to gaze resolutely at their monarch across the void.

Other features of the scene had a contrary effect. The set, which was used in both productions for most palace interiors, was rather domestic than imposing in character: 'the apartments of the palace all look habitable . . . They are usuable and used.'[30] Pageantry must have looked a little out of place there. Like the orderly procession, Claudius's set-speech thanking his council for their support (I.ii.1–16) was a show staged to give a legitimate appearance to his dubious claim to the throne and to excuse his technical incest.[31] But in Irving's text the crisply conducted diplomatic business with Voltemand and Cornelius was cut and Claudius turned immediately to the private concerns of Laertes and his own family.

The theme that emerged most clearly here was that of fair-seeming. Three of the actors who played Claudius in Irving's revivals were 'plausible' and pleasant enough in this scene to attract comment.[32] Probably they were instructed to emphasize the apparent sincerity of the man. Hamlet refused to participate in the show: 'He sits while others stand, not apart, however, in isolation, but in the midst.'[33] Amongst all these seemers, his face and 'inky cloak' alone reflected the true state of his heart, and his separateness showed that he was conscious of the distinction. He answered the Queen with angry vehemence, '*Seems*, madam? Nay, it is. I know not "seems".' When the King left the room with his retinue, Hamlet remained in his seat, a living rebuke to his uncle's feigned pleasure at his 'loving and fair' obedience. His isolation was emphasized by business added sometime after 1878. Young John Martin-Harvey played a Fool who stood close to the King throughout the scene. Irving rehearsed him.

I was to be the last to leave the stage after the general exodus of the courtiers before Hamlet's first soliloquy. On either side of me were Rosencrantz and Guildenstern. I was to turn to them and point to the melancholy form of Hamlet alone and disregarded. In rehearsing this for me he took the fool's bauble from my hand, and as he pointed at the place where Hamlet would be seated, his face suddenly creased into a thousand quaint, satirical, quizzical, half-contemptuous wrinkles.[34]

The Fool is an ambiguous figure, but Irving's meaning here is clear enough: the King and court are a mocking travesty of real feelings such as Hamlet's.

Irving laid the foundation for his interpretation of Hamlet's character and mental condition in this scene. It was the only glimpse the audience would get of the Prince in something like his natural state; melancholy and suspicion had obliterated his former happiness, of course, but he had not yet seen the Ghost. Here Irving would establish the traits which were to drive Hamlet almost to distraction under the impact of the Ghost's message, and his comparatively normal behaviour here provided almost the only criterion by which the extent of the impact could be measured. Hamlet's long silence while Claudius and Laertes spoke gave Irving an opportunity to use his wonderfully expressive face in the kind of detailed acting in which he excelled. Oddly enough, witnesses disagree as to exactly what he did. To some he seemed abstracted while others thought he listened and watched closely; one critic says he sat motionless, while others comment upon 'the tearing at the handkerchief', 'pushing back of the hair', 'the nervous fidgety ways' and 'the constant play of expression of his face' (see plates 5*a* and 5*b*).[35] It does not matter much. The impression conveyed was one of melancholy so marked and picturesque that illustrators chose to depict him in this scene more frequently than at any other point in the play. The full extent and cause of his mood did not become clear until he was left alone.

Hamlet remained slumped in his chair as he began the soliloquy, crushed by the burden of living: his 'O God, God' was 'heart-broken' at the thought of the 'weary, stale, flat and unprofitable' place his world had become in his eyes. But as he spoke of the cause, he stood up and began to pace, leaning against a column[36] on 'Heaven and earth, / Must I remember?' (142–3) His overactive imagination conjured up, unbidden, the picture of his mother as she had seemed with his father:

> Why, she would hang on him
> As if increase of appetite had grown
> By what it fed on.
>
> (143–5)

Coupled with his conviction that Gertrude had even then been playing her husband false, this image was intolerable. Trying to thrust it out of

5 *a,b*   Two impressions of Hamlet's melancholy, I.ii: *a*, caricature by Alfred Bryan; *b*, statue by E. Onslow Ford, R.A. (*a*, Harvard Theatre Collection; *b*, Guildhall Library, London)

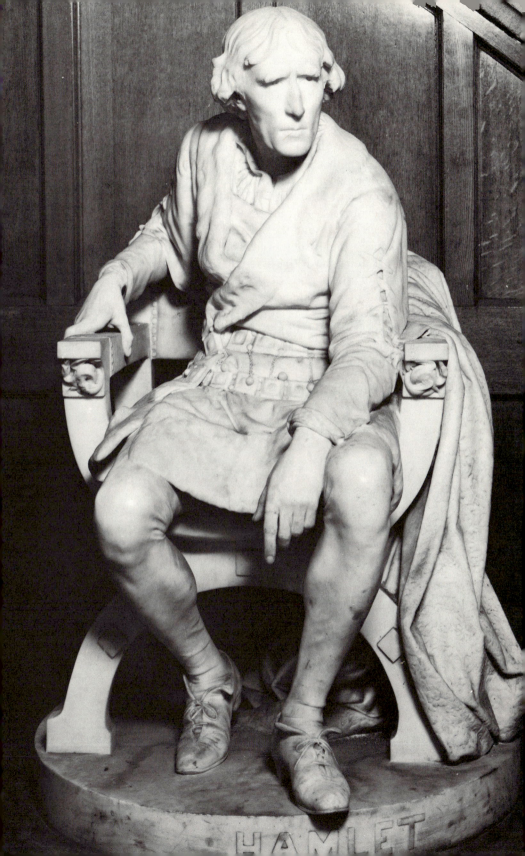

his mind, he 'slurred over' the usual 'point' at 'frailty thy name is woman' (146): Irving wanted his audience to listen to what Hamlet was saying, and he knew they could not do so if they were listening for their favourite quotations. He hesitated and groped for the comparison, 'no more like my father than I to – Hercules' (153) and then dropped another point in the last line, 'But break my heart, for I must hold my tongue.' As he concluded, Irving slumped into a chair again, to show that the soliloquy should be taken as an explanation of the melancholy reverie which he now resumed.

When Horatio and the others entered, he roused himself to give the audience a glimpse of the old Hamlet, friendly and gracious, automatically aware of the degree of familiarity appropriate to his own rank and to that of others. Soon he became abstracted again, barely seeming to follow the conversation when Horatio said he thought he had seen his father: 'Saw, who?' As Horatio replied, Hamlet awoke: at last events in the world around him had begun to relate to the reality which consumed his imagination. 'For heaven's sake, let me hear,' he urged, all attention.[37] He was appalled rather than amazed at Horatio's story; he had half suspected something of the kind. Passing out into the lobby upstage, he dragged out every syllable of the last lines,

> Foul deeds will rise,
> Though all the earth o'erwhelm them, to men's eyes,
>
> (257–8)

as though to suggest that 'there never could be an end to his horror and his rage'.[38]

The bogus domestic harmony of the throne room was mirrored by the scene of Laertes' departure (I.iii). There are two families in *Hamlet*, the fortunes of the lesser constantly reflecting those of the greater. Irving may not fully have understood this at first. In 1874, this scene was played, heavily cut, before a drop in the first grooves. It aroused no interest whatever. Isabel Bateman's Ophelia was 'sweet and gentle' but certainly nothing to spill ink over; Edmund Leathes (Laertes) was chiefly remarkable for 'an unfortunate habit of looking upwards like a fowl who has just drunk water'[39] and old W. H. Chippendale, who had played Polonius to nearly every Hamlet since Edmund Kean, was unlikely to offer any surprises. His precepts were omitted, but nobody complained. In 1878, however, Ellen Terry made

46

her Lyceum debut here and the scene came to life. She was thirty-one years old, but succeeded in conveying the suggestion that Ophelia was a girl of fifteen or sixteen. She used her unparalleled charm to give the character a winsome innocence which is seldom seen in our cynical times. Ophelia our contemporary has 'slept with' Hamlet;[40] she thinks Laertes' warning against him as priggish as it is belated, and responds with a subtextual irony which flatly contradicts her words. Her reciprocal advice is transformed into mockery. But Irving needed to establish a parallel between Hamlet's affectionate and trusting relationship with his family before his father's death and the apparent harmony in the Polonius household. For that he required an innocent Ophelia. Her countenance changed whcn Laertes first mentioned Hamlet; she paused shyly before she could speak his name: 'So please you, something touching – the Lord Hamlet' (89). When Laertes knelt for a blessing and to hear the restored precepts, Ophelia stood with her hand on his shoulder, 'gently enforcing with its delicate pressure' their father's words. At the mere suggestion that her brother might be involved in a quarrel (65–7) she gave 'a little frightened start'.[41] It was a touching family group. The children shared the father's fondness for moralizing, but it was neither fatuous nor comic: in an ordered society their small wisdom might easily guide them safely through life. But in the rotten state of Denmark they were all three doomed.

The next time the audience saw Polonius it would be as the betrayer of his family. Those few acting versions which retained II.i seldom went so far as to include Reynaldo. Irving cut the whole scene in 1874, but restored enough in 1878 to show that Polonius was setting a spy on his son. By contemporary critical standards the incident was an excrescence; it had no effect upon the action and introduced a superfluous character. Since Irving would hardly have broken with tradition, complicated the streamlined narrative of his acting version and paid an actor he did not need, without a very good reason, it is difficult to avoid the conclusion that in restoring this scene he displayed insight and a mode of critical thought that was considerably in advance of his time. Granville-Barker observed that Polonius's 'mean little embassy' establishes the tone of spying and duplicity that prevails in the next three acts.[42] In terms of Irving's interpretation, this duplicity was doubly significant because it occurred within the context of family life.

Polonius had last been seen as the centre of a family whose mutual love seemed to be founded upon trust; now, in the same room (the same set was used in both scenes) that trust was betrayed by the father. In the next scene Claudius would set spies upon his own 'son'. And in Irving's view, the basis of Hamlet's melancholy was the discovery that Gertrude, also a parent, had betrayed a family bond that was similarly based upon love and trust. The restoration in 1878 of Ophelia's account of Hamlet's distracted behaviour (77–100) reinforced this theme by focusing attention upon the emotional consequences of the Queen's falseness.

Meanwhile, however, the scene returned to the battlements for Hamlet's meeting with the Ghost (I.iv). Irving emphasized the son's love and reverence for his father, rather than his fear. Here Garrick gave a start of stark terror; his hat fell off, apparently dislodged when the hair of a trick wig stood on end. Irving swept his hat off as a sign of love and respect, and his cloak fell to the ground when he stretched out his arms as though to embrace the spirit. 'Angels and ministers of grace defend us!' (39) was whispered, and he went on to abjure the Ghost in 'tones of tremulous tenderness, filial reverence, and awe-struck submission'.[43] If the lines will not fully support such an interpretation, Irving was not the first to distort them; actors since Kean had stressed tenderness here, and it was traditional for Hamlet to kneel on 'I'll call thee Hamlet, / King, *father*, royal Dane' (44–5). Irving kept his feet, and reduced the rhetorical formality of the words by turning them into a series of separate pleas, 'each gathering strenuousness from the continued invincible silence of the apparition'. The climax was 'father'. A pause followed, and he began a new sentence, 'Royal Dane, O, answer me.' As the Ghost beckoned again and again, he seemed gradually to become hypnotized; 'I'll follow thee' (79) was spoken 'in the tones of one who is under a spell', as though there were supernatural power in the spirit's gesture (see plate 1).[44] Hamlet roused himself to shake off the restraining hands of his companions. Following the Ghost with his drawn sword, Irving avoided any definite business which could suggest suspicion that it might be a 'goblin damned'; Booth, for example, advanced his cruci-form sword-hilt. Horatio and Marcellus followed, picking up his hat and cloak on the way.

Irving was scholar enough to know that the stage direction which

48

locates the next scene (I.v) on 'Another part of the platform' is not Shakespeare's. He was probably the first English Hamlet to speak with the Ghost at a distince from the castle, reasoning that the lapse of time between midnight and dawn, coupled with the difficulty experienced by Horatio and Marcellus in finding their lord, suggests that he has been following the apparition for hours. This enhanced the supernatural effect. The Ghost seemed a spirit of great power; moreover, a new and impressively mysterious set could be used for the climactic scene. In 1874 this represented 'a close glen set in by mountains';[45] in the foreground two trees with a gauze stretched between them surmounted a rostrum disguised as a hillock (see plate 6a). At this period Irving never used a front curtain for scene changes, which took place in a blackout. At the beginning of a scene he could either bring up the lights to 'discover' actors who had taken their places in the dark, or they could make an entrance after the lights were turned on. The first method was seldom used in 1874; thus Mead had to cross the stage, mount the rostrum and take his place behind the gauze, all in full view of the audience. Under the limelight the gauze must have lent a ghostly blur to his appearance, but the effect was undoubtedly marred when he made his exit by climbing down from the rostrum and stalking off into the wings. This was all changed in 1878 (see plate 6b). The scene now took place on a rocky eminence suggested by Horatio's

> dreadful summit of the cliff
> That beetles o'er his base into the sea.

> (I.iv.70–1)

In the background was a wintry sea and, according to one witness, the distant walls of Elsinore.[46] Limelight glinted on the Ghost's helmet and dawn touched the sea. One unghostly scramble was avoided when the spectre was discovered already standing on the rocks, and the other when it sank from sight through a trap. After its exit an eerie effect was achieved by nudging the lights up a notch each time the Ghost spoke under the stage. Thus the gathering dawn brightened to emphasize each ghostly interjection.

In this scene Irving's efforts to communicate Hamlet's exhaustion, his love for his father and his mental anguish at the Ghost's message led him perilously close to melodrama. He adopted a crouching posture as he listened, and his exlamations were unrestrained: 'Alas,

Green Lime Light from 1st Flies, to remain till Ghost Exit

Gauzed tree

6 *a,b* The Ghost in 1874 (*left*) and 1878 (*right*), I.v, from the prompt-books (*a*, Harvard Theatre Collection; *b*, Shakespeare Centre Library, Stratford-upon-Avon)

poor ghost' was uttered as a sigh, 'Murder' as a yell and 'O, horrible! O, horrible! Most horrible!', a line borrowed from the Ghost on the authority of early editors, as a groan. When the spirit vanished, he collapsed on a fallen tree trunk and remained silent for an unconscionably long time before urging his sinews to bear him stiffly up (I.v.93–6). Rather illogically, some critics thought these lines made no sense unless Hamlet was standing up and striving to remain so. American reviewers in particular hated this business, and it is interesting to note that when Irving returned from his first transatlantic tour he no longer either crouched or fell.

In the Ghost scenes Hamlet's worst suspicions were confirmed. Love and pity for his father's spirit compelled him to redouble his condemnation of the adulterous mother whom he nevertheless loved. Aghast at this conflict of loyalties, he was at the same time exultant at the prospect of action against the hated Claudius. Enmeshed in a tangle of conflicting loves and loathings and bedevilled by his vivid

Hamlet

recollection of seeming love and trust treacherously betrayed, Hamlet worked himself up for the first time into a state of hysteria. In the soliloquy (I.v.92–112) and the dialogue that followed, Irving exhibited the psychological mechanism by which, in his view, Hamlet became distracted. It was a crucial moment if his reading of the character was to be understood. Hamlet would grow frenzied on several subsequent occasions, but here the process was plainest because he was free from the restraining presence of other people. In solitude Hamlet could express his emotions in extravagant behaviour which in turn redoubled his excitement. The grotesque business of entering his uncle's villainy on tablets snatched from his pocket was the climax of the outburst, and it showed how his mind was working:

Hamlet is evidently one of those who . . . find in solitude a licence and a cue for excitement, and who, when alone and under the influence of strong feelings, will abandon themselves to their fancies. Such men – though sane enough in society – will pace rooms like wild animals, will gaze into looking-glasses until they are frightened at the expression of their own eyes, will talk aloud . . . will do almost anything to find vent for emotions which their imagination is powerful enough to kindle, but not fertile or methodical enough to satisfy.[47]

51

Interrupted by the offstage cries of Horatio and Marcellus, Hamlet visibly composed himself, calling 'Hillo, ho, ho, boy! Come, bird, come' in a tone in which genuine anguish showed through the mockery. His agitation erupted at intervals through the mask of composure which he assumed before his friends. His mind was on the Ghost, and he was too exhausted to suppress either the 'wild and whirling words' or the dejection into which he suddenly subsided after uttering them. He was too preoccupied to make his apology to Horatio sound sincere,

> I am sorry they offend you, heartily;
> Yes, faith, heartily

(I.v.134–5)

but instead of being further offended, Horatio was 'very tender' in his reply, 'There's no offence, my lord.' Perhaps affected by this kindness, Hamlet sat for a moment and abandoned himself to grief. In 1874 he soberly stood in one place and made his companions swear a solemn oath. The wild gusting and backing of his moods was clearer in 1878 when Irving restored the quips at 'this fellow in the cellarage', and also Hamlet's rapid movements about the stage to escape the 'worthy pioner'.[48] The change deepened the sense of Hamlet's derangement; unable to control himself, perhaps he was disguising his instability beneath an 'antic disposition' which he was already trying out on his friends. By the time the oath had been taken, however, Hamlet had steadied. In the couplet,

> The time is out of joint. O cursed spite,
> That ever I was born to set it right

(188–9)

one critic thought he detected a new, sobering thought. Hamlet had remembered that he was a prince as well as a son; in avenging his father he would also be assuming responsibility for the State.[49] Irving showed that he was appalled by the burden, but he also took care to remind the audience of the filial love which forced Hamlet to assume it. 'Rest, rest, perturbèd spirit' was spoken with great tenderness; and as he made his exit, linking arms with Horatio and Marcellus on 'Nay, come, let's go together', he paused to look back at the spot where the Ghost had stood.

In Irving's view, Hamlet's moments of hysteria arose from the conflict of loyalties occasioned by the betrayal of love and trust. In the second act, more betrayals hemmed him in, isolated him, and emerged in his mind as a well-nigh universal principle of the deceptiveness of fair-seeming. Thus, after the Reynaldo scene in which Polonius betrayed his own family, Hamlet discovered the treachery of two friends he had loved. Rosencrantz and Guildenstern found him in a good humour, encouraged by the success with Polonius of his assumed madness. These two are often played as slimy rascals who could not possibly have been Hamlet's friends. Irving chose two pleasant young light comedians.[50] Hamlet greeted them joyfully, and affectionately put his arms around their necks as he asked why Fortune had sent them to prison in Denmark (II.ii.236). He frankly confided to them his melancholy, his bad dreams. But instead of returning confidence for confidence they flattered and chopped logic. Understanding came slowly, conveyed to the audience by a subtlety of inflection and mobility of expression which amazed many spectators. Suspicious now, Hamlet asked, 'Were you not sent for?' (280). Receiving no reply, he stamped impatiently, 'Come, come; nay, speak.' He read confusion in their faces, but could not quite believe that friends would prefer the King's favour to 'our ever-preserved love'. Drawing them to him he launched an appeal based on affection. Love demands honesty: 'If you love me, hold not off' (299). When they admitted that they had indeed been sent for, Hamlet gave a great sigh. Love and trust seemed to have won, and he returned to frank confession in the great prose speech on splendid creation and his inability to value it. No man would speak so before people he did not trust. And then he caught them smirking at each other. The critic who objected to his 'sudden and uncalled-for tone of insolence' surely missed the point.[51] In the sniggering of his schoolfellows Hamlet saw love and trust again betrayed; his response was directed against all the betrayers and false-seemers who surrounded him, at betrayal and false-seeming themselves. 'It is impossible to convey,' wrote Clement Scott, 'the effect of this change as indicated by the actor. It was electrical, and admirably effective.'[52] The rest of the scene was a rout, the two courtiers cowering before Hamlet's irony which extended beyond them to their royal patron: referring to the players, he said: 'He that plays the king shall be welcome; *his* Majesty *shall* have tribute of me' (328–9). The final welcome was spoken as an insult: 'Your hands, come then. Th'appurtenance of welcome is fashion and ceremony' (379–80). As Polonius approached to announce the players, Hamlet leaned upon his school-fellows' shoulders. The gesture recalled his affectionate greeting of a few minutes before; now, however, it denoted contempt.

Hamlet had been learning to distrust appearances, particularly of seeming love which may be feigned. He welcomed the little party of players both because it was their honest business to pretend to be what they were not, and because their genuine feelings at feigned situations served as a parody of life at court, where real situations evoked only false feelings. When Hamlet said, 'Dost thou hear me, old friend' (547), he waved away Guildenstern and indicated that he wanted the First Player. The Hecuba speech seemed to give him the idea for the Mousetrap stratagem, for while it was very indifferently delivered, he was much 'struck' by it and at the end remained 'abstracted'. Thus the final couplet of the soliloquy was pronounced as the natural culmination of a train of thought rather than a sudden idea. But Irving accompanied it with a famous and original piece of business. Upstage right there was a practicable column, solidly built and braced to prevent wobbling. Placing his tablets against it, Hamlet began excitedly to scribble ideas for the 'dozen or sixteen lines'. Martin-Harvey remembers that he seemed to use letters a foot high.[53]

The third act opened with a conference of the fair-seemers, intriguing against Hamlet. Rosencrantz and Polonius told the King and Queen about the entertainment scheduled for the evening. The room had already been arranged for the play, but if any critic noticed the redundancy he did not record it. Ophelia stood beside her father; her obedience and silence were plainly attributable to youthful innocence. She had no reason to doubt that these people meant what they said; like her, they seemed to have Hamlet's best interests at heart. In an article on this scene, Irving says that Ophelia should be unaware of the 'lawful espials', and reviews show that Terry played it that way.[54] The lines of Claudius and Polonius referring to that part of their plan were spoken aside (III.i.32–4, 43–4, 46–9). Ophelia left the stage, and the eavesdroppers withdrew – in 1874 to the wings, but in 1878, with an irony that was surely intentional, behind the curtains set up for the Players. Irving argued that since in Q1 and Q2 their 'exeunt' followed Hamlet's entrance, he must know of their presence. The moment when Hamlet becomes aware that he is observed must always be a moot point with actors, and many have used it to explain the apparent change of mood when he asks Ophelia, 'Where's your father?' (131). Irving's suggestion was novel, but it made little difference in his interpretation. He believed that Hamlet is so preoccupied with 'sublimer matters' that he forgets. 'It is when he perceives the spies that he remembers he is watched.' This occurred at the usual moment.

Irving sat in a chair upstage. There was no trace of declamation in the soliloquy, which was spoken in an undertone. Evidently Hamlet was going through another phase of depression and self-disgust, following the excitement of the previous scene. Ophelia's entry interrupted a new train of thought beginning 'Soft you now' (88); he broke off when he saw her, and his eyes lit up: 'The fair Ophelia.' It was already obvious that he loved her.

Romantics that they were, Victorian actors were inclined to play the 'love-interest' in *Hamlet* to the hilt. After Edmund Kean, few attempted to show that if Hamlet had ever loved Ophelia, he no longer did; Booth tried it, but nobody believed him. Irving was accused of turning the play into a 'love poem', and indeed the poses in plate 7 look like something out of *Romeo and Juliet*. But while love of Ophelia was important to his interpretation, another theme ran through this scene. A hostile critic observed that Hamlet so plainly longed to take Ophelia in his arms that Claudius's remark after his exit, 'Love? His affections do not that way tend' (165) made no sense.[55] Like Polonius, the critic had neither listened to the words nor noticed that Hamlet *did not* embrace Ophelia. To Irving, that was the whole point. Much shrewder than his counsellor, the King had observed that Hamlet was torn between two emotions. One of them was love, but the other had won. That was why Claudius was worried: what could it be, and was it a threat?

It was, of course. Hamlet rejected Ophelia because she hindered his vengeance. In her beauty and his love for her he saw a trap. Beauty destroys virtue, and thus betrays love and trust. Nobody can long remain both fair and honest. 'Hamlet's mother's beauty had been her snare, had tempted her adulterous lover,' Irving wrote.[56] Hamlet's discovery of the spies persuaded him that he was right; his feelings for Ophelia were dangerous. She must go to a nunnery where she could do no harm. The main theme of his words, then, emphasized by the reiterated 'Get thee to a nunnery', was not love but a revulsion so strong that his love gave way before it.

This was Irving's greatest scene. Taking advantage of his exceptional power in the portrayal of conflicting emotions, he stunned the audience with a hurricane of passion. Over the years he elaborated the effect by increasing Hamlet's longing for Ophelia and the effort of will required to tear himself away. When she offered to return the casket of remembrances, 'the hands that repulsed her petitioning hands trembled with passionate longing'; against his will, 'his soul goes out to her; his face is alive with passion'.[57]

Here Hamlet gave way for the second time to hysterical excitement. As in the scene with the Ghost, it was the thought, tragically mistaken but profoundly felt, that Ophelia's beauty and innocence were not what they seemed that again shook his reason. He loved her, yet she was false. The conflict was more than he could bear, and confronted with her he assumed the antic disposition as a defence. To her gentle enquiry, 'How does your honour this many a day?' he replied 'well, well, well' and tried to hurry away, only to be recalled by her next speech. Appalled by his own feelings when she gave him the casket, Hamlet put on his mad disguise: 'Ha, ha! Are you honest?' Irving wrote, 'It is at this point that the scene takes its sudden and violent transition.'[58] When Hamlet caught sight of Polonius he did not explode with fury as he had done when he detected the treachery of his schoolfellows, but asked with tears 'welling up' in his eyes, 'Where's your father?' The perfect innocence of her reply he misconstrued as evidence of her accomplishment in deceit. He loosed his shaft at the old man in his ambush and then, with a marked transition, his pretended madness became real hysteria. 'His first sudden "farewell" is a frantic ebullition of all-encompassing, all-racking pain,' wrote one observer. In later years, Irving elaborated here: 'with wild gestures and a burst of hysterical laughter' he rushed out of the room. A moment later he was back, 'laden, as it were, with a new armful of hastily gathered missiles of contumely'.[59] In 1878 his love was visible beneath the tirade; nevertheless, he worked himself up into an hysterical passion and chased her about the room with his abuse, making his final exit in a rush of invective. In 1885, however, he had reconsidered and adopted the Edmund Kean exit business which Hazlitt called 'the finest commentary that was ever made on Shakespeare': his last 'To a

7 Terry and Irving in the 'Nunnery' scene, III.i, 1878, by Edward H. Bell (Mander and Mitchenson Theatre Collection)

nunnery, go' was full of 'melting pathos'; when he reached the wings he paused and returned to fall at Ophelia's feet and kiss her hand. As Ophelia, Ellen Terry's reaction to the storm was a heart-broken lament for Hamlet's ruined mind: 'She thinks only of the wreck that fate has made of her beloved.'[60] No amount of self-pity would have carried such pathos.

The action flowed straight on to the play scene without a break. Hamlet returned with the First Player (not with three players as indicated in Qq). He was suddenly sane again, poised and at ease. Ellen Terry says, 'Nearly all Hamlets in that scene give away the fact that they are actors, and not dilettanti of royal blood.'[61] Irving 'button-holed' the Player and modestly offered his views on art; yet there could

8   The 'Mousetrap' scene, III.ii: Hamlet with Ophelia's peacock fan, 1875 (University of Victoria)

be no doubt that his instructions were commands. Night fell as he talked. There was a moment of stasis as he drew strength from Horatio, the only ally he had left, and then the court entered for the play.

This was another ceremonial occasion like the throne-room scene. Every available personage was used to swell the crowd, from the Fool to Francisco. Guards and noblemen carried torches, and harps again played the Danish march. The music reached a crescendo on Hamlet's 'I must be idle: get you a place' (III.ii.92) – already excitement was in the air – and continued *piano* through the preliminary cut-and-thrust with the King and Polonius.

In 1874 the improvised stage was erected in an archway upstage centre. The courtiers were ranged awkwardly against the wings on both sides as though the centre of the stage were a minefield too dangerous to venture upon despite the fact that it offered the best view. Hamlet lay at centre stage, his head towards Ophelia and his back to the play; thus the audience could see his face clearly so long as he watched Claudius and not the players. The King's face would also be visible when he averted his gaze from the disturbing spectacle upstage.[62] In 1878 the same set was used, but a trestle and rough proscenium were set up behind the dais at left, which served as a kind of forestage; thus the court could be grouped more naturally at right, and Hamlet could see the stage without changing his own position.

This was such a celebrated scene that small alterations in the traditional business attracted attention out of all proportion to their significance; while they are interesting, these have little direct bearing upon the core of Irving's interpretation, and it will be useful to dispose of them first. There was a tradition that has been traced back as far as 1735 that Hamlet takes Ophelia's fan and uses it as a screen, watching the King from behind it. Irving did this – plate 8 shows him shielding his face with it – but he astonished everyone by using a fan of peacock feathers, which are regarded as the worst of luck in the theatre. His motive is found in the second ballad-verse Hamlet recites after Claudius's exit:

For thou dost know, O Damon dear,
  This realm dismantled was
Of Jove himself; and now reigns here
  A very, very – peacock.

(287–90)[63]

59

The fan suggested the word, and then he threw it away in disgust.

Many Hamlets before and after Irving crawled and slithered towards the King during the climactic speech, "A poisons him in the garden for his estate . . .' (267–70), a 'vulgar trick' which Dover Wilson very properly condemns.[64] Irving adopted this business about 1883. But in 1874 he kept his place until the King rose and fled; then he leaped to his feet and flung himself into the vacant throne. This brought down the house, of course; but sensational effects aside, it was surely calculated to remind the audience that Hamlet remembered the burden which he had reluctantly assumed after meeting the Ghost: his duty as a Prince to oust a usurper who had 'Popped in between th'election and [his] hopes'. This may seem a side-issue, but in fact it concerned another aspect of the betrayal of love. Hamlet believes that Claudius has been able to succeed only because he has married the Queen. Thus she has unnaturally helped a 'cutpurse' to steal the diadem which belongs rightfully to her son.

Many thought this scene the climax of the play. Here the conflicts that were destroying Hamlet were seen in action. Excited by the project of exposing Claudius, he had also to contend with anxiety: would the plan work? The greatest hazard was his own tension, which he could scarcely keep in check. Success hung upon his ability to seem unconcerned. As usual he cloaked his jitters beneath an antic disposition. Before the court entered he was obviously anxious, but afterwards he seemed alternately bored and gay. His duty compelled him to treat Ophelia callously. The bawdy was all cut, but Isabel Bateman used the remaining lines to convey an impression of dejection which obviously derived from the nunnery scene. She was 'ill disposed for Hamlet's banter' and her 'you are merry, my lord' was reproachful. When Ellen Terry played Ophelia, Hamlet's gibes reduced her to tears. Commenting upon the Prologue, she said, ''Tis brief, my lord.' His reply, 'As woman's love', made her 'droop' and drop her fan; he offered it 'satirically' and saw her weeping. For a moment Irving showed how Hamlet's necessary cruelty was rending him in two; he pressed his face to the floor, 'giving vent to one heart-throb of grief'. Then the play began and instantly he was 'all attention, more highly strung to his purpose than before, more feverishly impatient of the climax'.[65]

The performance contained no surprises for Hamlet, because the dumbshow was omitted: Ophelia's 'What means this?' and the reply, 'Miching mallecho; it means mischief' probably referred only to the 'wail of music' which heralded the Prologue.[66] Hamlet's tension mounted as the heavily curtailed playlet unfolded; one observer noted that he seemed to be biting pieces out of Ophelia's fan.[67] He contained himself with difficulty until the King rose and fled. The courtiers all whispered 'Lights, lights, lights!' and vanished in a flash. Then the pent-up emotions exploded in a wild shriek of triumph, and he darted across the stage to the throne, shouting after the King, 'What, frighted with false fire?' This was the most violent outburst of Hamlet's hysteria in the play. As before it was a self-induced response to the intolerable conflicts of the situation, particularly with regard to Ophelia.

When Irving adopted the crawling business, Hamlet's self-control broke down earlier. The King's attention was arrested by Lucianus's speech; seeing this, Hamlet crept towards the throne, reciting the words along with the Player and sometimes, it seems, drowning him out. These were the lines which he had written. 'The story is extant, and written in choice Italian' was shouted. 'Innocence itself,' complained one critic, 'would fly in terror from the panther-like presence of the infuriated Hamlet.' But of course Claudius had already blenched. Irving mounted the throne, 'laughing and gasping in mad and reckless joy', and stood flourishing his sword. Then he chanted the doggerel 'in a tempest of delirium'.[68]

Rosencrantz and Guildenstern found him in a state of high excitement. In the scene with them and with Polonius, Irving had to make one of those crucial choices upon which the whole tendency of an interpretation turns. The tone of the soliloquy at the end is resolute, even (literally) bloodthirsty:

> 'Tis now the very witching time of night,
> When churchyards yawn, and hell itself breathes out
> Contagion to the world. Now could I drink hot blood
> And do such bitter business as the day
> Would quake to look on. Soft, now to my mother.
> (III.ii.396–400)

The contrast between this and the introspective self-contempt of the earlier soliloquies is hard to overlook in any performance. Hamlet speaks, however, not of immediate action against Claudius but of his mother. The question that must be answered is, has Hamlet allowed himself to be deflected from his purpose by his schoolfellows and Polonius with their summons from the Queen? If so, he has been betrayed by his excitement; the soliloquy is futile sabre-rattling, and his failure to kill the praying King is disastrous proof that he has lost his way. His attempt to correct this error results in the death of Polonius, which gives Claudius his chance to send Hamlet abroad and then, fatally, to turn Laertes' hand against him. This interpretation emphasizes the mechanisms by which the plot unfolds. Hamlet's character – specifically, his infirmity of purpose – is essentially subsidiary. Thus his state of mind in the fifth act, whatever it may be, is of secondary importance because it has no direct influence upon events.

Irving chose the alternative view. He was concerned before all else with the character of Hamlet, whose mental and spiritual state in Act V, and especially at his death, was therefore of the first importance. Gertrude's betrayal was the source of her son's misery, and in the closet scene they effected a partial reconciliation; the past could not be forgotten, but at least Gertrude repented. Above all, she demonstrated that her love for Hamlet was genuine, and that in the coming conflict between her husband and son she would be on the latter's side. There would be no more betrayals. Thus in the last act, Hamlet, if not at peace within himself, was relieved of the chief source of the conflict which had shaken his reason. Only Ophelia could disturb him now. The rest he left to the Providence which had sent him his father's ghost.

In the scene with Rosencrantz, Guildenstern and Polonius, then, Hamlet was not diverted from his purpose. His mother was the immediate objective: the King was in full retreat and could wait. Thus when the sycophants entered, insisting that he report to the Queen, he was as much amused as annoyed. He saw that they were trying to manipulate him, but with the aid of his assumed madness he ran rings around them: 'He plays, in brief, on them: and so far from showing violent resentment, he indulges only in careless banter.'[69] Indeed it was Guildenstern who lost his temper when pressed to play the recorder, only to be obliterated by Hamlet's explanation:

Why, look you how unworthy a thing you make of me! You would play upon me; you would seem to know my stops.

(III.ii.371–3)

Hamlet broke the recorder across his knee when he exclaimed, ''Sblood, do you think I am easier to be played on than a pipe?' and threw away the pieces when he concluded, 'though you may *fret* me, you cannot *play* upon me'. Then, angry for a moment, he proceeded to the passage interpolated from IV.ii, ominously warning them that when the King had used them up, 'you shall be dry again – you shall! You shall.'[70] 'Leave me, *friends*' was of course spoken sarcastically. At his exit Irving took a lighted torch from the practicable column, perhaps to symbolize the moral light he was bringing to his mother.

The short conference between Claudius and his confederates (III.iii.1–35) was played only in 1878, and then in an abbreviated form. It was usual to play in full the King's attempt to pray (III.iii.36–71), but Irving restored Hamlet's debate with himself, beginning 'Now might I do it pat, now 'a is praying' (73–91). This speech was so frequently omitted in the theatre that Tom Taylor thought it necessary to quote it all in his review. Taylor thought it a mere excuse for delay on the part of 'a disposition too kindly to do a cruel action, even when cruelty is demanded by justice', but E. R. Russell disagreed. There was no point in restoring the speech unless Hamlet meant what he said. Irving spoke 'in a tone of vehement savagery'[71] and it is likely that he intended it as a continuation of the mood established in the foregoing soliloquy: he still carried the torch. He would settle with Gertrude first. Initially the scene was played in red limelight, but moonlight was substituted in 1878. The drop representing the King's closet hung in the first grooves; meanwhile, carpenters erected the Queen's closet, the only box set used in the 1874 production. On opening night the unfortunate Swinbourne prayed to the accompaniment of 'a chorus of hammering and shouting behind'.

The scene in the Queen's closet caused great excitement because Irving invented new business to illustrate Hamlet's line 'Look here upon this picture, and on this' (III.iv.54). Since it had little real bearing on his reading of the scene, I shall dispose of this tempest in a teacup before proceeding. From the time of Betterton there had been dispute as to the form the counterfeit presentments of Gertrude's two husbands should take. There were two basic possibilities: portraits on the wall and miniatures. In Irving's time, Hamlet usually wore a miniature of the old King, while his mother sported Claudius's picture in little. Hamlet presented them side by side for comparison. Irving dispensed with portraits altogether; when he spoke of them he pointed towards the empty air downstage, allowing the audience to decide whether they were hung on the 'fourth wall' or painted by Hamlet's imagination.[72] The popular comedian, George Belmore, appearing at the Princess's in a burlesque pointedly entitled *Hamlet the Hysterical*, satirized this business by playing his closet scene with two empty picture frames.[73]

The closet scene was a great turning-point in Hamlet's life. Since his mother's remarriage he had been isolated from her, his over-vivid imagination tormented by the thought that she had been false to his father while he lived. How, armed with the certain knowledge that Claudius was his father's murderer, he burst into her room in a frenzy of indignation, uncertain perhaps of what he meant to do, but determined neither to use unnatural violence nor to let his love for her weaken his resolution to be cruel. He found Gertrude posed in a chair, clothed in the semblance of virtuous authority, ready to rebuke him for offending his 'father'. The hypocrisy of this fiction probed deep into the root cause of his agitation, and he burst out, 'Mother, *you* have my father much offended' (III.iv.11). Seeing that she persisted in maintaining the pretence, he rubbed her nose in ugly reality:

> You are the Queen, your husband's brother's wife,
> And, would it were not so, you are my mother.
>
> (16–17)

Now she was on her high horse. She swept towards the door to call 'those . . . that can speak'; the interview was in peril of ending before Hamlet could break down her pose. He interrupted and caught her arm, speaking calmly in order to give no cause for alarm; to some her sudden fear seemed unjustified ('Thou wilt not murder me?'). Unlike Macready and Fechter, Irving had made no implied threat by laying his drawn sword on a table when he entered. Now Polonius called for help behind the arras. They were spying on him again. He rushed diagonally across the room and stabbed the eavesdropper; one critic objected that Hamlet lifted the arras first and hence could hardly be in doubt as to the identity of his victim.[74]

As Hamlet began to wring her heart, Gertrude emerged as a 'weak, sensuous, affectionate' woman 'more sinned against than sinning'. Her amazement when she echoed 'As kill a king?' cleared her of complicity

in the murder. Her 'awe-stricken' face was 'charged with tears' when
Hamlet forced her to look objectively at her faults. Throughout his
tirade, his love for her was obvious; not that he moderated his
denunciations, for he felt a 'solemn obligation to say such things to
Gertrude as it must chill the blood of a son to think', but because it was
plain that he acted out of love. The conflict cost him great pain, which
Irving expressed in part by wringing his shirt bosom 'as effectively as
he does his mother's heart', a rather stagey gesture.[75] As always, the
strain imposed by his internal conflict nudged Hamlet towards hysteria; the 'hissing tones of invective' in which he began gave way to
fury as he grew more excited. Gertrude broke down on

> O Hamlet, speak no more.
> Thou turn'st mine eyes into my very soul
>
> (89–90)

but by now he was standing over her, too agitated to stop. Opposite his
next speech,

> Nay, but to live
> In the rank sweat of an incestuous bed,
>
> (92–3)

Ellen Terry wrote in her study-book, 'Working it up tremendous-
ly – excitedly – *The laws of Climax*'. Only the sudden appearance of
the Ghost forestalled an explosion; it must have seemed as though the
hand of Providence had intervened to bring about the reconciliation
which would set Hamlet free to act.

Irving meant the audience to be as certain of the Ghost's authenticity in the closet scene as on the platform, but his interpretation of 'his
habit as he lived' (136) caused some doubt. Following the Q1 stage
direction, 'Enter the Ghost in his night gowne', Mead wore a 'dressing
gown of dark stuff'.[76] In this domestic scene perhaps Irving meant to
remind the audience that the spirit had been father as well as king, but
the altered costume suggested a change in the Ghost; was it a hallu-
cination this time? If not, surely Gertrude should be able to see what
was visible to Horatio, Marcellus and Barnardo. Irving clarified his
meaning by introducing some really radical business at the Ghost's
exit. When Hamlet said, 'Look where he goes even now out at the
portal' (137), the Queen glimpsed the apparition and screamed. Even
this was ambiguous; *The Times* wondered whether the Ghost was
really there, or had Hamlet infected Gertrude with his hysteria?

Terry's study-book shows that this business was dropped in 1878; when Hamlet asked the Queen, 'Do you see nothing – there?', pausing before the last word, she replied 'Nothing at all; yet all that is I see' (132–3), turning and looking straight at the phantom. Perhaps Irving anticipated Dover Wilson in thinking that the Ghost is invisible to her because she is too sinful to see it.[77]

The Ghost's command that Hamlet step between his mother and her fighting soul calmed him. From now on he was tender, pleading rather than bullying. When he implored her,

> Mother, for love of grace,
> Lay not that flattering unction to your soul,
> That not your trespass but my madness speaks
>
> (145–7)

he knelt and buried his face in her lap like a child learning his prayers. She was his mother again. Gertrude wept bitterly when she said, 'O Hamlet, thou hast cleft my heart in twain' (157); and now, instead of scolding, he folded her head in his arms with 'an *ocean* of tenderness'.[78] Many earlier Hamlets had shrunk from the Queen's blessing, but Irving raised her when she kneeled at his line, 'I'll blessing beg of you' (173) and may have kissed her. Giving her a shaded candle (perhaps symbolic) he sent her to bed. His concluding couplet was thus spoken *solus*:

> I must be cruel only to be kind.
> Thus bad begins, and worse remains behind.
>
> (179–80)

He crossed to the arras and began to drag the corpse of Polonius towards the door.

Hamlet's attitude to Polonius in this scene drew some criticism. He did not seem to react very strongly when he discovered whom he had killed, but the lines spoken over the body of the 'wretched, rash, intruding fool' were spoken 'tenderly', and in the calmer mood before his exit he returned to the subject of the dead man with emotion: 'For this same lord, / I *do* repent' (173–4). It was probably Irving's intention that Hamlet should treat Ophelia's irritating father with some tolerance, but Chippendale made this difficult for him. Many of the old man's sillier speeches were cut, apparently out of deference to the actor's dignity.[79] In 1874 this made Hamlet's sarcasms sound like uncalled-for rudeness; but Ellen Terry, whose experience was limited to the 1878 revival, maintains that he was never rude to 'old Bromide', whom he treated as a 'dear, funny old simpleton'. Henry Howe, the old star actor who played Polonius from 1881, blended dignity with a delightful pottiness which allowed Irving to stress the eccentricity of Hamlet's lampooning rather than its bitter irony: he was even able to inject a note of 'tenderness' into his teasing on 'Am I not i' th' right, old Jephtha?' (II.ii.419). Polonius is a difficult character. If he is allowed to become a clown the audience misses the significance of his treacheries and is shocked by his death. Irving followed tradition by cutting Hamlet's 'I'll lug the guts into the neighbour room' in the closet (213), but he knew that a little sordidness went a long way with squeamish Victorians, and it must not be forgotten that the lugging itself was performed. Evidently he had no intention of either senti-mentalizing Polonius or softening Hamlet's cruelty; a Hamlet who could utter the 'Now might I do it pat' speech would not flinch at a few guts, no matter whose father they belonged to. And here, surely, was the point. Hamlet had been cruel to Ophelia. As a matter of duty it had been necessary, but the cruelty was no less damaging for being committed unwillingly. The same was true of the death of Polonius. To Hamlet it was only a regrettable consequence of the hysteria caused by his own suffering, but it meant pain and madness to Ophelia. The next act was concerned entirely with the results of that unconsidered act.

There can be no question that Irving's acting version was reprehen-sible in its omission of the first four scenes of Act IV. But *Hamlet* was too long for representation in full on the Victorian stage, and while these scenes did not necessarily contradict Irving's interpretation, they certainly would have complicated it. In his version, Hamlet did not appear at all in Act IV, but the spectator would scarcely have been aware that he had been sent to England until the King received the letter announcing his return (IV.vii.43–53). In his last version, even this was cut, which presumably indicates that Irving thought it inessential for his reading. If there is a change in Hamlet before the fifth act – if he abandons irresolution and self-disgust to commit himself to the guidance of Providence – it may take place during the voyage. He certainly believes that heaven has been ordinant in his safe and speedy return (V.ii.48). But even in the closet scene he seems to feel the hand of God:

For this same lord,
I do repent, but heaven hath pleased it so
To punish me with this, and this with me
That I must be their scourge and minister.

(III.iv.173–6)

As I have shown, the turning point was Hamlet's reconciliation with
Gertrude, an event prompted by the possibly providential interven-
tion of the Ghost. No second change of direction was needed unless
Hamlet should relapse into his former mood, and that is exactly what
he would have appeared to do in his soliloquy after meeting Fortinbras
(IV.iv.32ff). The whole episode seemed redundant.

The fourth act began with Ophelia's mad scene. Ellen Terry was
picturesquely pathetic rather than horrifyingly real; as Victorians liked
to put it, she was 'ideally' pathetic and beautiful. Clad in the simplest
of white costumes, which looked like and essentially was a bedsheet
trimmed with rabbit, with 'her fair, clustering hair, and a lily branch in
her hand' she resembled 'a Pre-Raphaelite saint or a Madonna by
Giovanni Bellini'.[80] Modern readers will no doubt react with contempt to such descriptions; madness, after all, is seldom pretty. But
Shakespeare does not call for ugly realism here; Ophelia must justify
Laertes when he says,

Thought and affliction, passion, hell itself,
She turns to favour and to prettiness.

(IV.v.186–7)

A sordidly realistic portrayal of Ophelia mad, if well played, can
temporarily turn an audience against Hamlet. Terry depicted a mind
'so shattered as to be beyond hope or help', but she took care to
exclude the squalid and painful. For Victorian tastes, this meant that
the bawdier songs had to be cut: her characterization was 'marred by
no touch of the sensuality which some students of Shakespeare insist
upon attributing . . . to the character of Ophelia'.[81]

Terry sought the form that Ophelia's madness should take in an
asylum. 'I noticed a girl gazing at the wall,' she writes. 'I went between
her and the wall to see her face. It was quite vacant, but the body
expressed that she was waiting, waiting. Suddenly she threw up her
hands and sped across the room like a swallow.' Sudden transitions
were the key. Ophelia's songs 'would begin with a bright rippling
laugh, and then suddenly fade into a plaintive wail of unutterable woe'.

One of these laughs can be heard on the recording she made of part of the scene in 1911: 'I would give you some violets: but they all withered when my father died. They say – th–they say he made a good end, a good end. [*Laugh then sings*] For bonny sweet Robin is all my joy' (IV.v.182–5).[82]

Her manner was gay when she asked, 'Where is the beauteous majesty of Denmark?' Then she sang quickly,

> How should I your truelove know
> From another one?
> By his cockle hat and staff
> And his sandal shoon.
>
> (23–6)

The last two lines were sung 'cunningly and *very* brightly shrewd'. The next song, two lines later, was sung slowly, with a sad wail. Her mood changed to suit the words: beside 'And there is pansies, that's for thoughts', Terry wrote 'Think – *Think* – Remember.' There were several 'fitful gleams of reason' when she seemed on the point of recognizing Laertes, and a touch of 'reason in madness' when she caught sight of the King and said, as though startled, 'Ha! It is the false steward [here she imitated a crude seducer "with becking and nods and wreathed smiles"] that stole his master's daughter' (171–2).[83]

Irving evidently regarded the remainder of the act as mere mechanism, and cut it more and more heavily in successive acting versions so as to give all the requisite information in the least possible time. The scene in which Horatio receives Hamlet's letter was omitted, and the last scene conveyed the broad outlines of the plot against him and the news of Ophelia's death. Its sole distinction lies in the fact that it was the only scene which passed entirely without critical comment.[84]

It is both fitting and ironic that the last scene of *Hamlet* should begin in a graveyard; fitting, because a death-theme pervades the play, and ironic because now Hamlet is free of his morbid preoccupation. The gravediggers discuss suicide, whereas Hamlet, when he enters, thinks of death but longs for it no more. The change in him is profound. In Irving's interpretation, the suicidal response to his situation had passed because the reconciliation with Gertrude had removed its cause. Now Hamlet would exhibit a new stoicism which was emphasized in the acting version, perhaps more than the text warrants. Perhaps Irving underestimated the clowns' importance; their dialogue before Hamlet's entrance was sometimes cut. But Lyceum audiences did not suffer Shakespearean clowns gladly.

At the graveside, Hamlet was brought for the last time to a state of hysterical excitement. Irving prepared this climax carefully. The scene was calm and beautiful; in 1874 a conventional set of wings and backdrop depicted a rural churchyard. It was noticed that this scene had been used the year before in *Eugene Aram*. The yew tree under which Aram dies was removed from centre stage, and the drop with its 'distant view of Knaresborough' was no doubt replaced by something more appropriate, but a church wing at left in the third grooves was a giveaway. A different church seems to have occupied the same position in the new arrangement adopted in 1878. Now the cemetery stood on a hill before a 'most picturesque' view of castle-capped headlands and the sea. Platforms upstage represented the hill.

'God's acre' is closed in by a simple country road, which rises up beyond it, and reaches its highest point at the gate from which the pathway descends almost to Ophelia's grave. Hamlet and Horatio enter along the road, the while the clown is singing at grave making, and it is at the gate, while watching the latter throw up the earth and skulls, the first words are spoken. Then saying 'I will speak to this fellow,' he approaches the grave-side. Could anything be more natural than this?[85]

Hamlet talked to the gravediggers with 'gentle philosophic melancholy lightened by a tinge of amusement',[86] indicative of his new peace of mind. The speech on Yorick's skull (V.i.185–97) was staged virtually as a soliloquy, since Horatio turned upstage and conversed inaudibly with the clown while Hamlet stood a little apart. This would emphasize the altered attitude to death, by contrasting this speech with the suicidal soliloquies earlier in the play.

The calm landscape was complemented by a ceremonious funeral; it cannot have been at all clear how Hamlet interpreted as 'maimed rites' this 'imposing representation of Catholic ceremonial'. The time was evening – the 1874 prompt-book contains the note 'red mediums on' – and in his Preface to the 1878 text Frank Marshall explained that suicides had customarily been buried at that hour, but not how the audience was supposed to know this. On the face of it, the funeral was bad theatre. Irving apparently indulged a gratuitous love of processions just when the audience would become impatient for the end, and indeed there were complaints. But perhaps he was subtly preparing a foil of calm scenery and ordered ceremony for Hamlet's graveside explosion. The procession, accompanied by a tolling bell and a hymn played on a harmonium, used all available members of the company as mourners and churchmen.[87] Claudius's position had never seemed so secure. The presence of so many priests and monks emphasized the fair-seeming order of his rule through the unity of Church and State.

Hamlet and Horatio were easily able to conceal themselves in the gathering night, to watch the funeral. Emerging from the shadows, Irving did not leap into the grave; instead, Laertes jumped out and grappled with him. This innovation won widespread approval. The eminent Shakespearean F. J. Furnivall wrote to him, 'As the *Academy* says that you've altered the leaping into the grave, I must call your attention to the enclosed lines of Shakespeare's great friend and actor, R. Burbage, who'll convince you, I think (at first sight at least) that *Sh. himself* authorized Hamlet's leaping into the grave. I've some doubt on the point myself.'[88] The crowd rushed forward, presumably to see the fight.[89] It has been said that Hamlet's outburst is prompted more by Laertes' rant than by grief for Ophelia, but this was not the case in Irving's interpretation. His grief was genuine, but since he still thought her false, he was also stung by the injustice of her brother's curses. As he saw it, another friend had betrayed him:

> Hear you, sir.
> What is the reason you use me thus?
> I loved you ever.
>
> (290–2)

All of Hamlet's earlier fits of hysteria had been linked to instances of love betrayed. Thus Laertes' behaviour turned grief into frenzied excitement. Irving stressed both Hamlet's sorrow and his renewed love for Gertrude by 'falling on her neck' after he said 'I loved Ophelia!' (271–3). The next scene began with this regret:

> I am very sorry, good Horatio,
> That to Laertes I forgot myself.
>
> (V.ii.78–9)

These lines with their implication that his reason had been temporarily unseated were thus given unusual prominence. The qualification that 'the bravery of his grief did put me / Into a towering passion' (79–80) was cut in 1874, no doubt because it offered a confusing alternative to grief and betrayal as motives.

71

In the scene with Horatio Hamlet was himself again, sanely amused at the waterfly Osric, 'Most generous and free from all contriving', and resigned to whatever Providence held in store. Irving played it before a cloth in the first grooves while the set for the duel was erected behind. A hall was represented in 1874, but in 1878 the scene was relocated outside the castle. Shakespeare's final scene was thus divided in two, the first concluding with a composite speech that was a forceful expression of Hamlet's new stoicism:

Not a whit, we defy augury. There is special providence in the fall of a sparrow. If it be now, 'tis not to come; if it be not to come, it will be now; if it be not now, yet it will come. The readiness is all.

(V.ii.220–4)

> There's a divinity that shapes our ends,
> Rough-hew them how we will.

(V.ii.10–11)

Thus Providence was doubly emphasized, an effect which was further enhanced by placing the speech at the end of a scene. Critics found it profoundly tragic.

The duel was a ceremonious occasion, accompanied by flourishes and cannon; the whole court was present. In 1874 the throne-room set was used, but in 1878 Irving substituted a hall with an open colonnade upstage, yielding a view of the orchard where Claudius had murdered his brother. Marshall touched on the poetic justice of this arrangement.[90] Everything was in readiness when Hamlet entered with Horatio: the scene was 'discovered' with everyone in his place. A table with goblets was set upstage right, and another at left with foils (see plate 9). It seems probable, therefore, that Laertes anointed his rapier before the audience. There was no hint that Osric was an accomplice.

Hamlet's apology to Laertes was offered gracefully 'with a smile of perfect confidence', but much curtailed, perhaps to avoid any suspicion of disingenuousness. The fencing was spirited and skilful; Irving was an excellent stage swordsman, and took care to cast as opponents actors who could keep their end up. He threw off his mission and his melancholy, rejoicing in the sport. 'Between the hits he talks merrily and self-complacently with his backers,' wrote one critic. 'All his troubles have not extinguished in him his liking for ribands in the cap of his youth. Probably he has begun to see that in great undertakings chance or Providence has more to say than we have.

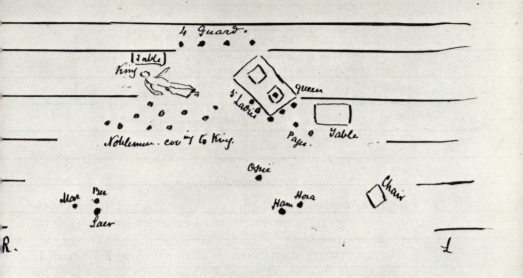

9 *Hamlet* V.ii, from the 1874 prompt-book (Harvard Theatre Collection)

At any rate he is free for the time.'⁹¹ He was courteous and charming; it was Irving's strategy to win the full sympathy of the audience now. When a little page offered him the cup, he let his hand rest for a moment on the boy's golden head before he said kindly, 'set it by awhile'. Such gestures win audiences as surely as kindness to puppy-dogs.

After the second bout, Osric as referee mounted the dais and spoke with the King. The Queen called for the cup, and was in the act of drinking when Claudius turned and saw her. His warning, 'Gertrude, do not drink', came too late; she replied, 'I *have*, my lord' (291–2).

And then the fatal third bout began. Readers of the play are frequently unaware how much carefully contrived action is required by the following terse dialogue:

> *Hamlet* Come for the third, Laertes. You do but dally.
>   I pray you pass with your best violence;
>   I am sure you make a wanton of me.
> *Laertes* Say you so? Come on.   *Play.*
>   *Osric* Nothing neither way.

73

Laertes	Have at you now!
	In scuffling they change rapiers.
King	Part them. They are incensed.
Hamlet	Nay, come – again!
Osric	Look to the Queen there, ho!
Horatio	They bleed on both sides. How is it, my lord?
Osric	How is it, Laertes?

(298–306)

Everything happens in five lines. At the beginning Hamlet is courteous and sportive; at the end he and Laertes are both dying. What happens in between?

The combatants must become 'incensed'. The foils must be exchanged. Both men are wounded. The Queen succumbs to the poison. Actors and directors must decide how and in what order these events occur. There are literally dozens of possible variations, but the basic choice lies between three interpretations:

The bout lasts longer than the others because Laertes is desperate; hence Osric interjects 'Nothing neither way.' At last Laertes slightly wounds Hamlet who, realizing that his opponent's weapon is unbated, attacks furiously, disarms Laertes, throws him the blunt foil and runs him through with the sharp one.

The bout is again protracted and grows heated as Laertes attacks fiercely. In the excitement Hamlet does not feel his insignificant wound, and the rapiers are exchanged accidentally.

Osric's remark signifies a drawn bout. Still unsuspecting, Hamlet turns away and Laertes, crying 'Have at you now!' attacks during 'time out', wounding him slightly. Hamlet is enraged, attacks furiously, disarms Laertes and stabs him.

Dover Wilson believes that the third alternative is correct and claims that this was how Irving did it.[92] If he is right, it was eccentric of Irving to cut the very lines which suggest time out and a foul, yet both his prompt-books omit them (302–3). Few reviews say anything specific, but certain inferences can be drawn. First of all, none mentions a foul; on the other hand, the *Graphic* refers to 'the gradual merging of courteous by-play in the serious business of the contest, till, as the struggle for mastery waxed warmer, an almost ferocious energy inspired the chief combatant'. Apparently the fencers simply

74

became exasperated when neither succeeded in scoring a hit. Several critics thought the exchange of weapons well managed considering the improbability of the event: 'Whom might it not move to laughter – to whom might not the change of swords seem impossible?'[93] One calls it an accident. We must infer that at this point Hamlet did not know that Laertes' foil was sharp. Another account says, 'Hamlet gets possession of his adversary's foil, and then throws his own to the adversary – by mistake, as we must suppose – and he neatly catches it.' Since Hamlet can only have received his wound before the exchange, it is clear that Irving selected the second alternative outlined above: incensed by the excitement of battle he did not notice the fatal scratch, accidentally disarmed Laertes, threw him the bated rapier at random, and ran him through without realizing that a hit with this foil would kill. It is probably significant that Frank Marshall called for business very much like this in his *Study of Hamlet*, published in 1875.[94]

The end came all in a rush. The exclamations of the onlookers were 'all spoken together'. Ladies gathered round the Queen, who had fallen on her throne, masking her from the audience. Hamlet became enraged as he heard Laertes' confession and the sentence of Providence: 'In thee there is not half an hour's life.' Shouting,

> The point envenomed too?
> Then venom do thy work

he rushed upon the King. But he did not stab him until he cried,

> Here, thou incestuous, murd'rous, damned Dane,
> Drink off this potion.
> Follow my mother.
>
> (326–8)

Thus Claudius's appeal, 'O, yet defend me, friends. I am but hurt', had to be cut and the meaning of 'Drink off this potion' was unduly strained. Apparently Irving wanted to eliminate the just but redundant business of killing the King a second time by forcing him to drink from the poisoned cup. There was no attempt to soften the savagery of Hamlet's revenge, however: 'Hamlet seizes the King by the collar of his royal robe as he might an intrusive scullion – runs him through as he holds him – flings him down backwards to the earth like carrion.'[95] Claudius had no doubt retreated before this onslaught, for he fell at some distance from the throne (see plate 9). Hamlet collapsed on the throne, an unmistakable visual parallel to the climax of the Mousetrap scene and hence a reminder that his duty as heir had been accomplished. Now he was King.

Hamlet rose once more to wrest the cup from Horatio. He died as he had lived, primarily motivated by love; suddenly overcome by the poison, as though effort had accelerated its action, he tried to embrace his friend. He raised an arm towards heaven as he spoke his last words:

> O, I die Horatio!
> The potent poison quite o'ercrows my spirit.
> The rest is silence.
>
> (353–4, 359)

Irving made two interesting points here. As Hamlet said, 'If thou didst ever hold me in thy heart . . .' (347), an oboe softly played the Ghost music. Of course this reminded the audience that he had fulfilled the Ghost's command, but it also suggested the unseen presence of the spirit whose supernatural agency had served as the instrument of Providence to guide events to this conclusion. Secondly, the only witnesses to the hero's death were Horatio and (apparently) Osric. The ladies of the court were still gathered around the Queen's body, while the men had crowded around Claudius. All had their backs turned to Hamlet and the audience. It was a daring stroke of stagecraft, used perhaps to stress Hamlet's isolation even in death and the essentially private nature of his tragedy. He was left alone with the one survivor of those he loved, and his longing for love had led to his death. But there was comfort in it. Horatio's love alone had been proven, beyond doubt, to be utterly free from false-seeming. The world, then, was not a 'sterile promontory'; in man, appearance and reality could sometimes be the same.

Style

The modern director, designer and actor in Shakespeare co-ordinate their work to present a highly selective and frequently novel interpretation of the text. They simplify by isolating and exaggerating a single theme which they thereby render dominant and unavoidable. Everything on the stage makes a direct thematic statement. Thus, for example, Hamlet speaks the Ghost's lines while gazing at his own face in a fragmented mirror which covers the entire upstage wall. Claudius speaks his first lines (I.ii. 1–39) holding a mask before his face. Appearance and reality are clearly the selected themes, and lest anyone should miss the point the performance begins with a voice-over tape which declares that the purpose of playing is 'to hold, as 'twere, the mirror up to nature'; meanwhile, Hamlet studies himself in the mirror. 'This means you,' the production says to the audience, who are entertained throughout by the spectacle of their own fragmented reflections. Ambiguity is swept away and the play becomes beautifully clear and simple. Unfortunately the baby has somehow been thrown out with the bathwater, because the performance, fine as it may be, is no longer *Hamlet*. This kind of selectivity suppresses as much as it emphasizes. John Russell Brown makes this point most clearly: 'As a response to the detailed demands of Shakespeare's texts with their ambiguities, suggestiveness, and very human variety, such a style is affected, simple-minded and unambiguous. It limits meaning and suppresses histrionic excitement.'[96]

Victorian actor-managers like Irving were among the first directors, and their practice carried the seeds of the modern approach. I have shown how Irving laid some emphasis upon the themes of love betrayed, appearance and reality, and Providence. Stage business and omissions reinforced the emphasis. But in practical terms any inclination which he may have felt to simplify and select was held in check by the prevailing naturalistic convention of his time. Claudius could not use a mask: the falseness beneath his fair-seeming could only be expressed by smiles and formality of speech. In other words, it had to be done by *acting*, and scenic arrangements could not help very much. Irving could marshal crowds of subservient courtiers to underline the spurious order of the court; but naturalism forbade him to costume them identically, or to move them by strings as though they were puppets. The throne room had to be believable; it could not be presented as a gigantic cage or playpen. Thus themes had to be inferred by the audience rather than directly stated on the stage. To modern eyes, Irving's production would probably seem indecisive and uncommitted; but then, so might a performance by the Lord Chamberlain's Men.

Naturalism, however, was in many respects the antithesis of Elizabethan stage convention. Plays written for the latter were not easily adapted to the late-Victorian stage, and inevitably suffered distortion at the hands of actor-managers who did not fully understand the problem. Irving's acting style was commended for its naturalness by progressive critics, but conservative spectators complained that he 'turned verse into prose'. This difficulty was highlighted in set-speeches such as Hamlet's soliloquies. These speeches on the Elizabethan stage were probably addressed directly to the audience, but in the 'theatre of illusion' the audience was conventionally supposed not to exist. Since there was nobody to speak to, why should Hamlet talk aloud? Irving had to make do with the fiction that he talked to himself. But a man who 'thinks aloud' does not harangue himself, so the actor interjected pauses and natural stresses which almost submerged the poetic and declamatory quality of the speeches: 'his longer passages are without the music of sustained elocution,' complained a critic of the older generation.[97] This clash of styles led Irving to abbreviate long speeches, particularly when they were written in a rhetorical fashion which his convention could not accommodate. Thus the King's speech in the throne room was reduced so much in length that its formal royalty was all but lost, and the effect of the transition to the more commonplace diction Claudius uses when not speaking *ex cathedra* was weakened.

Major movements could be encumbered by the same difficulty. In the nunnery scene Shakespeare obviously intends Ophelia to retire upstage or to the side when Polonius tells her, 'walk you here' (III.i.43). When Hamlet enters, it is conventionally supposed that he does not notice her. He delivers his soliloquy directly to the audience; when he is finished, he turns upstage and at last notices Ophelia: 'Nymph, in thy orisons / Be all my sins remembered' (89–90). But naturalism required that Irving give the audience the illusion that Hamlet was a real person, moving about an actual room and talking to himself. In the circumstances it was inconceivable that he should fail to notice an intrusive mouse, let alone another person. So Ophelia had to leave the room and re-enter when he had finished.

Convention in acting, however, is a subtle question. In Shakespeare, naturalism and artificial conventions co-exist in a state of continual transition.[98] Thus, while consistently naturalistic playing sometimes distorted or impoverished the dramatist's complex effects, it only occasionally required outright changes of meaning. But physical conventions are an entirely different matter. The Elizabethan stage was an extremely flexible acting machine. Action was unlocalized unless the dramatist required a specific location, which was then established conventionally. The late-Victorian stage, however, was completely inflexible. Naturalism required that every scene must be localized in terms of time and place. Each scene required a new set, and the changes could interrupt the flow of the action.

Naturalistic conventions of time and place created problems which did not exist on an Elizabethan stage. As I have shown, Irving made an important point out of the change in locale between Hamlet's scenes with the Ghost (I.iv;I.v). On a flexible stage there is no change because neither scene is localized: it is enough that Hamlet has shaken off his companions and is alone with the Ghost. Moreover, while Shakespeare can allow the passage of time between one o'clock and dawn to elapse in a few minutes of playing, Irving had to adopt the supposition that Hamlet had been following the Ghost for several hours between the scenes. The fact that he was able to turn this particular problem to advantage dramatically, does not alter the difficulty, which emerged very clearly in Act V. This was a trivial incident in which the clash of conventions did no great damage, but it was the occasion of much solemn debate which, in Shakespearean terms, was utterly pointless. When Osric comes to invite Hamlet to the duel (V.ii) Shakespeare gives no indication of time and place. The mourners at Ophelia's funeral have departed, and Hamlet has walked on with Horatio. His mood is so much altered from the fury of his exit that some time has evidently passed: that is all. Now Irving was obliged to choose a time and place for the Osric scene. Since the challenge must immediately precede the duel, he had to ask himself whether the duel was likely to have taken place on the same day as Ophelia's funeral. As soon as such likelihoods were raised, or course the answer presented itself: no. Irving used stage lighting as naturalistically as everything else. The funeral had taken place at dusk. Thus, unless the duel was to be a night affair, Osric had to approach Hamlet in the morning. Marshall says in his Preface, 'an interval of about twelve hours is supposed to elapse between Scenes 1 and 2',[99] and goes on to worry about a line in the Q1 graveyard scene in which the King tells Laertes:

> This very day shall Hamlet drinke his last
> For presently we mean to send him . . .

79

The theatre of illusion could not assimilate Shakespeare's frequently ambiguous use of time. Actors and naturalist critics like Marshall went to tremendous trouble to impose more or less rational time-schemes on plays whose chronology simply will not bear close scrutiny.[100]

The problem of place was even more awkward. Shakespeare gives no location for V.ii, but standard editions indicated 'A Hall in the Castle'. In 1878 Irving and Marshall found it 'inappropriate' that Hamlet should tell Osric to put his hat on if they were indoors. Even if they were aware of the Elizabethan custom of wearing hats indoors, the Lyceum audience could not be expected to share their knowledge. Besides, the subsequent discussion of the weather really does imply an outdoor scene (95–101). On the other hand, the duel must take place indoors because the cannoneer is 'without' (227) and Hamlet calls for the doors to be locked (312). Irving solved this problem by dividing the scene in two, the Osric sequence taking place outside the castle and the duel in the hall.[101] Even then there was a fly in the ointment. Hamlet says to Osric,

I will walk here in the hall. If it please his Majesty, it is the breathing time of day with me.

(174–5)

Marshall wriggles out of this with the conjecture 'that Hamlet, in saying this, indicates by a gesture the Castle which is close to them'. Here the whole debate founders under the weight of its own absurdity. The dramatist who gave us a hero who, after hobnobbing with a ghost, can talk of death as

> The undiscovered country, from whose bourn
> No traveller returns

(III.i.79–80)

was unlikely to worry about insignificant contradictions that an audience would never notice. Immediate effect was more important.

Supernatural events are awkward things to manage within a naturalistic convention. The contradiction in terms is not just semantic. While Irving's production style was sufficiently romantic to carry off Ghost scenes at night on the ramparts of a picturesque castle, some critics found the apparition incongruous in a well-lit box set. The Queen's closet was a comfortable boudoir (today it is usually a bedroom, a change for which the Freudian critic Ernest Jones is no doubt responsible), abundantly and realistically furnished to give it an intimate, lived-in look. Several critics viewed with distaste the mundane detail of a nightgown airing at the fire. In 1874 Mrs Pauncefort wore an 'unpicturesque kind of flannel dressing-gown' which was hastily replaced by a more majestic garment. The introduction of a ghost into such a room was improbable, especially when the spectre also wore a dressing-gown. *Blackwood's Magazine* complained:

Altogether ludicrous . . . is the appearance of the ghost in this very important scene. The convolutions of the Queen's night-drapery . . . so occupied our mind, that when, with a rush, a venerable gentleman in familiar domestic costume came on the stage, shaking it with substantial footsteps, the idea of the ghost did not present itself at all to our dull imagination; and it was impossible to avoid the natural idea that the lady's husband, hearing an unaccountable commotion in the next room, had jumped out of bed, seized his dressing-gown, and rushed in to see what was the matter.

In a classical play 'archaeological accuracy' was ordinarily a principle of the naturalistic convention. A modern-dress *Hamlet* was inconceivable: the scene was Denmark and the period mediaeval. But *Hamlet* is full of anachronisms, and Irving chose an essentially Renaissance atmosphere which suited the play. His sets represented architecture in a sparsely decorated Norman style which did not clash with the chain-mail and helmets of the soldiers, or the doublet and hose of the gentlemen. The *Theatre* thought he was right, since 'The Danish costume of the dark ages . . . was far from picturesque.' Beauty was a more important criterion than accuracy, so long as conventions remained unmixed. It was only in his own costume that Irving erred by mingling vaguely Renaissance dress with the traditional flummery of the stage. He wore black hose and a tunic loosely cinched with a jewelled silver sword-belt. Over this, in indoor scenes, he wore an open sleeveless jacket edged with black fur; outdoors, a long black cloak with brown fur trim was substituted. But in the exteriors he spoiled the rich but simple effect by donning a preposterous plumed hat obviously copied from the portrait of Kemble by Sir Thomas Lawrence. Many critics took issue with that hat as they had never done in Kemble's day; but Kemble's production had been uniformly of the stage, stagey, while Irving mixed his conventions. Nobody can do that without paying the penalty in inkshed.

Modern criticism

Morris Weitz has shown that *Hamlet* criticism, or indeed criticism of any dramatic work, can be said to describe, explain, evaluate or theorize.[102] The critic who 'theorizes' makes use of poetics and aesthetics: that is to say, he has, like Bradley, a conception of Shakespearean tragedy or whatever the genre happens to be, and a theory of the nature of art or *the* art. That Irving had an aesthetic concept I have shown in my discussion of his style; his Shakespearean poetics must wait until more productions have been discussed. 'Evaluation' was outside his province. He did not need to decide whether *Hamlet* was a great play, although his arrangement of the text might be regarded as a limited and indirect judgement. As an interpretative artist he was concerned with 'description' – what happens in *Hamlet* – and 'explanation' – why it happens, and what it means.

DESCRIPTION deals with issues which can yield factual answers. Does Hamlet delay? Is he mad? Does he love Ophelia? Does he know he is observed in the nunnery scene? Is the Ghost objectively real, and is it 'a spirit of health or goblin damned?' Is there a change in Hamlet, and when does it occur? Irving's answers to many such questions have already been described. Whether they are the right ones is not the real issue here; indeed, many of the answers are still as hotly disputed as they were in 1874. Take for example the nunnery scene. Dover Wilson uses his textual scholarship to postulate a missing stage direction which would allow Hamlet to overhear Polonius and the King planning to 'loose' Ophelia to him (II.ii.159); this means that he is aware of their presence throughout the scene. Harry Levin uses stylistic analysis to argue that he discovers their presence when he abruptly switches from verse to the prose of the antic disposition at 'Ha, ha! Are you honest?' (III.i.103).[103] Others hold that Hamlet never detects the spies, or senses their presence from Ophelia's demeanour at the beginning of the scene. Irving, it will be remembered, saw them when he entered, forgot them, and then glimpsed Polonius just before he snapped, 'Where's your father?' (131). There is still a sturdy minority who maintain that Hamlet does not delay at all,[104] and the dispute over his madness continues, fuelled by modern psychology – Ernest Jones and others have found him neurotic – and by the vast increase in knowledge of Elizabethan life and thought – Lily Campbell shows that Shakespeare's audience might have taken Hamlet for a sufferer from 'melancholy adust'.[105] Historical studies have complicated the issue of the Ghost. In Irving's interpretation it was the messenger of an ultimately beneficent Providence, and Hamlet's doubts were vague and short-lived. But some historical critics believe that doubt about the Ghost is a major reason for his hesitation: is it a Catholic spirit released from Purgatory to make Hamlet an innocent 'minister' of Providence, or is it a fiend from a Purgatory-less Protestant afterlife, come to make him a guilty 'scourge'?[106] Factual answers to these questions are possible, but none has won universal acceptance as yet.

EXPLANATION is ground where angels fear to tread. Here lurk the questions to which no conclusive answers can be given. Why does Hamlet delay? Is he an ideal hero or a knave, cruel, kind, ambitious, lovelorn? Is he a symbol? If he is mad, why? What is the central theme? What imagery best expresses the themes? Like every director or actor, Irving had to attempt answers to most of these questions. His performance displayed a common-sense approach which can stand as a rebuke to a good many modern critics and directors of several distinct schools: he was prepared to admit that answers cannot always be given, that *Hamlet* is an ambiguous play. There are critics who have used this ambiguity to reproach Shakespeare with artistic failure. Irving would have thought such an attitude absurd blindness to the mystery which is seldom absent from great art. Whether the mystery, or ambiguity, lies in the 'darkness which enwraps Hamlet' or in his character is perhaps immaterial.[107] More than a century ago Dowden saw its importance in Shakespeare's method,[108] and modern audiences have learned its value, transferring their loyalty from the explicitness of conventional naturalism to 'puzzling' Pinter. 'The desire for verification is understandable, but cannot always be satisfied,' says Pinter.

The assumption that to verify what has happened and what is happening presents no problems, I take to be inaccurate. A character on the stage who can present no convincing argument or information as to his past experiences, his present behaviour or his aspirations, nor give a comprehensive analysis of his motives is as legitimate and as worthy of attention as one who, alarmingly, can do all of these things. The more acute the experience the less articulate its expression.[109]

Hamlet cannot give a simple account of himself, and the attempt to make him do so is often attended by disastrous results. There is no common ground between Irving and the sort of modern critic who claims – tacitly as a rule – to have found a key to *Hamlet* which has been hidden from everyone else for centuries. Madariaga, for example, has the advantage of Irving on points of historical fact: he knows that Elizabethan gentlemen wore their hats indoors. But when his knowledge of Renaissance court life leads him to interpret Ophelia as 'a flirt; a fast girl' and Hamlet as a repulsive egotist – a discovery which he modestly compares to the Copernican astronomy – he defies common sense and the natural sympathies of countless audiences. Indeed, no interpretation which gives Hamlet a bad character is likely to commend itself to anyone who knows plays in the theatre.[110]

Irving would have been equally unimpressed by those theories which ascribe the play's ambiguity to Shakespeare's imperfect assimilation of his sources, 'like some ostrich with tin-cans inside him', as Harrison puts it, or the complexity of Hamlet's character to the dramatist's immature failure to objectify his protagonist. Nor is an actor likely to have much time for an approach which ignores the fact that *Hamlet* is a play, intended to be seen unfolding sequentially rather than viewed 'spatially' in the study.[111]

I do not say that Irving played Hamlet as Kenneth Muir thinks Shakespeare should be played, 'straight, without cuts and without gimmicks'. But as John Russell Brown has pointed out, it is not quite that simple: 'the text is a most complicated, difficult and inexhaustible clue, a clue that becomes a labyrinth as soon as we approach it at all closely'.[112] There are questions to be answered, choices to be made, an interpretative 'line' to be chosen through the innumerable alternatives offered by the script. Irving simplified, chiefly by cutting the text, and he 'explained' where choices were offered. But he did not oversimplify by subordinating everything in the play to a single dominant theme. In other words, he did not claim to possess a unique 'key' to *Hamlet*. Thus his production relates to a wide variety of modern critics of several different persuasions whose work, properly regarded, can be applied to the play as what Francis Fergusson calls 'Jamesian "reflectors", each lighting a facet of the whole from his own peculiar angle'.[113] None holds the unique key, and those who seem contradictory mostly respond – if their views are well-considered – to the ambiguity of the play.

Gareth Lloyd Evans explains the play in terms of Hamlet's character, in which he discovers an artistic temperament compelled by events
to come to terms with an unsympathetic reality. 'Hamlet is called upon
to avenge the wrong deed.'[114] Whereas the Ghost requires him to
avenge a murder, his nature is outraged by Gertrude's violation of 'the
order of love'. Like Irving, Evans believes that 'love, in terms of order,
fidelity, honesty, truth and indeed beauty (witness his description of
his father) is an all-enveloping and governing element' in Hamlet's
personality. Consequently, Gertrude's offence against love has 'taken
away from him his zest for life itself', even before the Ghost's
revelations. This is as exact a statement of Irving's starting-point as
Irving himself could have made. But here actor and critic part company. Irving's production emphasized Hamlet's former love for all
around him, and his betrayal by almost everyone he had trusted: not
just his mother, but also his schoolfellows, Polonius, Laertes and
(apparently) Ophelia. The lost order of his father's reign and its
affectionate domestic harmony were travestied respectively by the
ceremonious court under Claudius and by his mother's hypocrisy.
Both were aspects of false order, both fair seeming tricked out to cover
a foul reality.

Modern critics deal with both of these themes. A few seem to think
order in Denmark more important than Hamlet, who resembles an
overcomplicated Oedipus seeking the source of a regular plague of
disorder. Thus what Stanislavsky called the 'super-objective' – the
ruling idea or inner aim which directs and unifies the 'through-
action' – is 'to find and destroy the hidden "imposthume" which is
destroying Claudius's Denmark'. These critics set great store by
Fortinbras as a bringer of order, while Irving, whose super-objective
might be expressed as 'to kill the King', left him out.[115] But most
moderates incorporate something not unlike Irving's interpretation of
order as a subsidiary of the dominant theme of appearance and reality.
Order is restored when evil reality is identified, stripped of its fair-
seeming, and destroyed. Anne Righter, for example, takes the
'Murder of Gonzago' as 'the focal point from which a preoccupation
which appearance and reality, truth and falsehood, expressed in
theatrical terms, radiates both backward and forward in time'. In this
scene Hamlet uses the illusion of the play to distinguish truth from
falsehood in the real world. Others show how this theme is reinforced

by imagery or 'key terms' of seeming, clothes, harlotry and cosmetics, acting and play, and of course the dominant imagery of corruption and disease,[116] particularly when illusion

> will but skin and film the ulcerous place
> Whiles rank corruption, mining all within,
> Infects unseen.
>
> (III.iv.148–50)

Irving knew nothing of imagery, but he saw the glittering exterior of the court, and the rottenness underneath, and he knew that the foul reality neither originated in Hamlet nor corrupted him.

Hamlet's hysteria came from his horror at the corruption of those he loved; as Evans puts it, he is 'a perfectionist in thought and feeling', puzzled by the imperfection of love as he finds it.[117] In Irving's interpretation, he resolved his confusion step by step in the Mouse-trap, closet and graveyard scenes. In the first, evil reality was exposed and the antagonists declared themselves; in the second, Hamlet's reconciliation with Gertrude removed the prime cause of the internal conflict that had disturbed his mind; and with Ophelia's death, his reluctant love no longer held him back. Before the duel he was a changed man, willing to accept whatever came: 'The readiness is all.' Some modern critics do not perceive any change in him, but the majority see the abortive voyage to England as the turning-point. Hamlet has felt the guidance of Providence in the series of improbable accidents which foiled the King's plot and returned him safe to Elsinore; he has 'submitted to the will of God, and in this very act of submission he has attained his victory'.[118] But Tillyard agrees with Irving that the psychological turning-point is the closet scene: 'Once Hamlet can face his mother and share with her the burden of what he thinks of her, he can at least begin to see the world as something other than a prison.'[119] To Irving it was even more important. The Ghost's appearance was a providential intervention which brought about the crucial reconciliation that Hamlet's excited behaviour would other-wise have prevented. His reading agrees with those in which the Ghost is a divine agent sent to make Hamlet a 'minister' of justice, but is incompatible with those which hold that his failure to kill the King and his murder of Polonius show that he has lost his way and is trying to play God, to decree who shall be damned.[120]

But to Irving, Hamlet's mental state was the crux. He could not act against the King before he had settled with his mother, and Providence acknowledged the need by intervening to effect it. Thus Hamlet spared Claudius because he had more urgent business elsewhere, and the 'Now might I do it pat' speech was neither a rationalization nor an expression of spiritual arrogance based on doubt of Heaven's justice, but a promise to return to the King at a more convenient moment. At any rate, Irving must have known what several modern critics have seen: Hamlet cannot stab an unarmed man in the back and remain a hero.[121] Audience sympathy follows the very elementary 'Lone Ranger Principle' whereby a hero forfeits his heroism if he shoots before being shot at.

Irving Ribner is surely right when he says that in *Hamlet* Shakespeare 'affirms a positive order'.[122] Like the *Oresteia*, it is a tragedy which explores the problem of evil, and asks why the innocent must suffer and die. To Aeschylus and Shakespeare the answer was never really in doubt: evil and suffering lead ultimately to good. God is just. Shakespeare did not have to write a thesis play to prove a standard article of faith, and Irving did not have to perform it for that purpose. He too lived in an age of faith. It is modern man, tormented by the absurd gap between the justice he expects and his perception of the Eternal Injustice of Things, who takes Hamlet for his spokesman. Irving never explored this thematic pattern because for him and his age it was not a vital issue: the audience would not have understood. To him, Hamlet was *a* man, not Man. There was no question that he doubted, but truth immutable existed to be discovered and rediscovered. It was to be demonstrated, not called into question. The demonstration was secondary to the individual experiences which occasioned it. Irving's production was a tremendous success: perhaps one reason was that he shared with the dramatist an assumption that metaphysical doubt is mistaken. But when Shakespeare himself doubted and almost despaired, in *King Lear*, Irving's Victorian certainties betrayed him. He made Lear another mistaken individual, and failed.

3

Macbeth

25 September 1875
29 December 1888

Theatrical context

After his triumph as Hamlet, Irving needed another success in tragedy to prove that he was more than a melodramatic actor who had fooled the multitude with his tricks. *Macbeth* was the obvious choice: it was popular, but there had been no really successful new production for twenty years. Macready still reigned in popular memory, despite the efforts of Charles Dillon, Charles Kean and Samuel Phelps to supplant him during the 1850s; and a series of Lady Macbeths which included Ellen Tree, Mrs Warner, Isabella Glyn, Fanny Kemble and Helena Faucit had been powerless to shake the reputation of Mrs Siddons.

There is a theatrical superstition that *Macbeth* is an unlucky play. The Lyceum opening, originally scheduled for 18 September 1875, was postponed for a week for reasons described as technical in Mrs Bateman's apologetic advertisement.[1] Perhaps the new manageress had sensed that the anticipated triumph was not materializing and that her leading man was not working harmoniously with Kate, her eldest daughter. In the event, Irving was unable to carry out his unconventional conception, which in any case clashed with Kate's conventional reading. Nevertheless the production ran for eighty performances.

The leading roles remained unclaimed when Irving revived *Macbeth* in 1888. Tommaso Salvini and Ernesto Rossi made some impression in 1876, and Adelaide Ristori was acclaimed at Drury Lane in 1882, but no foreign star could become seriously identified with a Shakespearean part. Irving's reputation was secure and his dearest partner of greatness was Ellen Terry. The revival was eagerly anticipated: would he change his interpretation, and, if not, was his mature talent capable of carrying it off? What would Terry do with a part that was so conspicuously outside her normal range? The production was

88

most lavishly mounted. Charles Cattermole, a well known water-colourist, designed archaeologically correct costumes and props; sets by Hawes Craven, Joseph Harker and three contracting studios were revolutionary in their three-dimensional massiveness; and new music was composed by Arthur Sullivan. André Antoine saw *Macbeth* and was impressed by the 'incomparable' *mise en scène*, particularly the lighting 'of which we have hardly any idea in France'.[2] The production ran for 151 performances and was revived for an American tour in 1895.[3]

Text

In the first draft of Irving's 1875 acting version we glimpse the actor as greenhorn scholar. Many of the cuts and rearrangements are traditional, but the intrusive songs from Middleton's *The Witch* are banished. In his zeal for textual purity, Irving purchased the latest authoritative edition – that of Clark and Wright[4] – and, alas, read the introduction. The editors were 'disintegrators': claiming that Shakespeare's text had been retouched and adulterated by another hand, they condemned several hundred lines as spurious; most of these Irving obediently cut, including the report of the bleeding Sergeant (I.ii). He could not foresee that the critics would accuse him of cutting lines whose praise of Macbeth's valour conflicted with their mistaken impression that he intended to portray Macbeth as a coward, or that posterity would repeat the nonsense for a century. Faith in Clark and Wright led him into folly again in 1877, when he published an article identifying the mysterious Third Murderer (III.iii) as Macbeth's Attendant earlier in the play (III.i). Unfortunately, much of the 'evidence' Irving offered was drawn from stage directions which were editorial rather than Shakespearean, as the *Athenaeum* swiftly pointed out.[5]

After a draft in which either disintegration or tradition accounted for nine-tenths of the cuts, Irving prepared a more independent acting version. In defiance of tradition and Coleridge, for example, he restored the Porter's first speech. *Macbeth* is a short play: less than a quarter of the lines were cut,[6] but the original twenty-nine scenes were reduced to nineteen, partly by omission (I.ii; II.iv; III.v, vi; IV.ii) and partly by traditional combinations which he retained in all subsequent

90

texts (II.i–iii; III.i and ii; V.vi–ix). The acting text of 1888 divides the play into six acts, Act V beginning with the meeting of Malcolm and Macduff in England (IV.iii) and Act VI with the mustering of Macbeth's enemies.[7] The Sergeant is restored, but the murders of Banquo and Macduff's family are cut, presumably because they were narrated elsewhere. In omitting Lady Macduff, Irving sacrificed an important counterweight to Lady Macbeth; but the consequent isolation of the latter as the only woman in the play may have served his interpretation better. The Middleton songs are reintroduced on the grounds that they are 'clearly indicated in the first folio',[8] but since the Hecate scene is cut (III.iv), 'Come away, come away' is inserted as a spectacular choral scene at the end of Act IV. Apart from some cranky emendations[9] the text is reasonable. Glen Byam Shaw's Stratford prompt-book (Laurence Olivier and Vivien Leigh, 1955) shows many identical cuts, and improves upon Irving's notion about the Third Murderer by identifying him and the confidential Attendant with Seyton.[10]

Contemporary criticism

The traditional image of Macbeth was a burly, claymore-swinging Highlander like Rob Roy. The provincial star Barry Sullivan was a fine Macbeth of this order: 'He had great strength, great voice, great physique of all sorts; a well-knit figure with fine limbs, broad shoulders, and the perfect back of a prize-fighter.'[11] Irving's slender figure and ascetic appearance disqualified him from following the stereotype. Similarly, a contemporary paper said, 'The stage Lady Macbeth has muscles of iron and nerves of steel. She is a woman to make men tremble, and to frighten the wits out of women and children.'[12] The hard-favoured Kate Bateman could hope to follow convention (see plate 10), but Ellen Terry could not: charm, pathos and femininity were her long suit. In a satirical interview, Shakespeare's ghost said, 'genius can do anything – it made Pritchard genteel and Garrick six feet high – but, other things being equal, I'd back a thirteen-stone woman against a seven-stone sylph in the part'.[13]

The traditional interpretation is classical. Like a Greek hero, Mac-

10 Kate Bateman and Irving in *Macbeth*, I.vii, 1875 (Crown Copyright, Victoria and Albert Museum)

beth is destroyed by an inescapable necessity, and like the Aristotelian protagonist he is one of ourselves, neither very good nor very bad, but rather better than worse, 'by nature mild and noble'. Until he meets the Weird Sisters he has no thought of crime; they are potent as they are supernatural, 'Northern Fates' who not only tempt but *impel* Macbeth towards sin. His wife, 'a great bad woman, whom we hate', hustles him so decisively towards his fate that 'Little more than the mere execution falls to the share of Macbeth.' Of course the poor fellow hates the whole business; conscience tortures him before the murder and remorse afterwards. In the catastrophe, all his crimes 'cannot altogether eradicate the stamp of native heroism'.[14]

The alternative interpretation lays the blame upon Macbeth himself. Because it emphasizes the individual, his responsibility for his actions and his torment as he wrestles with the darkness in his soul, we may call it romantic. Appropriately enough, it was proposed by the co-author of *Lyrical Ballads*. The Weird Sisters instigate nothing: Macbeth has already conceived and brooded upon the murder, 'So surely is the guilt in its germ anterior to the supposed cause.' Other romantic critics elaborated Coleridge's idea. Macbeth has discussed the murder with his wife, and the witches, who 'tend on mortal thoughts', are summoned by the contemplated evil. His conscience afflicts him with 'horrible imaginings' which he mistranslates as fear of failure, and after the murder he mistakes his remorse for terror of consequences.[15] Macbeth's tragedy comes from his failure to understand himself: the Weird Sisters and his wife are mere accessories.

It was inevitable that Irving should have been drawn to the romantic interpretation: he was a romantic himself. Characters which were complex, introspective and individual to the point of eccentricity were as natural to his style as statuesque grandeur had been to classical actors like Siddons. He did not avoid the conventional interpretation of Macbeth because he was incapable of playing it; he avoided it as utterly foreign to his artistic nature. He must have been aware, however, that Coleridge's idea of the protagonist's 'cowardice of his own conscience' would be exceedingly difficult to convey. After all, if Macbeth himself mistakes conscience for fear, an audience may be excused for doing likewise.[16]

By 1888 Irving had changed his mind. The Coleridge theory was too complicated, and he turned to an essay by George Fletcher, a relatively obscure critic who had influenced Helena Faucit. 'Macbeth does not project the murder of Duncan because of his encounter with the weird sisters; the weird sisters encounter him because he has projected the murder.' He holds back, not from conscience but 'from fear of *retribution in this life*'. Despite great physical courage, Macbeth is a 'moral coward'.[17] Irving boldly called him 'one of the most bloody minded, hypocritical villains' in Shakespeare.[18]

'Our Romanticists,' says Gervinus, 'have made Lady Macbeth a heroine of virtue, and Goethe rightly condemned the foolish way in which they stamped her as a loving spouse and house-wife.' To classicists, she is 'of all the human participators in the king's murder the most guilty'.[19] But Fletcher interpreted Lady Macbeth as the actresses saw her: 'decidedly and even softly feminine in person' but endowed with that 'masculine firmness of will' which her husband lacks. Siddons took this view in the famous essay in which she stressed Lady Macbeth's beauty: 'it is of that character which I believe is . . . generally allowed to be most captivating to the other sex, – fair, feminine, perhaps even fragile . . . Such a combination only, captivating in feminine loveliness, could have compassed a charm of such potency as to fascinate the mind of . . . Macbeth.'[20] In performance, however, Siddons followed a thoroughly classical reading: 'We can conceive of nothing grander,' says Hazlitt. 'It was something above nature . . . Power was seated on her brow, passion emanated from her breast as from a shrine; she was tragedy personified.'[21]

Ellen Terry wrote in her copy of Fletcher's article, 'I cannot understand why Mrs. Siddons shd write *down one* set of ideas upon the subject and carry out a totally different plan.' But fair frailty was as foreign to the nature and physique of Siddons as majesty was to Terry, who remarked, 'It is no use an actress wasting her nervous energy on a battle with her physical attributes. She had much better find a way to emphasize them as allies.'[22] Irving's Macbeth would probably have killed Duncan even over his lady's protests; thus Terry was free to play pretty much as she liked. In her reading, Lady Macbeth's motive is love: 'she *loves her husband* – Ergo – she is a *woman* – and she knows it and is half the time *afraid* whilst urging M not to be afraid, as she loves a *man* = women love men'.[23] It is her tragedy that successive crimes isolate the criminals from each other. As the *Illustrated London News* observed, 'her participation in the crime is punished by utter loneliness, by the forfeiture of her husband's love, and she dies, maddened by remorse, of a broken heart'.[24]

Performance

The curtain rose on darkness, thunder and rain. Lightning revealed the Weird Sisters silhouetted against the sky, standing on a 'rocky eminence'. With their gaunt bodies and thin beards, the female voices seemed uncanny as they chanted their incantation. A shriek was heard, the First Witch cried 'I come, Graymalkin' and familiar spirits summoned the others. They concluded with an exultant couplet; darkness descended again, and 'a network of vivid lightning' revealed the witches actually flying 'through the fog and filthy air'.[25] Thus began Irving's 1888 production. Despite the supernatural effects, the witches had little occult power over Macbeth. The spectacle was designed to combat a tendency on the part of the audience to see the Sisters as a joke, an attitude encouraged by stage tradition, which assigned these parts to male low comedians who irresistibly reminded Victorians of pantomime's Widow Twankey. In 1875 Irving had cast a woman as the Third Witch, but now three 'tragic actresses of considerable repute in the provinces' wore the scraggly beards (see plate 15).[26]

In the earlier production the witches proceeded without aviation to meet Macbeth; but in 1888 a gauze was withdrawn to discover 'a green and whin-clad hillside, with the tents of Duncan's army in the middle distance, seen through a group of Scotch firs overreaching the fore-ground'. The bleeding Sergeant's sonorous messenger's-speech, spoken by 'an old elocutionist with more cannon balls than pepper-corns' in his voice, raised a joyous commotion amongst Duncan's followers. Then as the gauzes closed in again, distant thunder muttered and the sky grew lighter: the storm was passing.[27]

Sullivan's music accompanied the witches' 'sublimely wicked' speeches in the melodramatic manner. 'The witches declaim, they do not sing,' said *The Times*, 'and their voices in juxtaposition and contrast with the musical sound are of the wildest and uncanniest effect.'[28] Gradually the rhythm developed into a march with *pianissimo* drum, heralding the approach of Macbeth:

> A drum, a drum!
> Macbeth doth *come*.[29]

94

Then the generals entered together. In 1875 Irving wrote in his study-book a description of the impression he intended to convey: 'Lofty, manly, heroic. Living to command. The grief, the care, the doubt not of a weak – but of a strong man, of a strong mind . . . A man of action – of overpowering strength and resolution.'[30] In the revival, however, his melancholy was transformed into slouching villainy. 'This Macbeth is from the first "a man forbid." His lined and haggard features, his restless movements, his wild and wandering eye' gave him such a thoroughly unreliable look, accentuated by a wiry red moustache, that it was hard to imagine how he could have won Duncan's confidence.[31] He was even now contemplating murder as a means to the throne which his victories had brought almost within his reach. 'So *foul* and *fair* a *day* I have *not seen,*' he said, echoing the witches. Their greeting startled him:

> All *hail, Macbeth! hail* to thee, *Thane* of Glamis!
> All *hail, Macbeth! hail* to thee, *Thane* of Cawdor!   *start*
> All *hail, Macbeth!* that *shalt* be *king* hereafter.   *start*[32]

His agitation contrasted sharply with the innocent calm of Banquo, who asked with a smile,

> Good sir, why do you start, and seem to fear
> Things that do sound so fair?

Ellen Terry answered him in her study-book: 'Because he had longed for it before & here's his secret thought revealed.'[33] He dissembled his excitement, betraying himself for a moment by the intensity of 'Would they had stayed.' Ross's announcement that he was indeed Thane of Cawdor aroused such a series of emotions that Macbeth's companions noticed his abstraction. Awe gave way to exultation as he contemplated 'the swelling act / Of the imperial theme' and to terror at the thought of murder. Fletcher points out that the Weird Sisters mention no such means to the throne: 'a man who was *not* already harbouring a scheme of guilty ambition' would merely 'wait quietly the course of events'. This came to Macbeth only as a second thought:

> If Chance will have me King, why, Chance may crown me,
> Without my stir.
>
> (I.iv.144–5)

He spoke 'with a sigh of such relief as is felt only by the irresolute when

11　Macbeth's troops crossing the heath at sunset, I.iii, 1888 (University of Victoria)

they see a hope that events may spare them the dreaded necessity of making up their minds.'[34]

Now came one of those moments of lyrical stage management for which the Lyceum was famous. To a wild march, Macbeth's barbaric soldiers followed their general across the heather (see plate 11). 'They swarm along almost at a "double," in the most open order, or rather disorder, their spears, carried at all possible angles, forming a sort of fantastic fretwork against the fiery sky.' Their weariness could be felt

rossing the Heath
WM.

and shared; each man individualized, they seemed to number thousands.[35]

The novelty of Irving's first appearance as Macbeth so effectively diverted attention from Kate Bateman that little can be learned of her playing in the invocation scene (I.v). She was known for efficient rather than passionate acting in melodrama, and she seems to have played Shakespeare the same way: few thought it worked. Most found her charmless, and if 'a better representative of the character could not readily be found', then 'it would be difficult to illustrate more forcibly the poverty and impending bankruptcy of the English stage'.[36] Ellen

Terry's first scene was eagerly awaited, and applause followed the discovery of Lady Macbeth in her cosy sitting-room, reading the letter by firelight (see plate 12). She looked lovely: 'long plaits of deep red hair fell from under a purple veil over a robe of green upon which iridescent beetles glinted like emeralds, and a great wine-coloured cloak, gold-embroidered, swept from her shoulders'. The hair was complemented by a pallid complexion highlighted by ruddy cheeks, intended to 'mark her as a raw-boned daughter of the North', a Saga-heroine.[37] The costume was exotic, 'suggesting the Queen of Sheba rather than the Queen of Scotland'. Oscar Wilde remarked, 'Lady Macbeth seems an economical housekeeper and evidently patronizes local industries for her husband's clothes and the servants' liveries, but she takes care to do all her own shopping in Byzantium.'[38] The same incongruities were apparent in her acting. Ellen Terry classed Lady Macbeth with Shakespeare's 'pathetic' women, the pathos arising from her ultimate estrangement from the husband she loved too well. Her task in this scene, then, was to make her motive clear, but she substituted conventional sentiment for love: when she had finished reading the letter, 'she threw herself back in the long oaken chair to dream of the arrival and the fortunes of her king and lover'. She addressed the soliloquy to his miniature:

> Yet do I fear thy nature:
> It is too full o' th' milk of human kindness,
> To catch the nearest way
>
> (I.v.16–18)

– the affectionate, half-regretful tone clashing with the fearful meaning of the words. She concluded by kissing the miniature.[39] It was charmingly done, but unconvincing here and throughout the first two acts. 'What on earth,' the *Spectator* asked of the murder scene, 'is this graceful, amiable, and picturesque woman doing in these shambles?'[40]

She was unsurprised but pleased by the letter, which she read so naturalistically that grandeur in subsequent speeches would have seemed false. The invocation was illogically conceived. 'Surely she called the spirits to be made bad, because she knew she was not so very bad?', Terry said to Clement Scott; and in a study-book she wrote, 'she feels she has only a woman's strength – & calls on "spirits"'.[41] But nowhere was there any hint of demonic possession. The speech was mere hyperbole, and consequently the strength she exhibited later had

12 Ellen Terry as Lady Macbeth, reading the letter by the fire, I.iii, 1888 (Crown Copyright, Victoria and Albert Museum)

to come from within herself, which implied that she was quite bad enough. Resolutely she averted her mind's eye from consequences and remorse: beside '*Stop* up th' *access* and passage to REMORSE,' Terry wrote. 'She dreads THAT – action of pushing it away.' Her voice faltered at the awful words, and few critics were convinced that such a woman could ever summon enough wicked resolution to prompt a dastardly murder. The actress admitted, 'When I called on the Spirits to unsex me, I acted that bit just as badly as anybody could act anything.'[42] At Macbeth's entry she rushed forward to greet him with a long embrace. 'Duncan comes *here*, to*night*,' he said, averting his eyes and speaking 'with an affected indifference that obviously covers a guilty thought'. Placing her hand eagerly on his breast, she asked 'And when goes hence?' He replied with a meaningful pause, 'Tomorrow – as he *purposes*.' Drawing back, she touched her left shoulder with her right arm to denote inspiration: 'Ah,' she breathed, 'never / Shall sun *that* morrow see!' The remainder of her speech she marked 'Bright! Quick! Aflame! Alert.' Still talking, they went out with arms around each other's necks, she full of spirit, he dejectedly.[43]

Duncan's arrival at Inverness has attracted little comment except as a celebrated example of Shakespeare's verbal scene-painting. This was redundant in the theatre of illusion, and ironically Irving chose this scene for a display of revolutionary technique in scenic naturalism. It was played by moonlight, a circumstance which made Banquo's observations on the temple-haunting martlet a little awkward.[44] Craven gave Irving a massive built-up castle, rough-textured to represent stone. As Duncan and his followers approached the cavernous gate they climbed a great sloping bridge, which suggested that the castle was indeed situated on a rocky summit. Retainers lined the ramp, lighting the scene with torches; women bowed as Lady Macbeth swept down to meet the King, 'welcoming the Gentle Duncan to that murderous keep with words of poisonous honey dripping from her great, red, cruel mouth'.[45] There was no melodramatic hint of duplicity in her greeting. 'She is making him "quite at home",' remarked *Punch*, 'and in another few moments, after supper, you feel that the courteous old King will, with Macbeth's kind permission, kiss his charming wife under the mistletoe.' He was a 'dear old man', Terry thought.[46] The entire scene was accompanied by 'serene and beautiful music' which reinforced her interpretation. 'Of the treachery underlying the words of welcome no warning note rises from the strings of the harp which accompany the dialogue to the close.'[47]

No actor can expect to resolve all the ambiguities of a great Shakespearean role, but he must assimilate them in a unique characterization which convinces because it is a living creation. The supreme test in *Macbeth* comes in the series of scenes which now faced Irving and Terry. Classical and romantic interpretations were equally unsatisfactory. If Macbeth is driven to commit murder, why do his conscientious objections evaporate when his wife shows that he can get away with it? But if he mistakes conscience for fear, how is the actor to avoid looking like a poltroon? In 1875 some journalists praised Irving's 'remorse, which looks like cowardice, perhaps, to an indolent and vulgar spectator' but the majority were vulgar enough to share Mr Punch's opinion that 'the exhibition of physical terror and cowering, shrieking remorse . . . becomes repulsive'.[48] Lady Macbeth's strength of character when she urges her husband to screw his courage to the sticking-place, or bloodies the faces of the grooms, is difficult to reconcile with her weakness when she wastes away and dies. She scarcely seems the sort to suffer from the vapours, yet audiences are so unwilling to accept her faint as a 'feint' to distract attention from Macbeth that actresses of the classical school simply did not appear in the discovery scene.[49] If she is feminine and tender, however, what indeed is she doing in these shambles?

In 1888 Irving played Macbeth as a villain with no real conscience. The soliloquies, the decision to 'proceed no further in this business', the air-drawn dagger and the apostrophe to sleep were all insincere: his resolution never really slackened. Irving explained:

He was a poet with his brain and a villain with his heart . . . He loved throughout to paint himself and his deeds in the blackest pigments and to bring to the exercise of his wickedness the conscious deliberation of an intellectual voluptuary . . . Macbeth – hypocrite, traitor, and regicide – threw over his crimes the glamour of his own poetic self-torturing thought . . . playing with conscience so that action and reaction of poetic thought might send emotional waves through the brain while the resolution was as firmly fixed as steel and the heart as cold as ice . . . the man of sensibility and not the man of feeling.[50]

Like Hamlet, he had 'a trick of fostering and aggravating his own excitements', and a review saw this Macbeth as 'a more resolute and unscrupulous Hamlet'.[51] Of course, as a reading of the play this is bunk: there is not a shred of real evidence that supports, and a great deal that denies it. But it permitted a coherent characterization which was not only accepted as truth, but contained much truth as well. The central fact was Macbeth's extreme selfishness, which is well supported by the text: it is this which brings him to damnation, and alienates him from his wife. Ellen Terry's reading complemented Irving's. Lady Macbeth wanted the crown for her husband because

she believed him worthy of it, and her love for him lent her a degree of fierce resolution which did violence to her real nature. His apparently conscientious weakness seemed to prove that he needed her. But in the discovery scene she began to understand that this was untrue. Disillusioned, useless and isolated, she began the decline which led her to repentance and salvation.

Macbeth's soliloquy while Duncan feasted (I.vii.1–28) was the first major occasion when he indulged his lurid fancy, and his wife treated his decision to proceed no further as cowardice. Attempting to show enough courage for two, she described how she would have plucked her nipple from her child's boneless gums,

> And dashed the brains out, had I so sworn
> As you have done in this.

This was the most horrible image she could conceive, and she furtively brushed away a tear. The climax came when Macbeth asked, 'If we should fail?' Terry knew that Siddons's reply had been a fatalistic 'We fail!' with 'a strong downward inflection', but her own answer was a 'cry of defiance'. He sat as though dazed while she spoke slowly and charmingly, kneeling beside him and playing with his hands: 'Now see,' the actress wrote, 'here is a beautiful plan which your wifie has thought all out (the Hell-cat).' When he saw that her plan was safe, Macbeth brightened: 'His expression of countenance here sheds a flood of dry, accurate light on the very heart of Macbeth's idiosyncrasy.'[52]

The courtyard set of 1888 may have been Craven's most ambitious to date. At right stood a round tower containing a spiral staircase to Duncan's room; upstage centre was the outer gate which the Porter would open, and to its left a stair leading to a practicable gallery that ran along two sides of the yard (see plate 13). The windowless space with its flat timber roof ensured an appropriate sense of oppressive entrapment, but it tempted Irving to violate convention by introducing an impossible beam of moonlight.[53] Alone after bidding Banquo goodnight, Macbeth looked towards Duncan's door, evidently intending immediate murder. The invisible dagger stopped him in his tracks:

13 *Macbeth*, the 'Discovery' scene, II.iii, 1888. Irving at left, Terry at right, Wenman (Banquo) at centre. Design by Hawes Craven (Shakespeare Centre Library, Stratford-upon-Avon)

if this apparently supernatural weapon marshalled him the way that he was going, he realized with a start, perhaps it pointed the way to danger. Then, with a hollow laugh, he pulled himself together: 'There's no such thing.' Irving wrote, 'Fear, which takes hold of him, he refuses to acknowledge.'[54] His exit was a marked contrast to Terry's entrance: Macbeth 'reels and yawns and rocks, a very abyss of moral terror and sickened horror', but his wife entered firmly, with a 'horrible smile'. His offstage voice made her 'quite savage for a moment in the face of a possible defeat'. Furious that weakness on her part had jeopardized their enterprise, she gave her reference to Duncan's resemblance to her father a 'tone of impatient contempt'.[55] Macbeth's return was a huge relief. This gradually turned to alarm as he agonized about his inability to pronounce 'amen' and about the voice that cried 'Sleep no more.' Ellen Terry wrote, 'Why he is quite ill! Come come – the danger's *past* now – Consider it not so deeply / This last NOT stern and angry, but with some feminine consideration mixed with alarm.' But as he raved 'in the broken and gasping accents of a man under the influence of mortal affright', she began to lose patience: 'You want *shaking*.' What was the man talking about? 'Who was it that thus cried?' she asked, with practical common sense.[56] Then she noticed the daggers. Snatching them, she explained 'with cool and perfect sincerity' that 'The sleeping and the dead / Are but as pictures.' But it was a façade. 'If he do bleed, / I'll gild the faces of the grooms withal' was whispered to herself as she clung with outstretched arms to the tower wall. Macbeth scarcely heard the knocking, he was so absorbed in his bloody hands. Returning red-handed, Terry picked up his cloak with her fingertips and led the way offstage, but finding him oblivious of danger, she came back to '*Push* him *pull* him off the stage.'[57]

Macbeth's demoralization seemed so complete that his reappearance three or four minutes later, calmly and graciously greeting Macduff and Lennox in the cold light that entered the open gate, surprised his wife when she entered. She watched him tensely throughout the uproar which followed the discovery of Duncan's corpse, fearing and expecting a relapse. The still figures of the murderers commanded attention, standing at opposite sides of the court while an excited crowd swirled around them (see plate 13). 'This scene shd look a strange and wild affair,' Ellen Terry wrote, 'half torch light

– half day-light & frightened half dressed people huddled together.'
Irving's notes are vivid: 'Torches, swords etc. . . . some putting clothes
on . . . all pale . . . horns outside . . . raw bodied men & women.'[58]
Macbeth was imperturbable, even when Macduff asked him menac-
ingly why he had slain the grooms. The cool effrontery of his reply
staggered Lady Macbeth:

> Who can be wise, amaz'd, temperate and furious,
> Loyal and neutral, in a moment? No man:
> Th' expedition of my violent love
> Outrun the pauser, reason. – Here lay Duncan . . .
>
> (II.iii.108ff)

She stood behind Banquo, 'nervously assenting by unconscious nods
and gestures and inarticulate lip-movements to her husband's story'.
When he finished, she fainted. 'Strung up, past pitch, she gives in at
the *end* of his speech – when she finds he is safely through his story *and
then* she faints really.' After she had been carried out picturesquely,
there was a stir, the crowd gathering around Macbeth to question him.
The rest of the scene was abbreviated. Standing apart, Malcolm and
Donalbain conferred briefly, decided to fly and suited the action to the
word. Banquo declared, 'In the great hand of God I stand'. Macbeth
proposed that they meet in the hall together, and the crowd rushed
eagerly away as the act ended.[59]

Macbeth enters a new phase in Act III. The first two acts deal with
temptation and crime, the remainder with consequences. In his Victorian optimism, Irving interpreted it as a *de casibus* tragedy, a
demonstration of the inevitable fall of wicked tyrants. This reading
was only fully realized in 1888 with the co-operation of Ellen Terry.
The growing isolation of Macbeth and his wife allowed their careers to
take opposite courses. While he became confirmed in evil and followed
the primrose way to th' everlasting bonfire, she could repent because
her motive had been fundamentally unselfish. But Macbeth's ambition was utterly self-centred; he used his wife, and virtually discarded
her when she ceased to be useful (selfishness is the basis of Macbeth's
villainy in Fletcher's reading). Selfishness damned Macbeth because it
prohibited compunction while crime could yield any advantage, which
meant, in effect, while life lasted; thus there could be no repentance in
this life and, hence, no salvation. Irving rested his case on Macbeth's
declaration, after the Banquet:

For mine own good,
All causes shall give way: I am in blood
Stepp'd in so far, that, should I wade no more,
Returning were as tedious as go o'er.
Strange things I have in head, that will to hand,
Which must be acted, ere they may be scann'd.

(III.iv.134–9)

Here, he believed, Macbeth 'announces his fixed intent on a general career of selfish crime . . . How any student, whether he be of the stage or not, can take those lines . . . [and] torture out a meaning of Macbeth's native nobility or honour, I am truly at a loss to conceive.'[60]

Act III opened with visual reinforcement of Macbeth as usurper: the scene was Duncan's own palace at Forres, and Irving entered royally attired, but he was 'nervy, careworn, sleepless'.[61] The falseness of his cordiality to Banquo was thinly veiled by a sickly smile. The soliloquy showed that, with his accession, Macbeth's ruthlessness was now unhindered even by the fiction of conscience. 'Intensely selfish,' Irving wrote, and 'No need of his wife now.' The crown was his alone, with the burden of keeping it: his isolation had begun. When he needed help, he turned to common cut-throats. Their colloquy was cut very short (from 67 to 33 lines), but Irving achieved one memorable effect. Speaking of Fleance (III.i.134) his voice became 'white and flute-like . . . giving for the fraction of a moment a picture of youth and innocence'. Then it deepened with a veiled menace that was simply appalling.[62]

Just before the banquet the alienated couple met informally, dressed but without their crowns, in a futile attempt to comprehend each other's misery. Ellen Terry's notes are very complete. Lady Macbeth was apathetically wretched: 'Express here (when *alone*) a "rooted sorrow" – a half-dulled knowledge of the fact of her husband having been deceived in her. She sees clearer now, knows she has missed what she had hoped to gain.' No pathos was intended: 'Beware of showing the pathetic result of trouble upon a *good* woman. Lady M is not too good. Grief and trouble softens I think a *good* nature, but hardens a bad one.'[63] The short soliloquy was the cry of an overcharged soul:

Nought's had, all's spent
Where our desire is got without content:

'Tis safer to be that which we destroy,
Than by destruction dwell in doubtful joy.

(III.ii.4–7)

She tried gallantly to ease Macbeth's trouble, but the unselfishness of the gesture was the measure of her estrangement from this selfish man. His woe frightened her because it was unrepentant. His solution was more blood, though she did not yet realize it. 'Thou know'st that Banquo, and his Fleance, lives,' he said suggestively. If this was a test, she failed; she was no longer a suitable henchman. 'But in them Nature's copy's not eterne,' she answered lightly, meaning 'Don't trouble so, for they cannot live forever – that fellow Banquo may die any day – *why not*! and the boy may have whooping cough in such a climate as this.' She was alarmed and puzzled but he dismissed her with a kiss, saying 'Be innocent of the knowledge, dearest chuck.' The last line of the scene, 'So, prithee, go with me', was omitted to allow her to remain uselessly behind while he went off to do she knew not what. 'She drops her head standing alone,' Irving wrote, and Terry noted, 'She sits wondering and frightened.'[64]

At the banquet, Lady Macbeth's isolation was translated into the suffering which would lead to her salvation. Inevitably, it was a scenic extravaganza, but the star attraction – Banquo's ghost – remained technically intractable. In 1875 the usual 'bulky person splashed with blood' was replaced by a shadowy, transparent, greenish silhouette; there is no clear evidence to show whether this was a painted gauze or some form of optical illusion like 'Pepper's Ghost'.[65] Most critics disliked it, and in 1888 Irving reverted to tradition. The ghost first rose through a trick chair (see plate 14) and later emerged from the crowd. It departed 'positively crouching down in order to escape notice', according to William Archer, who complained, 'a spectre that dares not hold its head up is certainly not a credit to its class'. The effect required darkness, however, and Irving violated convention to get it. The feast was ostensibly lit by torches held by a row of gillies upstage. Whenever the ghost appeared, they turned their backs and lowered their lights. This motivated the darkness, but nothing motivated the gillies. The business met such a howl of critical execration that Irving changed it soon after opening night. In 1895 the visible apparition was replaced by a shaft of blue limelight.[66]

14 Banquo's ghost rises from the trick chair, 1888 (University of Victoria)

Cattermole's scholarship and Irving's love of pageantry met in the banquet. 'Before the action of the scene begins the rough soldiery enter, hang up shields and drink; then a procession is formed . . . of a score attendants and a number of cooks to set the table, each man bearing viands or furniture for the table.' Cattermole's designs for costumes, weapons, 'wine-cups, ivory cups, salt-cellars, Anglo-Saxon wine-pots, besides cakes in the form of castles' were based upon painstaking research.[67] In 1875 Irving played for sheer terror as he had in *The Bells*; quailing before the ghost, he flung down his coronet as though repudiating the fruits of his crime. Crying 'Unreal mock'ry, hence!' he crouched beside his wife's chair and covered his face with his cloak; 'he was scared,' said Oxenford of *The Times*, 'as never man was scared before'. Macbeth was still afraid in the 1888 production, but the stage business was less extravagant. While notes in the earlier prompt-books stress 'mental terror', those dating from 1888 call for

108

desperation, perhaps because even death cannot suppress Macbeth's foes. Unlike Hamlet's ghost this spectre is dumb, but it was no figment of Macbeth's imagination: Irving wrote, 'Guests feel instinctive terror as in the presence of Something.' No doubt Lady Macbeth sensed it, too, but with an effort that drained her last emotional reserves she put up a brilliant façade, moving amongst the guests, smiling and gracious, calming them down. Ellen Terry tried to show the audience that the strain was terrible: 'Think of this, good Peers, / But as a thing of custom' was to be spoken 'sweetly but with a ghastly mouth – the *mouth* tells all – the pain, the effort, and the madness'. When the guests had retreated in disorder, signalling thereby the failure of Macbeth's attempt to establish himself as ruler of an orderly kingdom, she sank into the throne at left while he collapsed on a seat at right: the physical distance symbolized their moral isolation. 'I think she feels pretty sad,' Terry commented, 'and that her *reason* here, begins to be shaken.'[68] Macbeth's returning vigour frightened her. 'He to go off full of vigour, *blood – more blood*,' wrote the actress. Later she told Clement Scott, 'I do believe that at the end of that Banquet, that poor wretched creature was brought through agony and sin to repentance, and was for-given.'[69] This was the final stroke of isolation: he was to be damned, and she saved. Irving adopted a piece of melodramatic claptrap to bring down the curtain: 'Macbeth takes a torch from behind a pillar, but suddenly, in a paroxysm, hurls it blazing to the ground. He shrouds his face in his robe as he leans rapidly forward and rests against a pillar. The Queen as swiftly kneels behind him, and remains clinging to his skirts, with an upturned face full of tragical solici-tude.'[70] The tableau marked the end of the act. Irving's reading of his last line, 'We are but young indeed', called attention to his solution to the play's confusing time-scheme: there was a 'lapse of years' between the acts. 'Change all beards,' he wrote in his study-book.[71]

In the six-act text of 1888, Acts IV and V illustrated Macbeth and his Queen travelling along the sundered paths where their sins had led them. He walked with the coolness of habit amongst infernal spirits,[72] whilst she trod a *via dolorosa* of penitence in her sleep. The witches' cave was the expected scenic triumph: Macbeth faced the bearded ladies across a rocky defile amongst mountains (see plate 15). Their cauldron was a hollow in the rock. Every device was used to intensify the effect: there were 'lurid exhalations, flashes from the nether fires, blood-dripping skies, and other meteorological eccentricities'; the procession of kings glided grey and shadowy through a mist, and an American critic said that he had never seen baboon's blood of a better quality.[73] Of course, Sullivan's music attracted attention. An introduction *andante maestoso* foreshadowed a 'strangely demoniacal' incantation theme, the thrice-repeated couplet being treated as a refrain:

> Double, double toil and trouble
> Fire, burn; and cauldron bubble.

Hecate entered with an electric star on her forehead and an offstage chorus sang the traditional ditty from Middleton's *The Witch* to 'a fine wild melody'.

> Black spirits and white,
>   Red spirits and gray,
> Mingle, mingle, mingle,
>   You that mingle may.[74]

The music and effects were so arresting that nobody paid much attention to the acting until Macbeth's closing speech. Irving marked with a 'great change' the decision to surprise Macduff's castle, and carefully underscored for emphasis:

> From this moment
> The very firstlings of my heart shall be
> The firstlings of my hand. *And even now*
> To *crown* my *thoughts* with *acts*, be't *thought* and *done*.
>
> (IV.i.146–9)[75]

These lines recalled the key couplet at the end of Act III which Irving found so damnably selfish:

> Strange things I have in head, that will to hand,
> Which must be acted, ere they may be scann'd.

The set was quickly replaced by 'an undulating, far-reaching, aëry mountain-top landscape' with a moonlit sea in the distance. Some sixty witches in gauze draperies appeared, apparently flying so that they seemed to 'people the wind'. The whole preposterous charade was simply a vehicle for Sullivan's choral setting of the other Middleton song,

> Come away, come away,
> Hecate, Hecate, come away!
> Over woods, high rocks and mountains,
> Over seas, our mistress' fountains . . .

15 The Weird Sisters and the Third Apparition, IV.i, 1888 (Library of Congress)

Most critics thought the music exquisite, though *The Times* found it 'loud and operatic' and remarked that evil-tongued persons might term it 'Pinaforean'. Dawn was breaking, and the witches vanished with unearthly shrieks.[76]

Irving's lighting emphasized the gloom of Macbeth's unhappy kingdom, and the sunny English lane revealed by the rising drop 'came as a relief to the first-night audience after so long a sojourn in Caledonia stern and wild,' Archer said. 'Good old England!' shouted a pittite, and there was a patter of applause. Sullivan reinforced the atmospheric change with a fresh and 'idyllic' prelude during the brief interval. The long dialogue between Malcolm and Macduff has great thematic significance, but it is also a bore and Irving cut it to bits.[77]

The lane must have been a shallow set, because the sleepwalking scene which followed required a massive anteroom in Dunsinane Castle with a cloistered corridor upstage, from which a short flight of steps descended. Bateman had botched this scene pretty thoroughly, but Ristori set a high standard, and Ellen Terry's performance was eagerly anticipated. This was the climax of Lady Macbeth's separate tragedy. Years of repentance and grief for the loss of her hell-doomed husband's love had expiated her crime. Her plain white hooded gown suggested a mantle of contrition, and the straggle of faded auburn hair framed a haggard face: the great red braids had been changed at the same time as the beards.[78] Terry played explicitly for pathos, but there was mystery and grandeur, too, as she passed through the cloister carrying the traditional lamp, and descended the stairs. She held the audience in 'a state of absolute, almost painful, stillness'. Sullivan wisely held his fire: a music critic remarked that a less experienced composer might have spoiled the effect with 'some "slow music" of the approved pattern'. She adopted a real somnambulist's 'long-drawn, almost whining utterance, and the breaking-up of words into their syllables'; walking in a natural, unselfconscious way, swaying slightly as she grieved, Terry whispered, 'Out, *damned* [pause] spot [pause]. Out, I say.' Spectators were much moved as she said 'Here's the smell of the blood still', rubbing the palms of her hands together. 'Trembling hands – she is *very* weak,' Terry wrote. William Winter told Irving, 'Ellen is very great at the line "All the perfumes of Arabia".' She seemed to fade away, her exit 'soft as peach bloom'.[79]

The last act was carefully paced to present an accelerating action that paused for a breathless moment at the climax and then plunged into the short, sharp duel. In 1888 five rapid scene changes alternated between the ramparts of the castle (Irving's VI.ii and iv) and four admirably realistic exteriors. Crowds of supernumeraries were skilfully manipulated, troops crossing and recrossing the stage at shorter and shorter intervals to cover scene changes and speed the pace. The scale of the movement can be guessed from that fact that 165 costumes were made for soldiers (designed in batches of 10), 115 Scottish and 50 English.[80] Irving was at his best in the last act in 1875, when several critics thought he based his reading on Caithness's report, 'Some say he's mad' (V.ii.13), but the study-books refer only to 'a deadly heart-sickness' and 'increasing irritability'. Beside the great 'tomorrow' soliloquy, Irving copied out Wordworth's 'My heart leaps up'.

> The Child is Father of the Man;
> And I could wish my days to be
> Bound each to each by natural piety.[81]

The relevance of the sentiment must be left to the reader's ingenuity. Perhaps Macbeth had an unhappy childhood.

In 1888 Irving denied Macbeth the dignity of courage or even madness; there was only a base fierceness growing into fear. With the Doctor (V.iii) his gait was unsteady and he was 'very grim', for the arrival of the detested English epicures had been a great blow to him. He seemed to be trying merely to maintain a show of courage. There was no pathos in his reflections upon honoured old age, and nothing but dull indifference in his elegy upon his wife's death, emended to begin 'She *would* have died hereafter.' Here Irving wrote, 'she'd have died another time, if not now'; after all, he had long ceased to care for her or for any living soul beside himself.[82] Irving wanted the attackers to sing as they came, an eerie effect at which Sullivan flinched: 'I am in despair about the last act,' the composer wrote. 'Your idea about the wild chant or war song going on all the time is splendid in theory, but at present it is impossible in practice, and I do not see my way to overcome the difficulty.' In the end, Irving got his way, and 'The soldiers "off" sang as they fought. Simulated distance made it a kind of hum, but there was a distinct tune in it.'[83] Nothing could have been more evocative of the inevitability of Macbeth's fall.

He met Macduff on the open moor out of sight of the castle.[84] In the warning,

> But get thee back; my soul is too much charg'd
> With blood of thine already
>
> (V.viii.5–6)

there was none of the tone of pity which, in 1875, had won Macbeth some sympathy at the last. In 1888 a hostile critic thought Irving presented 'a repulsive picture of the usurper, unbraced, undignified, and wholly demoralized and hysterical'. Friendly reviews corroborate the interpretation, but find the meeting his finest moment: 'the dominant impression left upon the mind is that of a wild, haggard, anguish-stricken man, battling for his miserable existence with the frenzy of despair'. He was old now; with his grizzled hair and gaunt face, 'he looked like a great famished wolf'.[85] The fight was a rouser in 1875; crying 'before my body / I throw my warlike shield' (V.viii.32–3), Macbeth *threw away* his buckler and, wielding his claymore two-handed, 'hurled blows at his adversary with a blind fury which evidently precipitates his fate'. In 1888 the line about the shield was cut because he threw it away earlier, at 'I'll not fight with thee.' There are no descriptions of the duel, probably because it was unspectacular. Perhaps he died almost without a struggle. Macbeth had not drawn his sword since he fought the merciless Macdonwald for his king; the dagger had become his weapon and, dying, he threw it point downward at Macduff's feet. He fell upon his face, and the soldiers gathered 'to execrate the prostrate tyrant in shouts'. Malcolm was raised shoulder-high to a general shout of 'Hail, king of Scotland', and the curtain fell.[86]

Modern criticism

Ask a modern critic or director what *Macbeth* is about, and he will usually offer you a theme: appearance and reality, Nature and unnaturalness, order and disorder; it is a fertility myth, a Christian allegory, a play of damnation. If you had asked Henry Irving the same question, he might have replied, 'Haven't ye read the play, then, me boy? It's – er – uh – about a man and his wife, ye know. Who – uh – kill their king, d'ye see – uh – and what comes of it. Has to come of it, ye know.' If you had explained the themes, he would probably have agreed with you. And if you had showed him that Shakespeare's audience saw Lady Macbeth as a woman who deliberately invites demonic possession, he would have acknowledged your superior familiarity with Jacobean life, and asked with mild irony whether you knew enough about Victorian life to suggest how he could convey that interpretation to *his* audience. A sophisticated crowd at Stratford-upon-Avon in 1972 might have enough chic occult knowledge to understand Lady Macbeth's meaning when she inverted her crucifix for the invocation;[87] but a Lyceum pittite in 1888 would have thought it a damned sacrilegious gesture and demanded his money back. The difference between Irving's meaning and ours is largely one of vocabulary and focus. Translate his interpretation into modern critical language, and you meet a sound explication in which many images contribute to the theme, but the central metaphor is found in the psychological state of the central characters. To see Lady Macbeth as a symbol is perfectly legitimate, but that is no reason why she must be a psychological impossibility. The actress who plays her must believe in her part or the play falls dead. This does not imply, as Irving Ribner would have us believe, that she will preoccupy herself with counting Lady Macbeth's children:

Much nonsense has come from attempts to treat her as a real person, to analyse her motives, account for her children and in general assign to her a share in Macbeth's tragic downfall to which her dramatic function does not entitle her. The moral choice which destroys Macbeth is his alone; her function is merely to second him in this choice, to counter-act those forces within him which are in accord with nature and in opposition to evil, those very forces represented by Banquo.[88]

'Very good,' Irving might say. 'My conception exactly, ye know – uh – er – but infinitely better said. Except – er – for the foolishness at the beginning.' He might have added that anyone who has faced the unenviable task of breathing life into a dramatic nonentity like Banquo is aware that a world-order in which he must counterbalance Lady Macbeth must be a lopsided order indeed.

If Irving had possessed our critical vocabulary, he might have summarized his interpretation like this: *Macbeth* is a play about the intrusion of evil into a cosmic harmony. Nature is an ordered system which is good in itself because it reflects the perfect harmony in the mind of its Creator. Evil is unnatural, life-denying and barren; because it stands apart from God's creation, it can neither find a place in the natural order nor create an order of its own. It is the principle of disorder. But evil exists both in 'pure' form (the Weird Sisters) and in fallen man, who can resist it and remain in harmony with nature, succumb to it and disjoint the frame of things, or sin and repent. If disorder remains unresolved, nature ultimately asserts herself and expels the alien thing, returning of her own accord to synthesis.

Stated in these abstract terms *Macbeth* sounds like a dead allegory illustrating a commonplace truth. It is a great deal more than that because it is a work of art. Thus it is an intricate complex of images and metaphors which express this theme, but it is also enriched with a host of images whose apparent irrelevance is the secret of its power because their mysterious wholeness is almost infinitely evocative. It is like a note from a great violin which, when analysed, turns out to be a fearful ruckus of overtones and yet has a miraculous life which is utterly denied the same note when it is electronically purged of its impurities.

The central metaphor of *Macbeth* is the protagonist, but he only works as a living metaphor (instead of an allegorical figure) because he is human. I do not say that he is an entirely knowable human being, since that would be a contradiction in terms; it is his complexity which makes him real. He is a mystery, even to himself. No actor, no critic can explain all of his ambiguities; to do so is to belittle him. But in the main, Irving saw Macbeth as a man in whom evil expresses itself in ambition for a crown which is not his by natural right. The crown is good in itself – Duncan is a symbol of order and right rule – but evil has twisted Macbeth's natural love of order into a selfish will to possess it for himself. His wife turns love into evil because she loves the image of order in a man who is a distorting mirror. Seeking a closer union with Macbeth, she urges him to seize the crown by murder. Disorder is the inevitable result. In the central metaphor of the tragedy, this expresses itself in the rift which grows between her and her husband, a rift which becomes absolute when he is damned while she repents and is saved. Many images converge upon this theme: Macbeth is a dwarf unnaturally dressed in a giant's robe, natural sleep has been murdered, feasts are broken, honour and duty violated. The cosmos is in turmoil: the earth shakes, Scotland is diseased, the heavens storm and give birth to prodigies, the sun is extinguished, the fowls of the air and beasts of the earth rebel against natural degree. ''Tis unnatural, / Even like the deed that's done.' Macbeth finds that he cannot possess the crown in peace, and since it is the symbol of peaceful order, this means that he cannot possess it at all. Led by the evil Sisters he commits more crimes in search of peace, but discovers that only his victims find it, while he continues to live in torment.

> Better be with the dead
> Whom we, to gain our peace, have sent to peace,
> Than on the torture of the mind to lie
> In restless ecstasy.
>
> (III.ii.19–22)

4

King Lear

10 November 1892

Theatrical context

Ten years after closing night, Irving's *King Lear* was well on its way to becoming a legendary failure. Legend, however, has a way of distorting the truth, and the facts must modify the traditional judgement. Indeed the production only ran for seventy-six performances, but *King Lear* has always been 'caviare to the general' and even this run was a record.[1] Reviews were mixed, but the great majority were favourable. Nevertheless, Irving never revived or toured the play, and his only published remarks imply a sense of partial failure: 'I may candidly say that I doubt whether a complete embodiment is within any actor's resources.' He explained what had happened: 'On the first night I had a curious experience. As I stood at the wings before Lear makes his entrance I had a sudden idea which revolutionized the impersonation and launched me into an experiment unattempted at rehearsal. I tried to combine the weakness of senility with the tempest of passion, and the growing conviction before the play had proceeded far that this was a perfectly impossible task is one of my most vivid memories of that night.'[2] The change cannot have been very sweeping because there is no hint that the rest of the company was caught wrong-footed. It is probable that Irving merely assumed a 'characteristic voice' which he was unable to sustain. The strain made him almost inaudible at times and brought out his old mannerisms (see above, pp. 11–14), so that blind Gloster's recognition, 'The trick of that voice I do well remember', raised a titter. But by 1905 a journalist who ought to have known better asserted that it had been 'like listening to the nocturnal noises in the Zoo'.[3] Accounts of subsequent performances show that Irving swiftly abandoned the experiment; he dropped the special voice and made the King younger and stronger, even altering his make-up. By the fifth night, 'Irving's rendering was magnificent, its pathos terrible'.[4] But it was too late: the legend had been born.

The critic of the *Referee* attributed Irving's difficulties, in part, to acute first-night nerves.[5] He had reason to be nervous. No actor since Garrick had enjoyed an undisputed success in *King Lear*, and Garrick had played Nahum Tate's recension in which Lear survives to regain his kingdom and Cordelia lives to marry Edgar. In 1823, Kean's boast that the public could have no idea of his full power until they had seen him beside Cordelia's body, proved empty. Macready restored much of Shakespeare's text in 1835, and Phelps achieved fifty-nine performances in repertory at Sadler's Wells, but public response was never enthusiastic. Shakespeare's other tragedies were always more popular, and even in 1892 there was still a prejudice that *Lear* was gloomy, full of horrors and, in unaltered form, unactable.[6] Tate's opinion that it was 'a Heap of Jewels, unstrung and unpolisht' found echoes in the press. 'Shakespeare is, as a poet and playwright, at his worst in *King Lear*,' said the *Idler*; the *Illustrated London News* explained why: 'As a play *King Lear* is – well, it is not. If all the lines that Shakespeare wrote were spoken, there would still be neither unity of action nor adequacy of motive . . . *Lear* would not be tolerated for an hour if produced without the name of Shakespeare.' From the 'general playgoer's point of view' it was 'distinctly lacking in the kind of interest possessed by dramas like *Hamlet*, *Macbeth* and *Othello*'.[7]

Text

Accordingly, Irving sat down to cut and rearrange. His acting version sought refuge from tedium in an artificial brevity: of the original 3,275 lines, some 1,507, or 46 per cent, were cut.[8] Unity of a kind was imposed by altogether eliminating six of the original twenty-six scenes (III.iii, v, vii; IV.iv, v; V.ii), and transposing or combining others to produce a sixteen-scene version. Much of the sub-plot was suppressed, the scenes on the heath were all run together without relief,[9] and Gloster's flight to Dover, his attempted suicide, and the meeting with the mad Lear, were likewise made into a continuous narrative. These arrangements reflected the practical expedients of the theatre of illusion: since each scene required a localized set, the shorter scenes – V.ii is eleven lines long – were simply not worth setting.

The ingenuity of Irving's acting version goes a long way towards compensating for this ruthless surgery, but nothing can adequately replace the dramatist's delicate juxtapositions or the disrupted patterns of imagery. The only scene of great intrinsic importance to be lost, however, was the supremely evil blinding of Gloster, together with the intimation of compensating good in the outraged reaction of Cornwall's servant. Here Irving gave way before public opinion, shared by most of the academic critics of the day, that such violence was too shocking to be represented upon the stage. The ubiquitous Mrs Grundy accounted for some predictable cuts. Lear's crazy obsession with sexuality vanished, to the ruin of a major theme: no small gilded fly would lecher in Irving's sight, and if copulation were to thrive, it must do so unseen and unmentioned. The Fool suffered heavily, of course: some of his most significant lines were cut, together with the response which they elicited:

Lear Dost thou call me fool, boy?
Fool All thy other titles thou hast given away; that thou wast born with.
Kent This is not altogether Fool, my lord.

(I.iv.154–7)

And again:

Fool If thou wert my Fool, Nuncle, I'd have thee beaten for being old before thy time.
Lear How's that?
Fool Thou should'st not have been old 'till thou hadst been wise.

(I.v.42–5)

In view of these enormities, it is tempting to exclaim with Goneril, 'The text is foolish' – another line which Irving cut, understandably enough in the circumstances – and to dismiss the whole production as a travesty. But the only alternative was not to play Lear at all, and if much was destroyed, more, and much greatness, remained. Most of the damage lay in the disruption of subtleties of structure and imagery which Irving never perceived because they have only been discovered by twentieth-century criticism.

Contemporary criticism

In 1892, critical attention was focussed upon entirely different issues.

The assumptions of the theatre of illusion were virtually unchallenged: actors and scholars agreed that scene, action and character must be believable. Unlike *Hamlet* and *Macbeth*, *King Lear* is neither readily adaptable to this style of production nor satisfactorily explicable by the corresponding critical tradition. The difficulties began with the opening scene. How can we believe, critics asked, that a king who has ruled long and successfully would divide and give away his kingdom, disastrously misjudging in the process the worth of the recipients? Coleridge comments upon the 'nursery tale character' of the scene, and adds: 'It may here be worthy of notice, that *Lear* is the only serious performance of Shakespeare, the interest and situations of which are derived from the assumption of a gross improbability.'[10] Most scholars tried to explain away this improbability, and an actor who needed a plausible characterization had to address the same problem. Two solutions were regularly offered. One school of opinion held that Lear is so impetuous that he acts without thought or self-control. A second argued that he is already beginning to go mad. Gervinus took the former view: Lear is a barbarian king in a 'heathenish time' when civilization and Christianity have not yet imposed their controls upon men's passions. 'The best of this race know of no inner strength, of no noble will, of no calmness and self-command, of no moral principle, whereby the power of the blood can be broken, the impulse of passion controlled and immoderate desires bridled.' Lear should be played as 'a man still endowed with the strength of passion which makes him not only the child but the very king of that heroic age'.[11] But most writers thought Lear was mad: the Variorum edition, which appeared in 1880, contained a section in which critics and medical men discussed his behaviour as symptoms.[12]

Victorian taste favoured pathos, and neither interpretation ruled out a pathetic performance, but there was greater potential for pity in a Lear who suffers through no fault of his own. Schlegel said that 'the science of compassion is exhausted' by the spectacle of an old man tormented for 'the childish imbecility to which he was fast advancing' when he divided the kingdom.[13] Morally, however, the play is more palatable if Lear is responsible for his own woes: 'fate in Shakespeare,' said Gervinus, 'is nothing else than man's own nature'. Thus each play contains a warning against a specific vice, and each catastrophe can be construed as the retribution of a just heaven. Dowden realized that if Lear is unbalanced he is morally innocent. In this case the play has implications which Victorian commentators were reluctant to face; it cannot 'reach or inculcate moral truth' because it represents the universe as a grotesque and morally disordered place in which the innocent suffer. Bradley saw the same implication; to him Cordelia's death was a 'sudden blow out of the darkness', and he heartily wished it away.[14] Both scholars scanned the text for evidence that Shakespeare had not really intended anything so blasphemous, and Irving adopted the solution Dowden summarized in an article timed to accompany the Lyceum production.

In no other tragedy are the dissonances so violent; yet, if we enter into its spirit aright, we feel that its dissonances are subdued and there is a solution at the close. The moral motives of the drama may be expressed in a few words: they are the blind rejection of love – love made an alien and an outcast; the temporary triumph of unnatural hate; the onset and the victory of love; love's trial and cruel testing-time; its ultimate conquest, and the seal of death set upon that conquest. Lear dies upon the rack; but he dies as a believer in that which is best and most real in human life . . . Cordelia lies dead in his arms; but she has achieved something higher than the restoration of her father to his throne; she has restored him to love; she has accomplished the good work of a life; even in his agony it is love that delivers over the afflicted old man to the great calm of death. And in spite of all the material suffering and the rending of the heartstrings, this is the truest sense is victory.[15]

Note that Lear is not a heartless tyrant who at last discovers love: he is *restored* to love. Irving perhaps recalled Schlegel's suggestion that the old man gives away everything he has 'out of a foolish tenderness'.[16] In his production, this foolishness was symptomatic of the senile decline of previously formidable mental powers. The decline was hastened and transformed into true madness by the betrayal of his doting tenderness for his daughters. Irving's Hamlet had been driven to the verge of madness by similar betrayals: his Lear was Hamlet grown old. Interpreted thus, he is a man for whom love is the currency of an ordered world. Secure on his throne and at the head of his family, he has freely given and accepted affection, never asking whether it was counterfeit. He is happy to give away wealth and power because he believes himself to be rich in love and secure in an order cemented by natural affection. When Cordelia refuses to feed his illusions, he rejects her because, if she is right, her sisters' love is sham, and order becomes chaos. Betrayed by Goneril, he fears he will go mad; betrayed again by Regan, he learns that the basis of his sense of order is illusion and his mind crumbles into a proportionate disorder. As one critic put it, 'His brain gave way when all the love he had to bestow was turned to gall.'[17] In the purgatory on the heath, he earns the right to learn love's truth from Cordelia, and the play moves towards an optimistic synthesis of love and suffering in a better world.

Performance

Irving's entry was magnificent. The barbaric splendour of the court must have suggested, at first sight, that he intended to play the king of an heroic age, as recommended by Gervinus. A lofty hall was thronged with some sixty of Lear's knights, long-haired Viking warriors in 'horned helmets, skins, and clothing of rough material'. Trumpets sounded, and to a wild march a procession entered, down a flight of steps. Last came Lear, 'a grim, white-haired old chieftain, with fierce restless eyes flashing between dark heavy eyebrows, much of the warrior, more of the King in manner, look and movement'. He looked as patriarchal as 'Moses on Mount Sinai or Noah at the hour of the flood'.[18] The warriors greeted him with a great shout, clashing their weapons against their shields; Lear flourished his sheathed sword over his head. But when he mounted the throne and began to speak, one saw that the old man was wandering: not stark gibbering mad, but decidedly senescent and queer. He used his sword as a walking-stick, plucked at his beard and toyed with his hair. There was something foolish in the way he referred to his 'darker purpose'; his face wore a faintly irritable expression which foreshadowed the anger to come. One critic predicted, 'Years after, when the courtiers talk over the old time they will say, "Do you remember how strange his manner became, how impetuous he was, how fretfully he persisted in the importance of his own particular wishes? His mind must have been infirm, as his body was, then."' Only now did the spectator begin to notice that he was a little dishevelled, his hair and beard tawny rather than snowy white, 'as befits a very old man who is too much engrossed with his own misfortunes to be able to devote attention to his personal appearance'.[19] After its first magnificent impact, the set reinforced this interpretation: whereas scholars assigned the action to the eighth or ninth century B.C., Irving brought it forward to 'a time shortly after the departure of the Romans, when the Britons would naturally inhabit the houses left vacant'.[20] The king and his followers were squatters in a crumbling palace. The steps were worn, stones were chipped, creepers hung from the great arch. Like Lear, it had outlived its grandest days.

The period was chosen at the suggestion of the Pre-Raphaelite painter Ford Madox Brown, who provided designs from which the scenic artist Joseph Harker painted this scene and two other castle sets.[21] Irving sought Brown's help because *Cordelia's Portion*, painted in 1875, had influenced his characterization. Make-up, expression and posture were modelled on the painting; the Lyceum properties department copied the throne with its sprig of mistletoe, the table beside it, and Lear's sceptre (see plates 16a and 16b).[22]

Cordelia stood apart from her sisters, her simple sea-green gown a significant contrast to their red and purple embroidered dresses rich with jewellery.[23] Ellen Terry played for sympathy: in her silence there was no hint of priggishness or obstinacy, nothing to justify her death by making her share the blame. Natural reserve inhibited her from making a public exhibition of emotions as deep and personal as her love for her father, the love which was eventually to emancipate and redeem them both. The actress used her famous charm to soften Cordelia's attitude: 'her rich soft voice gave such a tender tone to the harsh words that any but the old man could have seen the love through it'.[24] Stage business was calculated to express this love: Cordelia's voice broke on 'love' when she said, 'I love your majesty / According to my bond, no more nor less', and Lear's reply, 'Mend your speech a little, / Lest it may mar your fortunes', was spoken 'coaxingly' and his arm stole round her waist.[25] When his rage burst out, she sank submissively to the ground. His anger arose from frustrated love. Terry avoided playing the scene as a confrontation: her portraits convey melancholy rather than anger or pride. The speech in which Cordelia asks Lear to make known the cause of her disgrace can be strong and rebellious (I.i.223–32): Terry played it on her knees. At Lear's exit she hid her face. Following the King, the Fool stooped 'with a quick, reverent motion' and kissed the hem of her gown, thus directing the sympathy of the audience: 'All hearts go with the act of homage,' said one critic, 'and not many eyes are dry.'[26]

Now Edmund worked Gloster against Edgar with such despatch and ease, owing to extensive cuts,[27] that the scene must have seemed a caricature of Lear's folly.

16a *Cordelia's Portion*, by Ford Madox Brown, 1875. The painting influenced Irving's interpretation (Fitzwilliam Museum, Cambridge)

16b *King Lear* I.i, by J. Bernard Partridge. Make-up and properties were copied from *Cordelia's Portion* (University of Victoria)

124

Edmund   . . . I found it thrown in at the casement of my closet. [I.ii.61–2]

Gloster   O villain, villain! [75] Go, sirrah, seek him; I'll apprehend him. Abominable villain!

Edmund   If your honour judge it meet, I will place you where you shall hear us confer of this, [92–3] and that without any further delay than this very evening.

Gloster   He cannot be such a monster.

Edmund   Nor is not, sure.

Gloster   —to his father, that so tenderly and entirely loves him. Heaven and earth! Edmund, seek him out. [95–101] These late eclipses of the sun and moon portend no good to us. [107–8] Find out this villain, Edmund; it shall lose thee nothing. [120–1]

Exit.

The critic who urged Alfred Bishop (Gloster) to 'show more of the struggle against belief' was rather unreasonable.

In Lear's subsequent scenes of conflict with Goneril and Regan, Irving emphasized the loving father whose affection is betrayed. Our attitude to Goneril is partly determined by the behaviour of Lear and his followers in her house. In the film version of Peter Brook's *Lear*, they responded to their master's furious exit by wrecking the premises. Charles Kean's knights were perfect gentlemen, astonished to hear Goneril describe them as

> Men so disordered, so debosh'd, and bold
> That this our court, infected with their manners,
> Shows like a riotous inn.
>
> (I.iv.250–2)[28]

Irving's hirsute hundred, returning from the chase (with real hounds) were unruly enough to show that complaint was not entirely unjustified: they echoed Lear's peremptory shout, 'Dinner, ho, dinner!' Their want of discipline seemed a symptom of his mental instability. But as Goneril, Ada Dyas was 'aggressively shrewish', powerful and tough: while many were dissatisfied with her performance, the desired effect was evidently to prevent the knights from alienating sympathy from Lear.[29]

Oswald, as Gordon Craig played him, was no commonplace stage buffoon, but a person of some consequence, a trusted steward modelled on Irving's own Malvolio. His rudeness carried weight because it represented the deliberate policy of his mistress. In Irving's acting version, the scene rushed to its conclusion much faster than in the original. Much of the Fool's dialogue was cut, and Goneril entered hard upon Oswald's exit at the toe of Kent's boot.[30] Thus Lear had

no time to cool down before his anger was further irritated by her
scolding. His confused mind was unable to take in the significance of
what was happening to him until the Fool explained:

> For you trow, Nuncle,
> The hedge-sparrow fed the cuckoo so long
> That it had it head bit off by it young.
> So out went the candle, and we were left darkling.
>
> (I.iv.223–6)[31]

Something in the allegory entered his consciousness where he had
been able to resist the evidence of his senses. As Goneril scolded, his
face showed his dawning understanding; Irving wrote in his study-
book, 'Agony of thought that he has dispossessed himself.' Then came
the explosion:

> Darkness and devils!
> Saddle my horses; call my train together.
> Degenerate bastard! I'll not trouble thee:
> Yet have I left a daughter.
>
> (I.iv.260–3)

Irving noted the emotions he would play for: 'Delusion – Incoherence,
uncontrollable rage.' The impotence of his position and the knowledge
that it was self-inflicted made him sob bitterly, beat on his head, and
throw down his staff at

> Life and death, I am ashamed
> That thou hast *power* to shake my manhood thus!
>
> (I.iv.305–6)[32]

And only then, transposed to the end of the scene, came the great
curse.[33] Every stage Lear makes his 'points' here: the first-night
audience were waiting for it as they would anticipate a new Hamlet's
'To be or not to be'. Irving followed the tradition of Garrick, Kemble,
the Keans and Macready by kneeling, but he stressed Lear's agony
rather than his rage. In his study-book he wrote, 'Invoking Nature –
with sweet images of child that lay in her father's breast.' No actor
could convey such an idea to an audience: Irving meant this as a
stimulus to his own imagination. Lear's deep and tender love for
Goneril had been betrayed, and in the curse he struggled to uproot it;
the unnatural violence of his words was the measure of the emotional
cost. The effort of this assault upon his own feelings shook the King's
frail old body almost beyond endurance. He gasped, choked, struggled

to express himself: 'the thin, eloquent hands, with every sinew stretched like a cord, trembled in response to the agony which all but severed soul and body'.[34] The horrible terms of the curse were a less severe indictment of Goneril than the state to which she had reduced her father. Lear broke down as he concluded with the hope

> that she may feel
> How sharper than a serpent's tooth it is
> To have a thankless child.
>
> (I.iv.296–8)

Goneril quailed before his passion, shrieked, and hid her face on Albany's shoulder; this business, the fixed attention of the throng of knights, and the emphatic position of the lines, transposed to the end of the act, all served to enhance their significance.[35] With those words ringing in their ears during the interval, the audience could not doubt that Lear's world was falling to pieces as he learned that paternal love can be repaid with filial contempt.

In the second act Irving established the link between Lear's disillusionment and his subsequent complete madness. In the moonlit courtyard of his castle, Gloster was duped by Edmund, Cornwall and Regan arrived, and Kent quarrelled with Oswald and was set in the stocks. After a glimpse of Edgar's flight across 'a windy hillside – purple black beneath the silver stars',[36] the scene returned to the courtyard (see plate 17). Dawn was breaking as Lear arrived with a few followers. He had been travelling all night. Exhausted, he was beaten from the outset.[37] The scene began with an interpolation from Act I (v.14–48) in which Lear began to repent his treatment of Cordelia: 'I did her wrong.' Several lines were cut here, so that the Fool's account of the use a snail makes of his house ('Why, to put's head in; not to give it away to his daughters') was juxtaposed with Lear's premonition:

> O! let me not be mad, not mad, sweet heaven;
> Keep me in temper; I would not be mad!
>
> (I.v.47–8)

As he spoke he threw his hat into a chariot which stood by, the eccentric business suggesting that he had reason to be afraid. The juxtaposition linked Lear's recognition that his generosity and love had been misplaced with the madness he feared. Transposed to Act II, it concentrated that fear in a single scene, where it grew as Lear fought against the knowledge that Regan was no better than her sister: the knowledge would be fatal to his reason.[38]

He met her coldly formal greeting with love. Irving noted, 'Regan now the only daughter left. All his tenderness goes to her.' He wept on her shoulder, perhaps at 'Beloved Regan, thy sister's naught', and there was pleading in his voice when he said, 'Her eyes are fierce; but thine / Do comfort and not burn.'[39] But her impatient 'Good sir, to th' purpose' forced him to face the truth. There was a pause. Then, with 'a terrible suggestiveness . . . Lear, transported from his momentary tenderness towards Regan, demands, with flashing eyes, "*Who* put *my* man in the *stocks*"'.[40] When the sisters combined against him there was 'a sudden revulsion – most pitiably depicted – as the King perceived that Regan was, if possible, more heartless than Goneril'. Again Irving stressed the old man's terror of the madness he felt scratching its way in: 'I *prithee*, daugher,' he begged, 'do not make me mad', and grotesquely he doubled his fists to his mouth. Lear's consciousness of utter betrayal and wretched sense of impotence turned his attempt to duplicate the curse of the first act into a fiasco. 'No, you unnatural hags!' was spoken incoherently. As he denied that they could make him weep, the storm broke overhead with a thunder-clap, and Lear burst into a paroxysm of sobs, falling upon the Fool's shoulder on 'O Fool, I shall go mad.' The rest of the act was cut. With this as the curtain line, the significance of the scene seemed unambi-guous: again Irving had cut his text so that a line which reinforced his interpretation was heavily emphasized.[41]

In the heath scenes the actor must choose between two paths, both strewn with mines and mantraps. Modern criticism insists that *King Lear's* universal themes transcend the personal tragedy of the father and king. The storm is perceived as a convulsion of the cosmos which is emblematic of the chaos in Lear's mind as illusions come crashing down before the sledgehammer of reality. Performance and produc-tion must somehow convey to an audience this transcendant signifi-cance, and Lamb's assertion that 'the Lear of Shakespeare cannot be acted' expresses his conviction that it is impossible to convey. 'On the stage we see nothing but corporal informities and weakness, the

17 (*over*) Lear curses Goneril and Regan in the courtyard of Gloster's castle, II.iv
    (Shakespeare Centre Library, Stratford-upon-Avon)

Scene III
Act II — No, you, vnnatvral
hags,
I will have svch revenges on you both,
That all the world shall —

impotence of rage; while we read it, we see not Lear, but we are Lear.'[42] Lear is us, Man; his experience matters to us because the reality his suffering discovers, however terrible, is Reality.

The actor's alternative is to emphasize Lear the man: this was Irving's choice. Victorian criticism and stage tradition, with their concentration upon character, assumed that this was the true interpretation, and that only perfect illusion could make it work. Lamb's sneer at the 'contemptible machinery by which they mimic the storm' could, it was thought, be answered by perfecting the machinery and hence the illusion. Lear ought to be played as a believable case-history, and his symptoms delineated as realistically as the storm.

Irving's tempest would have astonished Lamb: 'No such realistic representation on the stage of a storm is within our recollection,' said a typical commentator.[43] But because it was naturalistic, the storm existed on an entirely literal and prosaic level, quite independent of the tempest in Lear's mind. This storm would have occurred had Lear been at home in bed. In similar fashion, Irving characterization was made of the stuff of life, not of poetry: the mad scenes were based upon study of real lunatics in an asylum.[44] Thus the terrible vision of the human condition could be taken as a symptom of madness, to be pitied by the audience but not to be shared. The old man might as well have imagined he was Cleopatra: the important thing was to play his madness well and truthfully. Such an interpretation obviously emphasizes pathos; the danger is that it easily degenerates into domestic melodrama. Irving tried to redeem it from sentimentality in two ways: he emphasized Lear's dignity in madness, and he gave the pathos significance by incorporating it in a thematic synthesis at the end of the play. Most of the critics who admired the production were satisfied with pathos, which was all they expected. Of the remainder, a few agreed with *The Times*: 'He is something more than the old man Lamb saw turned out of doors by his daughters on a rainy night ... His sorrows and wrongs ... assume a grandeur that seems to lift the whole conception beyond the purely theatrical.' Others, however, insisted that 'It is a father's agony, rather than a king's humiliation that we see', and that he was 'hopelessly outplayed by the storm'.[45]

Irving continued the psychological developments of the first two acts: Lear's obsession with his daughters, his fear of madness, and the causal link between them. Beside 'My wits begin to turn' he wrote

'Shivering'. 'That way madness lies' was spoken with 'shuddering truth' and 'a sudden wayward rush forward as of a man in dream-horror fleeing an inevitable fate'; it 'almost stops the breath'.[46] Full madness came with Edgar's entrance as Poor Tom; Lear instinctively linked madness with daughters: 'Didst *thou* give all to thy daughters? And art thou come to this?' In the hovel, his reference to 'The little dogs and all; / Tray, Blanch and Sweetheart' expressed a 'disconsolate note of madness' and 'let them anatomize Regan . . . Is there any cause in nature that makes these hard hearts?' drew comment for its 'terrible bitterness' and was 'thrillingly delivered'. There was pathos at the end as 'he crouched by a rude bed and played idly with its furnishing of straw'; and when the Fool and Poor Tom carried him off, 'many of the audience wished that, like poor Gloster, they had no eyes to weep with'.[47]

William Terriss played Poor Tom as a 'dilapidated coxcomb', and the newspapers vied with each other in ridiculing his costume: *Punch* thought he looked like the Good Fairy in a pantomime. Successful enough as Edgar at home, on the heath Terriss was empty, his lines 'loud, rotund, insignificant'. He saw his part as comic relief in 'a damned dull play'.[48] Irving wisely rejected the temptation to prettify the Fool by casting a woman – there is a story that Ellen Terry volunteered for the part – and chose William Haviland, whose 'delicacy of finish' excited universal admiration: 'playing the part seriously, he contrives to bring out more fully than could otherwise be done the grim poetic significance of the play'. His slight figure in coxcomb and motley suggest a boy, but his face was that of a sad-eyed man whose fidelity 'enhances the poetic aspect' of his master.[49]

Pathos mounted at a dangerous pace in Irving's abbreviated acting version. Three pathetic scenes followed with scarcely a break. Gloster, blinded offstage, attempted suicide with almost perfunctory brevity but at least without absurdity. Then, against an ironically sunlit landscape, the two old men met. After rehearsing this moment alone, Irving wrote to Ellen Terry, 'I went over it yesterday . . . hobbling about, half looking on the ground and talking to myself, and when I came unconsciously on Gloster was startled and exclaimed . . . with a downward inflexion "Ahh! – Goneril with a white beard." I quite frightened myself – there is no necessity to *shout* this part – It's frightful from its intensity.'[50] As he predicted, 'Every inch a king' made a great impression: 'he deliberately avoids the conventional trick of a sudden return to a momentary youth: he gives it with the air of an uncrowned king wandering in his wits, to whom the very word "king" suggests, but only for a moment, the memory and glory of a former kingdom. He says it as one in a dream.' As he spoke he brandished the traditional handful of wild flowers over his head as though it were a sceptre.[51] Surely to the observant this business recalled the flourished sword with which he had acknowledged his soldiers' roar of greeting in the first scene. He spoke with deep anguish:

> I know thee well enough; thy name is Gloster:
> Thou must be patient.
>
> (IV.vi.179–80)

His exit became famous: 'Lear scampers from the stage at the words "you shall get it by running", as only a lunatic could run – with utter indifference to appearances, to grace, to everything', fleeing imaginary dangers 'with wild, suffering, pathetic eyes'.[52]

Many found the scene of Lear's awakening more moving than his death. Musicians onstage played a *pianissimo* 'melodrame' as Cordelia approached her sleeping father, who lay on a couch, dressed in regal robes. The recognition was pure pathos: it can hardly be anything else without perverse misinterpretation. 'I can still see him,' one spectator recalled, 'sitting on his couch and staring at the daughter he had banished as she bent tenderly over him. "You are a spirit, I know – when did you die?" he whispered, and I can almost weep now when I recall his voice.'[53] The great moments came thick and fast. Any competent actor can make the tears flow with

> Pray, do not mock me:
> I am a very foolish fond old man,
> Fourscore and upward, not an hour more nor less;
> And, to deal plainly,
> I fear I am not in my perfect mind.
> Methinks I should know you and know this man;
> Yet I am doubtful: for I am mainly ignorant
> What place this is, and all the skill I have
> Remembers not these garments; nor I know not
> Where I did lodge last night. Do not laugh at me;
> For, as I am a man, I think this lady
> To be my child Cordelia.
>
> (IV.vii.59–70)

Ellen Terry shed real tears here. Saying 'Be your tears wet?' Irving 'touched her with his long, wan fingers and put the salt drops to his lips' before he replied, 'Yes, faith.'[54] This business did great execution in the audience, but there was more to come: Terry was admired for her response to Lear's humble apology,

> I know you do not love me, for your sisters
> Have, as I do remember, done me wrong.
> You have some cause, they have not.
>
> (IV.vii.73–5)

Kneeling, she said 'No cause, Ah! Ah!' in a voice 'half choked with joy to see her father once again, half choked with sorrow at seeing him as he is'. Looking at her piteously, Irving said, 'Pray you now, forget and forgive. I am old and foolish', in 'the sweetest accents of wistful beseeching insinuation, as by a child who had quarrelled with his nurse', and he dropped his head on her shoulder as she supported him offstage. The audience exploded with appreciation of sentiments 'as beautiful in their wholesome tenderness as acting can make them'.[55]

The last scene was played on 'flowery down-lands' beside the sea, in front of a drop representing sheer chalk cliffs (see plate 18). The opening movements passed rapidly, accelerated by bold cuts which left the villains with little to say. Edgar came out to battle with joy and 'disposed of Edmund in a very few seconds' of rousing combat. The exposure of the bastard's villainy and his dying repentance were cut very short (100 lines were reduced to 17) and a messenger was dispatched to rescue Cordelia.[56] Then Lear's voice was heard off-stage: 'Howl, howl.' He continued, 'howl, howl' as he entered, carry-ing Cordelia in his arms. This was no mean feat, as Ellen Terry, at forty-five, was going through a plump phase: Kean had staggered here, and Salvini frankly gave it up, dragging the corpse on.[57] Kneel-ing, Lear tried to detect Cordelia's breathing, kissed and held her as though to bring her back to life; failing, he laid her on the ground. 'Cordelia, Cordelia, stay a little' was a 'pitiful wail', a 'despairing cry'. Then, in an instant, he was all hope and senile eagerness to hear her voice. 'I killed the slave that was a-hanging thee,' he said, brightening with childish satisfaction and a momentary vigour which showed how it had been possible. 'I am old now,' he added, lapsing again into a weakness that grew steadily; at the same time, his mind gradually

18 The death of Lear, by Hawes Craven (Shakespeare Centre Library, Stratford-
upon-Avon)

cleared. While Lear talked to Kent, he toyed absently with the rope
which remained around Cordelia's neck.[58]

Now the sun was symbolically setting, its slowness keeping time
with the 'slow loosening, one by one, of the cords of life'; in that red
light, 'the face of the dying stands out, very fine, mortally pale'.

> Thou'lt come no more,
> Never, never, never, never, never.
>
> (V.iii.307–8)

Irving's reading left no hope: 'It is impossible to translate the intona-
tion of the five successive "nevers" which descend, which bury
themselves in the deepest depths of human despair,' said a Parisian
critic. With his last words he bent to kiss Cordelia, then fell back gently

136

in Kent's arms, 'pointing his gaunt fingers to her dead body as he . . . gently expired'. Around him 'the crowd of barbaric warriors lowered their spears pointing to the dead king' (see plate 18).[59]

There can be no doubt that Irving played for pathos again in this scene: critics found it 'ineffably sweet – one of those bits which make strong men feel a lump in their throats'.[60] The business with the rope, the four long sighs with which Lear's twenty-five lines of dialogue were punctuated, the sunset which symbolized his ebbing life, the unmotivated incidental music which was played near the end, are all pathetic devices of an almost melodramatic order; it only wanted an angel choir. Nevertheless, there was a sense of anticlimax. The real resolution of the play as Irving interpreted it was the awakening scene: stripped of illusion by betrayal and suffering, Lear learned from Cordelia the real nature of love. Her death brought him to despair, but it did not deny the truth he had learned. With the last link broken between the real world and the world as he had once imagined it to be, the old man was no longer a part of life or interested in it: he simply ceased to live. Dying, he accidentally found a state in which love thrives immutably; the implied reunion in heaven redeemed all suffering. Irving's audience went out into the night consoled by a resolution which suggested the existence of a benevolent Providence. They did not pause to wonder what all the agony was for.

Style and criticism

If this bland response denoted failure, the blame was not entirely Irving's. The conventions of the theatre of illusion obscured the play's significance. Lear and his world were rationally and realistically conceived: his behaviour was psychologically explicable, the storm was a meteorological phenomenon, time and place were concrete, and safely remote. There was no sense of ambiguity or mystery. Nothing in the play implied any significance beyond itself. Cordelia's goodness was as accidental as the wickedness of Edmund or Goneril: if there were any cause in nature which made these hard hearts, it was heredity or environment. Suffering was caused by human action and bad luck. Thus if the sufferers were innocent, there was no need to question the justice of the universe: the audience were merely invited to blame the villains and pity the victims. *King Lear* became a pathetic melodrama which touched the heart-strings, but left the vital organs undisturbed.

Cordelia's death is not redundant: it alters everything. On the heath, Lear has expiated his blindness. He awakes regenerate and clear-sighted. Had Shakespeare stopped there, *King Lear* would have been his *Oresteia*, a splendid vindication of the ways of Providence: 'From suffering comes wisdom.' But the death of Cordelia turns regeneration into irony. She dies through a mischance too pointed to be accidental. 'The gods defend her!' cries Albany, and immediately her corpse is 'brought in like a Christmas present', as Wyndham Lewis says, to show us 'the vanity of human supplications, and notions of benevolent powers'.[61] This is what Lear's painful education has been for: to render him fully vulnerable to this exquisite agony, to make him see quite clearly the malignity of the cosmos.

> This feather stirs; she lives! if it be so,
> It is a chance which does redeem all sorrows
> That ever I have felt.
>
> (V.iii.265–7)

The point of these lines is surely that Cordelia is *not* alive, and that therefore Lear's sorrows cannot be redeemed. Significantly, his last words revert to this theme:

> Do you see this? Look at her, look, her lips,
> Look there, look there!
>
> (310–11)

His meaning is often debated: is Lear expressing his despair, or is it vain hope? In either case, the question is not whether Shakespeare is twisting his ironic knife, but merely how many times. If Lear dies in despair, he has been killed by his horror at the unjustifiable death of innocence. But if he dies in hope, it is a *false* hope which he has deliberately embraced rather than face reality. He knows better:

> I know when one is dead, and when one lives;
> She's dead as earth.
>
> (260–1)

If he dies happy, he is self-deluded. He returns, in short, to illusion, and returns voluntarily. All the suffering of the past five acts has been utterly vain. Truth is too much to bear.

Irving's experience with *King Lear* suggests that the conventions of the theatre of illusion are too earth-bound to realize the cosmic implications of such a play, and too inflexible to accommodate its structure. They turned it into a dull and ill-constructed melodrama. It must be remembered, however, that these same conventions allowed him to achieve some admirable and legitimate scenic effects which would have been impossible in the presentational convention for which the play was written. Irving's convention encumbered the action with scene changes, prevented the use of a single strong visual metaphor, and ruled out the kind of thematic reinforcement which can be achieved with a unit set, by echoing the groupings of the first scene in the last, for example.[62] But I have noted that Irving was able to turn Lear's crumbling Roman palace into a powerful metaphor for his mental state. An important visual theme ran throughout the production. Gradually, scene by scene, Lear moved from protected enclosure to naked exposure. The abdication was played in an enclosed hall with a single doorway through which the outside world could be glimpsed. As experience exposed Lear to cruel nature, the scene moved out of doors: the clash with Goneril took place in an unroofed atrium, while the confrontation with Regan occurred in an open courtyard. The scenes on the heath conveyed a sense of utter nakedness to the sky: sets depicted treeless plains broken only by standing stones, symbolic relics of a bygone age. The interior scenes were elaborate, built-up sets of solid appearance, while the exteriors were created by the simplest traditional means, using only painted drops and wings: it was as though the rich spectacle of the theatre had been stripped away from Lear with his other illusions, leaving him alone in the void.

5

Four Tragedies

Othello,
Richard III,
Romeo and Juliet,
Coriolanus

> Excellent wretch, perdition catch my soul,
> But I do love thee, and when I love thee not,
> Chaos is come again.
>
> (III.iii.90–2)

Othello sums up the key principle of Shakespearean tragedy as Henry Irving interpreted it: love, order and salvation stood in antithesis to lovelessness, chaos and perdition. Their conflict propelled tragedy, and catastrophe was their synthesis.

Irving understood tragedy in terms of the individual. His Lear failed because it had no cosmic dimension. Every coherent play creates a world with its own moral laws; today we are inclined to believe that it is the *sort* of world which is created, and the kind of moral laws it follows, which makes tragedies. The inhabitants and their deeds will be tragic because they live in a tragic world. The theme of *King Lear* is the same as that of *Love's Labour's Lost*; the protagonists have the same illusions; but in the park of Navarre a fool can discover his folly without meeting grievous harm, whereas folly kills where boy-gods run amok with fly-swatters. The forces that rule a tragic world are irresistible, possibly malevolent, indifferent at best to human desert; and there is no refuge from them.

Irving's interpretations were never tragic in this way. His Shakespeare never questioned the justice of a moral order which was *a priori* unquestionable, and when Lear or Hamlet did so they were to be pitied for their mistake and set straight before they died. The laws of the tragic world were the same as those of the real world as Irving perceived it: they were just. And since Providence was not seriously questioned, the conflict could not be cosmic: it had to be personal or social.

Because Irving was a romantic actor, his tragic heroes were frequently eccentrically individual; indeed, the dramatic interest largely derived from what Victorian critics called their 'idiosyncrasy'. It was tragedy of the uncommon man. In a providentially ordered world evil can only come from a man, who might be at the centre of the play, like Richard III or Macbeth, or more or less to the side, like Iago, Claudius or the Edmund–Goneril–Regan menagerie. This man was evil in himself, an intruder who inevitably came into conflict with the world upon which he trespassed, and his equally inevitable expulsion was the propulsive force of tragedy. Order manifested itself in love, but the 'kindless villain' was isolated, selfish and loveless. He was a dissembler who usually brought chaos by making his victims incapable of distinguishing between the appearance and the reality of love. His victims – Hamlet, Lear, Othello, Lady Macbeth – often suffered mental disorder: it was no accident that Irving restored to the stage the scene of Othello's epilepsy (IV.i.35–9).

Most of the tragedies boiled down to a conflict between a villain and his victim, either one of whom might be the centre of interest. The restoration of order could never be really in doubt because it was the will of Providence; this gave the action inevitability, but it meant that the resolution did not depend upon the sacrifice of a Hamlet or a Romeo. Thus tragedy could not be justified by pointing to renewed order, because it would have happened anyway. But oddly enough, there was no sense of waste either. Obviously, nobody felt anything of the kind when Richard Crookback fell on Bosworth Field, or when Irving's thoroughly evil Macbeth was slain; but even the deaths of the victim-heroes yielded a sense of satisfaction or exultation rather than a feeling of anything so futile as waste. This experience is common in the theatre. Irving's remarkable achievement was to elicit this response whether he played the hero or the villain, Hamlet or Richard.

In assessing this reaction the natural exhilaration of an audience witnessing a great performance should not be discounted. But perhaps there were other reasons. In the first place, Irving treated the two types of Shakespearean tragedy as essentially one type with differing emphases. And in the second, his tragic performances seemed to assert that even great evil can affirm the significance of the individual. If we try to console ourselves for the deaths of Romeo and Juliet with the thought that Verona will now enjoy tranquillity, we shall become aware of the difference between theoretical effect and dramatic experience. The only people we care about are dead: Verona can make itself a shambles, and welcome. Hamlet, Lear, Romeo and Juliet only achieve significance because they suffer and die, and a Macbeth or a Richard matters *because* he is evil. That is why their stories are worth telling. Romeo and Juliet in middle age, squabbling over the tradesmen's bills, old King Hamlet the Undecided, General Macbeth (Rtd) boring his cronies with army stories: these are visions of horror because they are insignificant.

In suffering and death the tragic hero and tragic villain alike attain a self-realization which is unique and imperishable. The victims can fulfil themselves only because the villains create the chaos which is the crucible of their significance; and the villains earn the dignity of completeness with the challenge they hurl at the unchallengeable and their defiance in the face of inevitable defeat.

Othello   14 February 1876, 2 May 1881

Here the lover and the violator of order are almost equally prominent, and Irving tried his hand at both parts. In October 1875 Salvini's volcanic Othello conquered London. He combined the myths of the Noble Savage and the Wild Man. Tremendous natural dignity gave way to animal passion when Iago stripped away his veneer of civilization. He backhanded Desdemona across the mouth instead of striking her with the letter as more gentlemanly Moors had done and he cut his own throat with a scimitar, realistically and messily.[1]

When Irving played Othello four months later, he tried to divert attention from the accident of race as the source of disorder. In his characterization, said Joseph Knight with disapproval, 'there is more of European culture and refinement than of African imagination and heat of temperament'. He startled the audience by wearing a light bronze make-up and Venetian uniform instead of the traditional turban and *djellaba*.[2] Outraged prejudice and tradition no doubt accounted for some of the critical abuse he encountered, but the first performance was deeply flawed by mannerism. Incoherent speech and extravagant gesture marred his scenes of high passion: critics condemned a 'curious habit of violently nodding while the right foot is planted firmly considerably in advance of the rest of the body'.[3] Worse, Irving indulged in old-fashioned 'illustrative business'. 'I'll tear her all to pieces,' he cried, and 'his fingers not only perform with the perfection of a machine the comminuting process, but also appear as if they were distributing the fragments among the audience'.[4] Othello should have dignity and repose. His authority is usually established when he quells an incipient brawl with his cool command, 'Keep up your bright swords, for the dew will rust 'em' (I.ii.59). Irving stood with his back to the audience, 'throwing up his arms in an excited manner' and speaking petulantly.[5]

None of Shakespeare's tragedies yields so readily as *Othello* to the sort of interpretation Irving preferred. The Moor is so emphatically a protagonist for whom reason, poetry and order are founded on love and trust, that the actor's failure seems almost perverse. In the first act, Othello ought surely to be triumphant and joyous in his fulfilled love, but Irving gave him a melancholy predisposition to jealousy. Facing Brabantio before the Senate, he started when the old man accused him of seducing Desdemona with drugs and spells (I.iii.104–5), and bowed gratefully when the Duke said there was no proof.[6] He went out to meet Desdemona and brought her in, treating her throughout with an almost obsequious uxoriousness that was evidently founded on insecurity: at Brabantio's warning,

> Look to her, Moor, have a quick eye to see:
> She has deceiv'd her father, may do thee
>
> (I.iii.292–3)

he started and cried 'No' as though 'to banish a rising doubt'.[7]

Henry Forrester, an actor of subordinate reputation, impressed everyone with his unconventional Iago. 'He stands up before us square and fair, manly of form, pleasant of voice and face . . . and it is precisely because he seems of such honesty that we find nothing incongruous in the success of what we know to be so outrageous a piece of treachery.'[8] Significantly, Irving chose Forrester to play the smiling Claudius in his 1878 *Hamlet*; Iago was such another loveless fairseemer. Like many earlier Othellos, Irving was writing at a desk when Iago got to work (III.iii.35). His jealousy was easily aroused, 'the mine of passion . . . sprung too soon and too suddenly'. He neither rejected nor suppressed his suspicion: 'It transfixes him with horror. He gazes into vacancy, open-mouthed and in a daze.'[9] Left alone, he gave way to excessive passion at,

> I had rather be a toad,
> And live upon the vapour in a dungeon
> Than keep a corner in a thing I love
> For others' uses.

(III.iii.274–7)

When Iago returned, Othello seized him by the throat and threw him down, demanding 'ocular proof' (365–9), then cast himself full-length on a couch. At the climax, he fell in a 'realistic semblance of an epileptic fit'. Mind and body were disordered by passion, and he became 'incapable of connected speech and movement'. Irving was not yet equal to such a display of emotion, however, and most critics substantially agreed with the wag who said that 'his appearance and manner are those of a sham Indian about to perform his war dance in a booth at a county fair'.[10]

Irving restored Desdemona's scene with Emilia (IV.iii) and her 'willow' song, perhaps to give himself a rest before the last scene, where he regained a measure of composure and stillness. The bed was hung with heavy curtains, which he discreetly closed before murdering Desdemona. The last speech was weakened by a tendency to 'illustrate' his narrative by enacting his anger against the imaginary Turk, but the suicide was dramatic: stabbing himself, he fell and crept across the floor to die beside the bed.[11]

Irving began to think about playing Iago soon after *Othello* closed. In a public reading in 1877 he attempted a characterization that was much more complex than either the traditional rascal or Forrester's honest gentleman with a heart of brimstone. He was a man with a 'conscious devotion to evil, a wide-ranging intellect and great ambition as a destroyer' hidden beneath an 'alternating surface-personality' which offered each victim a deceiver fashioned to expoit his individual weaknesses.[12]

The opportunity to try out his new idea came in 1881, when he revived *Othello* with Edwin Booth. This was a hasty and inexpensive production: the Senate scene used the courtroom set from *The Merchant of Venice* with the dais at right instead of left, and the production account amounted to less than a tenth of the cost of *Romeo and Juliet*.[13]

Iago followed the lines established in the reading. Deceiving every-one 'in right of his superior intelligence', he changed his masks with dazzling virtuosity: 'to Roderigo, a fantastic trifler; to Cassio, the best of good fellows; to Othello, a complex composition made up of cynical philosophy and bitter truth'.[14] Instant transitions underlined his duplicity. Making his plans at the end of the first act, he paused in thought at 'how, how? ... let me see' (I.iii.392) and 'covered his brooding brow with his long lean hand, then as the fiendish solution occurred to him, he suddenly withdrew his hand, and discovered a face expressing triumphant malignity'. As the speech ended he heard guards approaching, and instantly he became the light-hearted soldier of fortune.[15] Alone with Roderigo, Iago spoke contemptuously of 'the Moor' and expressed disgust at the thought of Desdemona's love, but to Othello's face he was 'cunningly deferential'.[16] Irving ingeniously turned his own honest emotions to dramatic account: when Ellen Terry (Desdemona) appealed to him,

> O good Iago,
> What shall I do to win my lord again?
>
> (IV.ii.150–1)

he wiped away his real tears and blew his nose 'so that the audience might think his emotion a fresh stroke of hypocrisy'.[17] Brilliant costume set off his pose as a gallant adventurer: 'a crimson and gold jerkin, with a mantle of dull or faded green, sometimes alternated with a short cloak and a red mantle worn on one arm' (see plate 19).[18] His humour was as brilliant as his clothes, and spectators frequently found themselves caught up in a laugh, unwillingly and at times insidiously, because they seemed to be sharing a joke with the devil: 'the flavour of grim comedy . . . is effectively exhibited, and the audience is moved in the most tragic scenes to a kind of merriment. The asides are delivered in a gibing, acrimonious, yet self-contented spirit, the effect of which is indescribable.'[19] Watching Cassio welcome Desdemona to Cyprus (II.i), he commented sardonically on their innocent actions while 'he leaned against a vine-clad archway, plucking and eating the grapes' and spitting out the seeds 'as if each one represented a worthy virtue'.[20] The shocked laughter with which an audience responds to dexterous hypocrisy was deliberately courted by Irving's management of the scene in which Roderigo is killed (V.i). It was played in a dark street running upstage between tall houses. Iago left Roderigo in ambush, only to emerge during the fight, stab Cassio, and vanish again. He re-emerged, killed Roderigo, and was on the point of finishing off Cassio when the Watch entered through an arch upstage. Darting indoors, he appeared at a window with such an air of innocence that, according to *Punch*, 'it was unanimously declared that the climax of the fun had been attained, and that nothing more intensely humorous had ever been seen on any boards'. *The Athenaeum* added, 'We can recall no picture finer in its way than that of the saturnine ruffian turning over with his foot, in indolent and mocking curiosity, the body of Roderigo to see if life were extinct.'[21]

Bradley says that the great question about Iago is *why*. The explicit motives are numerous but unsatisfactory.[22] Rejecting the melodramatic stereotype of an habitual villain who makes mischief his sport, Irving seems to have played Iago as a vulnerable, insecure cynic who committed dreadful crimes, probably for the first time, when the promotion of an honest fool like Cassio threatened his anarchic vision. If he could pervert and smash the lives of the honest fools, his power and their impotence would prove their ordered world an illusion. Real hatred was as foreign to his nature as real love. To Iago, 'love' was a polite word for lust and 'honesty' for self-interest. Emilia meant nothing to him: Georgina Pauncefort played her as a matronly and respectable person who seemed unlikely to have been guilty of promiscuity. But by stressing Iago's sexual jealousy of both Othello and Cassio, Irving suggested the irrational paranoia behind his malignity.[23] He gave Iago a great deal of small, fidgety business which was no doubt meant to suggest his insecurity: 'he is never for an instant still, always playing with his cap, or his dress, or his moustachios, slapping Roderigo on the back, throwing has arm around his neck, . . . now sitting on a table, now leaning against a pillar'; he 'toyed with a pen, with his sword-belt and trappings, used a poignard as a toothpick, rumpled his hair incessantly, waved a red cloak about him bull-fighter fashion'.[24]

Irving's Othello of 1881 was such a contrast to his Iago that they might almost have been designed to be played together, like one of those recordings of a popular singer in a duet with himself. The new

19 Booth as Othello, Irving as Iago, 1881 (University of Victoria)

Othello had the dignity and repose that were lacking in 1876: 'He employs a stillness of pose which is perhaps more remarkable in him than it might be in some other actors; but the emotions which he feels are shown by the varying, but never exaggerated, expressions which flit across his face. His gestures are significant, but few and quiet.' He was 'the most civilized specimen of a Moor that has yet been seen in history and fiction,' complained a critic who missed the traditional 'animal and barbaric nature' of Othello.[25] But the bronze complexion was abandoned for the blackest make-up since the days of Macready, and the Venetian costume was replaced by native dress: he wore a small white turban in the first act, with 'a flowing amber robe over a purple brocaded gaberdine'. Each successive dress astonished the audience with its 'picturesque' richness: 'jewels sparkle in his turban and depend from his ears, strings of pearls circle his dusky throat, . . . and his richly-brocaded robes fall about him in the most lustrous and ample folds'.[26]

The most significant change, however, lay in Irving's interpretation of Othello's jealousy. It was no longer incipient in the scene before the Senate, where his confidence in his wife was as perfect as his love. He was still uxorious, but the great address (I.iii.128–70) was unclouded by premonition: towards the end 'he gradually departs from the somewhat formal dignity and reticence of the opening, not into loudness or violence, but into a poetical exaltation caused by the memories of his courtship which he is recounting. There is nothing in it the least unbecoming either his own dignity or that of the august personages he addresses; it is a natural and noble forgetfulness of the moment which seems to fit the noble, loving nature of the Moorish general.'[27] Ellen Terry remembered that he spoke, 'beaming on Desdemona all the time. The gallantry of the thing is indescribable.'[28] Tom Mead's Brabantio was 'just the sort of father who, while by his own coldness and want of sympathy he had driven Desdemona to seek sympathy elsewhere, yet was cut to the very heart when he woke up to find that she had chosen a husband and future for herself'.[29] This time, Othello was quite unperturbed at the old man's bitter warning.

Othello responded to Iago's insinuations much less readily than before. George Saintsbury pointed out that the omission of Bianca, a custom Irving followed in both productions, tends to make the Moor seem too easily persuaded of his wife's guilt, but Irving made it seem quite plausible'[30] The scene was a room in Othello's Moorish house, with 'a bright sunlit coast' outside. The General was too absorbed in business to pay much attention to his Ancient's feigned disquiet at the sight of Cassio (III.iii.35). He sat at a table to write, pausing, when Desdemona approached and kissed him on the forehead, to kiss her hand. He remained playful and untroubled until Iago's insistent coyness, 'Think, my lord?' (109), irritated him enough to arouse 'a vague suspicion of something being wrong, not with his own affairs so much as with Iago's state of mind'. He tried to resume writing, but Iago prodded him until he resolved to uncover what seemed to be 'some special ill known or suspected by the Ancient'. Rising with a smile and shaking his head, he said, 'By heaven I'll *know* thy thought' (166).[31] Othello was disturbed when Iago reminded him, 'She did deceive her father, marrying you' (211). In his study-book, Irving underscored the reply, '*And so she did*!!!!' Now he began to suffer and Iago pressed home his advantage. The study-book is full of notes like 'look pitifully at Iago' (241), 'head on back of chair' (244), 'hand to head – leaning on table vacantly' (260). He spoke the soliloquy (262ff) sitting on an ottoman; at the climax, Desdemona entered. There was a long pause and then, with a 'Great change', he rose and cried '*I'll not believe it*'·(283): this cry, 'so wondrously indicative of the thorough generosity and nobility of his nature, simply electrified the house'.[32] But now his jealousy grew of itself until some thought he became unbalanced. Shuddering when he said, '*Villain*, be sure thou prove my love a whore' (365), he attacked his tormentor, half-strangling him and kicking him when he was down. Othello was very still as he listened to the villain's account of Cassio's dream (419–32); and beside the subsequent discussion of the handkerchief, Irving wrote, 'very intense, terrible calmness, tremendous agony, assumed calmness' (438–53).[33]

On the evenings when Booth played the Moor, the bed in the murder scene stood to one side on the chamber, but Irving moved it to centre stage. A red lamp burned on the table. Othello's manner justified the assertion, '. . . nought did I in hate, but all in honour' (V.ii.296). To him the murder seemed 'a just and necessary execution'; his jealousy was forgotten.[34] Taking the sleeping Desdemona in his arms he kissed her, and rose 'intoxicated'. He did not grow angry until she asked for Cassio: then 'getting very savage', he said, 'No, his mouth is stopped' (72). There was no violence until the last moment, when Desdemona tried to run; Othello seized her, flung her on the bed and closed its curtains behind him. The curtains were traditional, but Irving turned them to advantage with a characteristically bold stroke: there was a long silence, 'broken by a loud knocking at the door, of which no notice is taken for a time'.[35] The audience sat gazing at the empty stage, nerves harrowed by the knocking, full of the knowledge of what passed behind those enigmatic curtains, waiting through the interminable seconds for the Moor to draw them aside. When Emilia entered and heard Desdemona's dying words, Othello slumped into a chair downstage right, his back to the audience; thus Emilia's face alone was visible when she reacted to 'thy husband knew it all' (140). When she confessed that Iago had begged her to steal the handkerchief, Othello shrieked. There was a fine, quiet moment after he stabbed Iago: Lodovico asked whether he had consented to Cassio's death. Othello paused, looked at his lieutenant, bent his head in shame, and said, 'Ay'. When Cassio protested, 'Dear general, I never gave you cause', Othello held out a hand to beg for pardon: impulsively, Cassio kissed it and the Moor turned away, 'agitated' (298–301). The play ended with his suicide, the curtain descending as he fell at Gratiano's feet (357). Booth stood over him, 'pointing triumphantly at the dead body and gazing up at the gallery with a malignant smile of satisfied hate'.[36] Irving's Iago was stoical in the last scene, enduring pain and punishment as though satisfied that his life was vindicated and fulfilled. When he refused to speak further (305) his manner implied 'a mystery that he disdained to unfold and which others could not comprehend'. Led away before the end, he looked round at Othello and shrugged as he went out.[37] The contrast between this, and Booth's melodramatic gesture, crystallized a difference in style which may be guessed from their postures in plate 19. Booth was old-fashioned and explicit: his interpretation was as sound as Irving's, but by Lyceum standards it was overstated. 'Unfortunately, fine actor as Edwin Booth undoubtedly was, his point of view and Irving's differed, and his performance was the only one not in harmony with the rest of the picture, not in sympathy with the dominating mind. It was as though a splash of crimson had been introduced in a delicate nocturne by Whistler.'[38] Nevertheless, while most critics preferred Irving as Iago, Booth's style served him better as the Moor. Irving was glad to drop Othello when the American went home, but he played Iago on his autumn tour.[39]

Richard III   29 January 1877,   19 December 1896

29 January 1877. A merry peal of bells cuts across the chatter of a first-night audience. The house lights dim and the rising curtain reveals a sunlit mediaeval street leading to a castellated stone gateway (see plate 21a). Five armoured soldiers cross; then through the gate limps Richard, a young, sensitive-looking man dressed much like Hamlet, but wearing a maroon cloak heavily trimmed with fur and a pointed Robin Hood hat (see plate 20a). The applause gives him time to reach the footlights.

> Now is the winter of our discontent
> Made glorious summer by this sun of York.

Few members of the audience have ever heard these words spoken in a theatre.

Colley Cibber's version of *Richard III* still held the stage in 1877: Barry Sullivan had played it at Drury Lane the year before. Phelps introduced Shakespeare's text at Sadler's Wells in 1845, but he failed to persuade either the public or other actors to abandon their preference for the traditional adaptation: indeed, he reverted to Cibber's version in 1861.[40] It is true that after the Lyceum production Cibber was seen no more in London, but the entire credit does not belong to Irving. The public and critical mood was ready for the change, authenticity was the vogue. Irving's venture received a puff universal that drowned the plaintive voices of the minority who thought that Cibber's was in some respects the better acting script, and of those who pointed out that '*Richard III* at the Lyceum is a much more satisfactory adaptation of the original play than Colley Cibber's. But it is none the less an adaptation.'[41] The reader may judge from the facts whether there is any substance to this charge.

Richard III is Shakespeare's second-longest play, and Irving cut nearly 1,600 of its 3,600 lines: even so, playing-time was two hours and forty minutes.[42] He omitted a number of minor characters, most notably Sir Thomas Vaughan. Victorians, like modern playgoers, had a limited appetite for cursing queens, and Irving prudently abbreviated the ladies' 'copious exclaims'. In limiting Queen Margaret's part to one scene (I.iii), however, his motive was probably a realistic assessment of Kate Bateman's capacities rather than anxiety that she might take the play away from him as Mrs Warner is said to have done with Phelps; when a first-rate Margaret (Genevieve Ward) was available in 1896, her part was largely restored.[43] In accordance with contemporary practice, Irving cut scenes enacting events narrated elsewhere, like the death of Rivers and Grey (III.iii), and short 'information' scenes like the Scrivener's.[44] There was less excuse for the omission of Richmond's first appearance (V.ii); and the death of Clarence (I.iv) was retained, unnecessarily by prevailing standards, no doubt for the poetry in which he describes his dream. His conversation with the Murderers (I.iv.166–271) was cut. The only major rearrangement was made in response to the intrinsic difficulties of accommodating an Elizabethan play to the theatre of illusion: Richard's tent could not believably share the stage with Richmond's, so V.iii was broken into four scenes alternating between the two locations, an arrangement which required some transpositions.[45]

Cibber's Richard had been played as a 'petulant, vapouring, capering, detonating creature', a 'coarse, loud, swaggering bully' who 'stamped about the stage in scarlet doublet and flapping, russet boots, with black ringlet wig and bushy eyebrows'.[46] This melodramatic villain proceeds from one mood to the next in a series of 'points': when his confidence is shaken by the ghosts, for example, he pulls himself together with the famous line, 'Conscience avaunt; Richard's himself again', a transition whose genuine dramatic value is brilliantly demonstrated in Olivier's film.[47] Shakespeare's subtler characterization suited Irving better; besides, as Clement Scott pointed out, 'No recollection of the superiority of some preceding tragedian in the delivery of a particular passage need trouble either actor or auditor. With the entire abandonment of all the speeches for which the audience used to wait in an attitude of applause, Mr. Irving has wisely cast aside all traditional accompaniments of the character.'[48]

In both Lyceum productions Richard's deformity was slight. The left shoulder was padded to suggest a low hump and he limped on shoes with heels of unequal height. But in 1877 he was young, while in 1896 Irving made-up beyond his own fifty-eight years (see plates 20*a* and 20*b*). Young Richard's motive was the deformity that isolated him;

20a Young Richard, 1877: caricature by Alfred Bryan (Shakespeare Centre Library, Stratford-upon-Avon)

20b Old Richard, 1896, by Arthur Rackham (Shakespeare Centre Library Stratford-upon-Avon)

in the opening soliloquy he spoke with 'savage bitterness' of the 'injustice of nature towards him'. He set out 'without anger or hatred, but without the slightest remorse' to prove his superiority to his better-shaped fellow-men.[49] Irving said he was 'a Plantagenet with the imperious pride of his race, a subtle intellect, a mocking, not a trumpeting duplicity, a superb daring ... a youthful audacity'.[50]

153

Many observers commented upon his courtly refinement and royal
bearing: 'He never lost nobility, the nobility of Lucifer.' The older
Richard of 1896 was less tragic because his motive was not so human
and accessible. He could laugh at his deformity; he seemed 'an elderly,
or at least a middle-aged fiend' who had outlived all pleasures but the
intellectual one of doing evil superbly, an 'artist in crime'.[51]

Like Iago, Young Richard was a skilful fair-seemer. He embraced
Clarence affectionately as he went to the Tower and joked with the
released Hastings without a trace of mockery. When he heard Henry's
funeral approaching he hid behind a stone cross and emerged as a
convincing lover, 'tender, pathetic, sportive and earnest'. The youth
and 'graceful weakness' of Isabel Bateman as Lady Anne made his
success quite plausible. She shuddered at the sound of his voice and at
his touch, but when she cried, 'Out of my sight! Thou dost infect my
eyes' (I.ii.141), she spoke as though she 'already felt herself giving way
to Richard's arts'.[52] The audience was permitted only the subtlest
reminders of his duplicity until Anne was out of sight; then the
transition to harsh command on 'Sirs, take up the corse' was instan-
taneous. His 'scornful exultation' when he asked,

> Was ever woman in this humour wooed?
> Was ever woman in this humour won?
>
> (I.ii.227–8)

produced 'a shout of derisive applause'.[53]

Only the little Duke of York's childish joke about the deformity that
had ruined his soul was able to shake Richard's composure:

> Uncle, my brother mocks both you and me;
> Because that I am little, like an ape,
> He thinks that you should bear me on your shoulders.
>
> (III.i.129–33)

With 'evil fire in his eyes', Irving spoke a transposed aside: 'So wise so
young, they say do ne'er live long' (III.i.79). Olivier made a similar
'point' without words: the terrible silence that followed the child's
gaffe lasted a skin-crawling twenty-five seconds.[54]

Richard's pious mask was impenetrable when he appeared to the
Mayor and Citizens, standing between 'two right reverend fathers' in
the gallery at Baynard's Castle (III.vii). When he had descended, and
graciously accepted the crown, the crowd cheered: holding a prayer-

book before his face, he shot Buckingham a grin of cynical triumph that was pure high comedy.[55] This was his moment of triumph. Now things started to go wrong, and Richard felt 'a fateful premonition of his end'. At first he retained his composure. When Buckingham failed him and claimed the promised reward, his refusal, 'Thou troublest me; I am not in the vein' (IV.ii.117), was not the sudden 'wild burst of passion' of a 'point', but dignified, 'admirable in its quiet contempt'.[56] Leading his army against the rebels, he met Queen Elizabeth and his mother at Tower Hill. Neither the old Duchess's maledictions, nor the Queen's initial refusal of her daughter's hand seemed to disturb him, but as the messengers hurried in with their 'songs of death' his anxiety began to show in a 'growing fierce irritability': instead of weakening, however, 'the wolf bayed by enemies becomes a tiger'.[57]

In his tent at Bosworth, the chaos Richard had made rose up and almost choked him. Only his predominant will could give him victory on the morrow. But remorse and fear caught at his throat. Like Mathias in the last act of *The Bells*, he was shaken by his conscience when he could least afford it. Left alone, Irving held the audience spellbound through fully two or three silent minutes. He sat beside a table, studying a map and warming his hands at a brazier. Rising with a groan, he gazed out moodily into the night where camp-fires burned under the stars. A distant bugle seemed to emphasize his isolation. Even the young Richard of 1877 seemed prematurely old and weary here; in 1896 his fatigue yielded a unique glimpse of the human being beneath the 'high-spirited, revelling devilry' he had shown the world, naked now when nobody was looking.[58]

The ghosts appeared only to Richard, and a number of them were omitted.[59] He woke in abject terror, slid from his couch and huddled at its foot, covering his head with his ermine cloak. The great soliloquy expressed agonized despair. The climax came at,

> There is no creature loves me;
> And if I die, no soul will pity me.
>
> (V.iii.201–2)

He clutched the crucifix that stood on the table, the business possibly inspired by the painted crucifix in Hogarth's portrait of Garrick as Richard.[60] The speech ended here. Irving intensified the pathos by cutting the next two lines:

155

Nay, wherefore should they, since that I myself
Find in myself no pity to myself.

Without Cibber's celebrated 'point' there was no suggestion that
Richard was able to shake the weight of destiny from his shoulders. As
he went out to spy on his army, 'the influence of dream is still upon
him'.[61]

In the battle Young Richard seemed 'to fight with the mere power of
his will after his physical strength is exhausted'. Beaten to his knees
and mortally wounded, he tore at Richmond's sword with hands and
teeth. Old Richard fought Richmond in a gathering ring of soldiers:
'Irving slashes and hacks and wields his sword as though he were in
reality defending his life.' Run through at last, and 'passionately
tearing his gauntlet from his stiffening fingers, he flings it defiantly at
the conqueror's feet'.[62]

The first production was mounted on a very modest scale. Only ten
sets were used, and of these, three were front scenes and two – Tower
Hill (IV.iv) and the sunset for the battle – cannot have been much
more than drops in the third or fourth grooves. A sketch in Irving's
1877 prompt-book shows how a fireplace inserted in a doorway made
one box set serve as two different rooms in the palace.[63] Wherever two
full-stage sets were used in the same act, Irving interposed a 'carpenter's scene': while Catesby was testing Hastings's loyalty in front of
a drop in the first grooves (III.ii), the stage crew had five minutes to
erect behind it the most ambitious set in the production. This was the
room in Baynard's Castle where Richard accused Hastings of treachery (III.iv) and was acclaimed King by the Mayor and Citizens
(III.vii); the scenes were run together as one. It occupied the full stage.
The gallery where Richard stood with the two divines ran across the
upstage wall, probably in the fourth entry. It was reached by a broad
flight of steps at left. The long council table stood at right centre,
below a large arch.

In 1877 the coffin of Henry VI was escorted by only twenty-two
monks and men-at-arms, but in 1896 supernumeraries innumerable
with a forest of inverted scarlet halberds formed a background like a
tapestry to the wooing of Lady Anne. The composition was based on a
recent Royal Academy painting (compare plates 21*a*, 21*b* and 21*c*).
Illustrations of other scenes from the later production tell the same

story of superior and more elaborate design, more accuracy and detail, more beauty and, above all, more realism.

With characteristic exaggeration, Shaw describes Irving's 1896 Richard as a version of Mr Punch. He played the Lady Anne scene 'as if he were a Houndsditch salesman cheating a factory girl over a pair of second-hand stockings'. This suggests that the assumed sincerity was vulgar and transparent, an opinion shared by most critics; others observed that 'Richard and Buckingham seem to treat the Lord Mayor and his associates as nincompoops, and are scarcely at pains to hide the tongue in the cheek.'[64] Indeed, Richard seemed to look upon his crimes as 'exquisite practical jokes'. Accordingly, 'the audience was inclined to take Richard as a comic character' and refused to accept his wickedness as a serious matter.[65] If audiences in 1877 took Richard seriously and those of 1896 thought of him primarily as a great joker, we must conclude that either the performance or the audience had changed. That the latter was the case is suggested by reviews which say, in one way or another, 'Richard III is not *now* a tragic role.' The play was no longer plausible. 'The thing suffers,' says Henry James, '. . . from everything to which . . . the present cultivation of a closer illusion exposes it. The more it is painted and dressed, the more it is lighted and furnished and solidified, the less it corresponds and coincides, the less it squares with our imaginative habits.'[66] Irving had done his work too well; the naturalism he had helped to create, both visually and by ousting Cibber's melodramatic script, had made Shakespeare's *Richard III* obsolete nineteen years later.

The significant changes in Irving's later interpretation were in Richard's motive, his age, and the manner of his death. Only the first was the result of an altered line-reading; the rest followed logically. As his interpretation of the opening soliloquy and the incident with the little Duke of York showed, Young Richard was embittered by a deformity one could pity, and there was pathos in his isolation and suffering. Old Richard's motive was less human; he wanted the crown, of course, but the dramatic emphasis lay entirely with his delight in the intrigues he used to obtain it. When the goal was reached, however, and rebels threatened to seize what he had won, Richard's ambition came into focus. This was serious: 'his character alters as though by magic,' said J. T. Grein; 'The courtier becomes a man of war.' To many he seemed more devil than man, comic at first as Mephisto-

21 *a*   *Richard III* I.i, from the 1877 prompt-book (Museum of London)

21 *b*   Irving and Julia Arthur as Richard III and Lady Anne, 1896 (University of Victoria). Compare the painting in 21*c*.

21 *c*   *Richard, Duke of Gloucester, and Lady Anne,* by Edwin Abbey, exhibited early in 1896 (Yale University Art Gallery, The Edwin Austin Abbey Memorial Collection)

pheles was comic, but ultimately a thing to be exterminated like 'some direful, furtive, deadly reptile'.[67] Thus when Richmond in his shining silver and gold armour entered like St George to slay the dragon, 'There was a really splendid effect in the introduction of this picture of youth and life into the gloomy atmosphere of age and doubt.'[68] Irving made Young Richard the protagonist of an eccentric tragedy. The major interest was the fate of a man whose isolation by a freak of Nature brought a terrible retribution upon the world that had conceived him. But Old Richard was a thing outside Nature, a scourge out of Hell, as Dowden says, who 'dashes himself to pieces against the laws of the world he has outraged . . . Richmond conquers, and he conquers expressly as the champion and representative of the moral order of the world.'[69]

Romeo and Juliet   8 March 1882

'*Hamlet* could be played anywhere on its acting merits,' Irving told Ellen Terry. 'It marches from situation to situation. But *Romeo and Juliet* proceeds from picture to picture. Every line suggest a picture. It is a dramatic poem rather than a drama, and I mean to treat it from that point of view.'[70] He deployed lavish expenditure, expert assistance and new scenic techniques to make his production a spectacular 'illustration' of the play, a step which he thought was 'justified by the better development of our present stage, of whose advantages the poet would doubtless have freely availed himself had his own opportunities been brought up to the level of our times'.[71] The production costs amounted to almost £10,000. Two eminent scenic artists assisted Craven with the eighteen sets, some of which were unprecedented in their solidity:[72] Juliet's balcony was a lofty marble loggia instead of the 'little wobbling cage' of tradition, and the subterranean tomb foreshadowed the designs of Gordon Craig. Irving's new lighting techniques displayed Juliet's bedroom in three different lights at different times of day, including a dawn that gathered and changed as the lovers parted. The costumes used rich new fabrics that were just beginning to come on the market. Walter Hann painted special tableau curtains that looked like embroidered cream satin, and Sir Julius Benedict composed romantic music for the big Lyceum orchestra and a 'selected choir'.[73]

Romeo and Juliet were forty-four and thirty-five years old, and the critics cut them up. The consensus held that while Terry was delight-ful in the play's lighter moments, Juliet's 'fire and passion' were outside her range. Irving suffered more. 'It is not possible to conceive anything more lamentably, more maddeningly bad, than Mr. Irving's Romeo,' said one critic. Lovers had never been his line, and in his love-making Charles Hiatt saw 'not a single moment of ecstasy'. He was deplorably bad, grotesque, laughable, a monstrosity: and he packed the Lyceum for 160 nights.[74]

There has always been a minority opinion that Romeo and Juliet not only precipitate the catastrophe, but deserve it: they are rash, or undutiful, or immoral. This view seldom appeals to actors, or indeed to anyone whose sensibilities retain their balance. But in the absence of a villain the alternative is to blame Fate, which is not a Christian attitude. Nevertheless, Irving emphasized it. He restored the Prologue where the lovers are described as 'star-crossed'.[75] When Romeo and the other 'sumptuous youngsters' prepared to gatecrash Capulet's ball, a symbolic 'Fate tree' overhung the torchlit street where they gathered, reinforcing Romeo's dark exit speech:

> . . . my mind misgives
> Some consequence yet hanging in the stars
> Shall bitterly begin his fearful date
> With this night's revels . . .
>
> (I.iv.106–9)

It loomed again over the 'dismal heart-chilling street' in Mantua where he heard of Juliet's supposed death and bought poison from the Apothecary.[76] Terry attributed Juliet's swift surrender to a sense of urgency prompted by a 'presentiment of sorrow':

> O God, I have an ill-divining soul!
> Methinks I see thee, now thou art so low,
> As one dead in the bottom of a tomb.
>
> (III.v.54–6)[77]

Irving's other productions maintained a sense of a beneficent Provi-dence which cannot be reconciled with an amoral or malevolent Fate. Here his treatment of the city of Verona is significant.

The beauty of Verona was like the fair-seeming of one of Irving's villain-heroes. The first scene was the market-place. A picturesque crowd of citizens and nobles, children and donkeys went peacefully about their business around a fountain in the foreground, which was shaded and gave 'a delightful feeling of repose'. Upstage, a sloping bridge crossed a walled stream and led to streets blazing with sunlight. But peace was an illusion. Under the pretty surface, the city was a hell of vendetta and sordid murder where tempers boiled over in the hot Mediterranean sun. The sunlight glared in the background like the violence behind the fair-seeming beauty and repose. Lackeys of the two factions began a quarrel that spread like a grass-fire. Capulets came pelting up and were getting the best of it. 'Then over the bridge came a rush of the Montagues . . . . They used to pour in upon the scene like a released torrent.' The fight was no aesthetic sword-dance: it was war, deadly and dirty.[78] This strife and the heat that made it grow were the villains.

The brawl was at its height when trumpets sounded, and the Prince appeared on the bridge with his retinue. Suddenly the crowd fell silent; then they dispersed, muttering. The remainder of the scene could not have been played convincingly in the sun, but Irving's novel scenic arrangement allowed Romeo and Benvolio to meet and lounge beside the shaded fountain in the foreground. Irving wore doublet and hose of pale greyish green and a low fez-like cap, crimson to bring out the melancholic pallor of his face.[79] He found the key to his interpretation of Romeo in his line to Benvolio, 'Thou canst not teach me to forget' (I.i.240). He spoke of Rosaline, whom Irving restored because 'Shakespeare has completely worked out his first baseless love . . . as palpable evidence of the subjective nature of the man and his passion.' Romeo was a victim of Queen Mab, a fantastic lover whose devotion was more constant than its object because he needed to worship an ideal. Reading Capulet's guest-list, 'his eye lights and his tongue lingers on the name of Rosaline'; he even kissed the paper.[80]

Irving chose a tall dark girl to represent Rosaline at the ball. She sat still and pale upon a 'sedilia of blue and silver', a cold contrast to the fair-haired, animated Juliet surrounded by adoring children. Romeo approached during the minuet: 'Can I ever forget his face,' says Terry, 'when suddenly in pursuit of *her* he saw *me* . . .'[81] In this moment the reality of love replaced illusion, but it also catapulted the lovers towards inevitable catastrophe. The instant transfer of Romeo's worship shocked those who were unaccustomed to the full text, and Irving was blamed as though he had written it himself.

Romeo speaks of his lips as 'two blushing pilgrims', and Juliet extends the metaphor, calling him 'pilgrim' throughout their first meeting (I.v.97–105). Irving wore pilgrim's costume to the masquerade, a scene of such visual splendour that some critics thought it swamped the drama. It is difficult to believe the report that five hundred actors and supernumeraries thronged the stage, but there was certainly a good-sized crowd in Capulet's grand loggia.[82] Costumes and movement were deftly arranged to ensure a continual grouping and re-grouping of harmonious colours and forms. After the minuet, dancers in 'light blue and white satin, in silver and in gold' performed a torch-dance.[83]

Romeo's new love was more serious than the old, but its rich, poetic expression eluded Irving. 'In the atmosphere of essentially youthful passion he is clearly out of his element,' said a typical review. If he meant to borrow rhetorical fire from Juliet, he was disappointed. Terry was subdued in the balcony scene: 'seldom have Shakespeare's words roused less attention. There was no variety . Each speech was delivered in the same manner; the mind did not dictate the tongue's utterance, and the new Juliet, save in one line, "Dost thou love me? I know thou wilt say – Ay" [II.ii.90], seldom gave her audience the impression that her heart was in her work.'[84] But some thought the scenery almost compensated for unsatisfactory acting. The balcony – a roofed marble terrace – overlooked an orchard in a ravine; the moon shone coldly throught the foliage, and Romeo stood on the lip of a raised stone flower-bed full of tall white lilies.

The Nurse (Fanny Stirling) found Romeo and his friends sheltering from the heat beneath a tree in an open space outside the city walls. Despite extensive cuts in her dialogue with Lady Capulet (I.iii) and in this scene (II.iv), she was a great success; indeed, reading between the lines we may guess that this venerable survivor of Macready's day knew little and cared less about 'support' as Irving understood it, and simply stole the show.[85] 'She was the only Nurse I have ever seen who did not play the part like a female pantaloon,' Ellen Terry wrote. 'She did not assume any great decrepitude.' Terry was at her best in the next scene (II.v) when she coaxed the Nurse to tell her news: 'nothing could seem more natural than the changes of tone and visage here employed'.[86]

Mercutio (William Terriss) fought Tybalt (Charles Glenney) in a sun-baked street that reinforced Benvolio's warning:

The day is hot, the Capels are abroad,
And, if we meet, we shall not 'scape a brawl,
For now, these hot days, is the mad blood stirring.

(III.i.2–4)

A glimpse of 'a cool passage in the distance beneath foliage-covered trellis-work' merely emphasized the heat. Terriss was boisterous and empty, Glenney attracted no notice, but Irving's interpretation was interesting: he addressed Tybalt 'with a sort of abject anxiety to avoid a rupture', as though 'Romeo's fibre has been weakened' by his love-melancholy. When his 'fussy and pottering interference' had caused his friend's death, he was shocked into seeing himself clearly:

O sweet Juliet,
Thy beauty hath made me effeminate
And in my temper soft'ned valour's steel.

(115–17)

He caught up Mercutio's sword, shading his eyes against the sun; he was past Tybalt's guard in a flash, and a crowd gathered around the body as Romeo fled.[87] This was an important turning-point, a step towards self-knowledge and maturity; and as Romeo matured, Irving became more comfortable with his part.[88]

To some eyes the luscious dawn breaking outside Juliet's window distracted attention from the lovers when they parted (III.v): 'Here we have, if anything, an excess of colour. The golden lattice, . . . the foliage in the garden, the sky showing the pinks, and oranges, and purples of a sunrise, and, at last, the golden sun itself, are all beautiful enough, but they are a trying background for the central figures.' Others thought this the 'most touching scene in spite of Irving's peculiarities', and that he played with 'a tenderness of passion and devotion that demands high praise', while Terry was 'instinct with charm and consistently natural'.[89] The window stood at left, and the bed which plays such a conspicuous part in some modern productions was tucked away at right, at the top of the long arm of the L-shaped room. Juliet's young courage as she faced her parents, and her 'moral revolt' when the Nurse advised bigamy, were touching. There was an underlying cold-heartedness in Mrs Stirling's performance that struck exactly the right note here. But Ellen Terry's 'potion scene' (IV.iii) was less successful. She was 'deliberate' where critics thought she should be excited and openly terrified: 'Nothing is called out of the depths.'[90] Friendly critics preferred to concentrate upon visual effects: 'The faint hues and lines of the dim room seem to blend with her imaginings in a spectral manner which is notably appropriate and thrilling.' An offstage wedding chant accompanied a procession of bridesmaids who entered in the morning and knelt around Juliet's bed. When the Nurse discovered the supposed corpse, her 'parrot scream' was 'horribly real and effective'.[91]

Terry wanted to show that Juliet matured when she accepted the potion, and that she excelled herself when she awoke in the tomb to find her worst terrors more than realized.[92] But while her art was not yet equal to the challenge of the later scenes, Irving's performance improved as Romeo matured and assumed tragic stature. In the Apothecary scene (V.i), rhetoric is abruptly replaced by understatement, and Irving was at once in his element. Granville-Barker says the scene calls for 'sheer acting'. The set was a drop in the first grooves, representing a picturesque but dilapidated street modelled upon one of Doré's illustrations for *Don Quixote*.[93] Irving received Balthasar's news in silence. 'His face grew whiter and whiter. It was during the silence ... that Henry Irving as Romeo had one of those sublime moments which an actor only achieves once or twice in his life.' His reply, 'Then I defy you, stars', was quiet: his fate was settled there, beneath the symbolic tree, and he accepted it.[94] George Augustus Sala paid Irving tribute for this scene: 'I have seen few finer things on the stage than the impression of complete self-mastery, of inexorably concentrated volition engendered by irremediable despair, conveyed to the mind of the spectator. ... The paleness and wildness of Romeo's looks do not alter by one whit his calmness and brevity of speech. ... His defiance of the stars is simply a cool and collected recognition of the *Ananke* – of the inevitable, of there being "no armour against Fate".'[95]

The last scene of *Romeo and Juliet* presents problems in the theatre of illusion because the action begins outside the tomb, but ends inside. Besides, Irving remembered Romeo's words, 'I *descend* into the bed of death' (V.iii.28), and insisted, 'I must go *down* to the vault.'[96] He solved the difficulty by dividing the scene in two. Romeo killed Paris in a gloomy churchyard; the door of the vault offered 'genuine resistance to the crowbar', but when it opened a flight of steps led down into the earth. Then the scene changed (V.iii.83) to the interior. William

Telbin's set was a masterpiece of solid construction. From the floor of the vault where Juliet lay, a stone stairway led in two flights to the entrance far above: moonlight shone down from the door which Romeo had wrenched open. There were at least forty practicable steps, reaching a minimum of twenty-five feet towards the 'flies.' Down them came Romeo, dragging the body of Paris. When the lovers were dead – the critics tell little about the manner of their death – Hann's tableau curtains met for a moment.[97]

Irving was more interested in the lovers than in the restoration of order in Verona. The city's human hatreds were the driving reality behind a purely symbolic Fate, and in death Romeo and Juliet effected a reconciliation which, but for human evil, could have been brought about by their love. This undoubtedly showed the hand of Providence, but in the Lyceum production the really significant compensation which the tragedy offered lay in the growth and self-fulfilment of the lovers. Behind the curtains the sound of an approaching crowd was heard. Then they opened once more. The stairs were thronged with people of both factions, all bearing torches. Prince Escalus made Montague and Capulet join hands, and spoke a four-line tag while they gazed in silence at Romeo and Juliet, imperishably united in tableau.[98]

Coriolanus   15 April 1901

The chilliness which has denied *Coriolanus* any real popularity does not derive from the character of the hero. Temperature is his problem: Caius Marcius has a very short fuse, and when ignited he goes off with a sustained *fortissimo* monotony that few audiences can endure. John Philip Kemble's statuesque interpretation appealed to the neo-classical taste of late-eighteenth-century audiences, but *Coriolanus* held little charm for Victorian playgoers. When Irving staged it in 1901, London had not seen a major production in more than forty years.[99] West End journals professed a keen interest, but a typical proletarian critic admitted that the play gave him a backache, and the public largely stayed away. Alma-Tadema, who designed the sets, found the Stalls 'little occupied' on the tenth night, and the run ended after only thirty-six performances.[100]

Marcius is an epic hero at odds with a tragic world where his heroic virtues – pride, integrity, valour – can lead only to disaster. His soul yearns for emulous combat with one beloved enemy, but Aufidius is a pragmatist like Achilles in *Troilus and Cressida*, prepared to exterminate his rival when the Homeric role becomes inexpedient. Marcius worships his own image of Rome, but scorns the Romans; because they are not a race of heroes, he fatally underestimates them, assuming that they have no pride at all. And the inhumanly simple code he has learned from Volumnia rends him when it comes into conflict with the human love that her teaching has inspired. An actor's interpretation may emphasize any of these three major conflicts.

In Irving's three-act text, Aufidius did not appear until the last act. Deprived of the battle scenes, he was little more than a sword to run upon. He welcomed Marcius with a show of cordiality, enviously plotted against him, and slew him like a villain. The significance of the 'political' plot was also reduced. The Lyceum mob was neither an idealized proletariat nor a debased rabble: they were costumed as honest tradesmen, and were not very tumultuous until aroused by Marcius' contempt. Some observers found them sympathetic, and all agreed that Irving grouped and individualized his fifty supernumeraries as never before.[101] They were civilians, not soldiers, and Marcius' contempt was based entirely upon his accurate but irrelevant estimate of their military value. He was a man of narrow sympathies 'who would not have been beloved even by his fellow nobles'.[102]

Irving entered unobtrusively, but he easily dominated the stage.

With every opportunity for extravagant gesture he stood, as the play seemed to foam about him, like a rock against which the foam beats. Made up as a . . . lean, thoughtful soldier, he spoke throughout with a slow, contemptuous enunciation, as of one only just not too lofty to sneer. Restrained in scorn, he kept throughout an attitude of disdainful pride, the face, the eyes, set, while only his mouth twitched, seeming to chew his words, with the disgust of one swallowing a painful morsel.[103]

There was humour in his invitation to the crowd to follow him to war: 'The Volsces have much corn' (I.i.248). He laughed when they stole away.[104]

The laugh was on Coriolanus in the second act, when he was obliged to stand in the Forum soliciting the 'most sweet voices' of the plebeians: in the margin of her study-book, Ellen Terry (Volumnia) wrote 'Fun', 'Funny' and 'Very Funny' beside some of his crankiest speeches. His ironies were wasted on the Citizens, who were 'puzzled asses' and 'a surprised donkey'.[105] Irving's son Laurence (Brutus) and

James Hearn (Sicinius) made the Tribunes mildly comic rather than villainous demogogues, and Coriolanus treated them with irony, scarcely troubling to look at them or their followers, 'confining his attention to the patricians, his equals' until Sicinius called him traitor. Then he responded with 'noble scorn', but there was no uncontrolled outburst. The famous exit speech, 'You common cry of curs ... I banish you' (III.iii.120–3) was a traditional 'point', but Irving underplayed it as a calculated insult. Turning to go, he took the skirt of his great, dull-red silk toga in both hands and swept it in their faces 'as though to whirl them away in the wind created by this superb gesture'.[106]

Irving took neither the 'political' plot nor the rivalry with Aufidius as the central conflict. Sir A. C. Mackenzie's Overture suggested the emphasis he would choose; it was 'a rather elaborate piece of orchestral music, mainly based upon two themes, one doubtless representing the imperious and scornful character of Coriolanus himself, and the other the gentler nature of his wife and mother. In the working out the two, by a happy idea, seem to be contending for mastery.'[107] For Irving, the tragedy revolved around the relationship between Marcius and Volumnia. This was a sound decision in view of Ellen Terry's obvious incapacity in the role of the traditional Roman matron. It would be difficult to imagine anyone less likely to encourage small boys in the mammocking of butterflies. She tried, but the critics could not believe in her: 'Oh, how bad it makes one feel to find that they all think my Volumnia "sweet",' she wrote, 'and *I* thought I was fierce, contemptuous, overbearing.'[108] Some accepted her performance as a new reading: 'Miss Terry's Volumnia substitutes softer and more appealing graces for the species of quasi voluptuous love associated with the memory of Mrs. Siddons. That a woman such as she should have stirred her son to heroic deeds is conceivable enough, but she prompts rather than participates in his greatness.'[109] Bram Stoker explained:

Neither women or men of today expect a strong man to take orders, no matter how imperiously the orders are given ... For this reason, as well as to suit her own ideas and purposes, Ellen Terry has given us a different Volumnia ... She has recognized that the force of such a mother was in her silence as well as in her speech; in the sweetness and common-sense of her domestic life as the mistress of a great household, as well as in those moments of haughty ambition in which she urged her great and victorious son to still greater and more victorious deeds.[110]

The loyal Stoker is rationalizing, of course, but there can be no doubt that this is how the public understood Terry's performance, and it may well have been Irving's purpose to give *Coriolanus* an interpretation which would be consistent with what his partner could be expected to achieve. He treated it as a tragedy of filial love; in his acting version, the climax of each act was a decisive scene between Marcius and Volumnia.[111]

Irving staged Marcius' homecoming from the conquest of Corioli as an 'Ovation', a procession only less splendid than a Triumph. Alma-Tadema's set depicted the Forum as it might have looked in Etruscan times. A backdrop showed the Capitoline hill crowned with the temple of Jupiter. At left, a triumphal arch decorated with bronze shields and bunting partly concealed another temple. A throng of Citizens and Senators, headed by Marcius' family, were on hand to hear the Herald (II.i.161–5). A troop of women entered through the arch, waving palm branches and walking backwards: 'one step to the right, one to the left, then twist right round and begin again'. They fell back upstage, and Coriolanus entered, riding in a gilded chariot drawn by four white horses. His soldiers were armoured, but he wore a plain toga and a wreath of oak leaves. Volumnia wore purple and a golden diadem, like a queen. Dismounting, he knelt and kissed her hands; she raised him, kissing his forehead. He led his wife and mother forward to share the acclaim, but it was Volumnia who took the centre of the stage and the full attention of Marcius (see plate 22).[112]

When Coriolanus quarrelled with the Tribunes, Volumnia used his love for her to make him apologize: bullying left him unmoved. Irving stressed the man's integrity: 'I cannot do it to the gods,' he said solemnly. 'Must I do't to *them*?' (III.ii.38–9). When she sensed that he was weakening, Volumnia tried to assert her own will. '*He must*' was 'sharp', and Terry wrote 'War' in the margin of her text. A pause; then seeing that this was the wrong tack, she added '*and* WILL' as an affirmation of her son's good sense: 'Peace, peace. Keep it up,' Terry wrote (97).[113] Capitulating, Marcius seemed inclined to blame her for making him compromise his principles. 'Well, *I must* do't,' he said with a sigh.

> Away, my disposition, and possess me
> Some harlot's spirit.
>
> (110–12)

22 *Coriolanus* II.i, 1901. Rome gives Caius Marcius an ovation and he shares it with Volumnia (State Library of New South Wales)

Volumnia would have none of this: 'At thy choice then,' she said with a 'great change' in her manner. It was a trick he knew well, but was powerless to resist. 'No doubt she always works upon him,' Terry noted. At first he seemed disposed to shout, albeit in assent: 'Look, I am going' (134). When she swept out of the room, saying '*Do* your will' (137), he submitted to the inevitable with affectionate humour: 'Mildly! Well, *mildly* be it then. Mildly!' (145).[114]

A great olive tree hung over Coriolanus when he stood outside the house of Aufidius in Antium. This was the symbolic 'Fate tree' that Irving had often used before, and at its foot stood a bronze Chimaera.

By taking a step which would inevitably bring him into conflict with Volumnia, Marcius sealed his own fate. Perhaps it is not too fanciful to point out that he was striving to turn himself into a monster of integrity impervious to love. Before the walls of Rome, Volumnia would prove that this too was a Chimaera.[115]

It was night when Menenius visited the Volscian camp. Behind a grove of trees, embrasured walls could be discerned against the sky.[116] Marcius was kindly but firm when he rejected his friend's plea, and the melancholy dignity of the old man's exit earned J. H. Barnes 'a hearty cheer from the whole house'.[117] The scene continued with a passage transposed from Act IV: Aufidius told his Lieutenant of his envy (IV.vii), and then Coriolanus returned. Ellen Terry was unhappy with his entrance: 'Weak and not convincing through his coming on *alone*'. By the time Volumnia entered, however, the stage had filled with Volscian soldiery.[118] Colour highlighted the conflict. Coriolanus wore a rich gold cuirass, a red tunic embroidered with gold, and the skin of a leopard. The Volscians, in superb, barbaric armour and 'tunics of gloriously rich colour' were gathered at left, while the suppliants entered at right, dressed entirely in black and white.[119] As they approached, Coriolanus spoke 'aside', revealing the struggle with which he rejected their entreaties and maintained his dignified reserve. He bowed coldly to Volumnia, but his voice was 'tender' as he spoke of 'the honour'd mould / Wherein this trunk was fram'd' (V.iii.22–3). Then he struck his breast – a quaintly conventional gesture – as he said, 'But out, affection!' (24). He weakened at the sight of his son: 'Breaking down at young boy'. He greeted Virgilia (Mable Hackney) formally and turned away:

> Like a dull actor now
> I have forgot my part and I am out,
> Even to a full disgrace.
>
> (40–2)

Then, 'striking heart before looking', he kissed her, 'keeping apart'. At the foot of the page, Irving wrote 'Great nature cries' (33), an appropriate summary of his interpretation of the scene.

Volumnia's speeches were so heavily cut that her appeal was simple and direct: Ellen Terry was sweet and gentle. When Marcius yielded, a tragic understanding passed between them: she asked him to give his life for Rome, and he assented for her sake.

171

O mother, mother
What have you done?
You have won a happy victory to Rome;
But for *your son* – believe it, O, believe it! –
Most dangerously you have with him prevail'd,
If not most mortal to him. But let it come. [*Long sigh*]

(182–9)

Taking her hand, he repeated the culminating gesture of the Ovation scene (see plate 22), implying that this too was a triumph, a victory for love. Volumnia cast open her black veil, revealing an embroidered gown of gold and pink; over the walls of Rome, the dawn was breaking.[120]

The last scene was played in the Forum at Antium. The drop represented a flight of steps leading to a squat, forbidding temple; a great bronze altar with a bull's head and horns stood before it. Coriolanus entered to music, surrounded by his soldiers. Aufidius's taunts provoked a retort which Irving originally intended to speak 'as if hysterical':

Measureless liar, thou hast made my heart
Too *great* for what contains it. 'Boy!' O slave!

(V.vi. 103–4)

In performance, witnesses agree that he faced Aufidius calmly and answered him 'with great disdain'.[121] Marcius gave himself to death with 'personal distinction and quiet pathos', coming out from amongst the soldiers as though to launch his taunt without their protection. His death was suicide, a sacrifice.[122]

6

Much Ado about Nothing

11 October 1882
5 January 1891

Theatrical context

On stage the 'merry war' between Beatrice and Benedick has too often degenerated into an unseemly fracas between stars competing for attention. A strong director can stop it; otherwise, actors must be found whose mutual esteem inhibits competition and whose powers are so nearly equal that one will not inadvertently overwhelm the other. With the possible exception of Garrick and Hannah Pritchard, the English stage produced no such partnership between comic actors of the first rank from Shakespeare's day to 1882, when Irving and Terry made *Much Ado about Nothing* one of the biggest hits of their career together. The play was then little known on the stage, its reputation eclipsed by *As You Like It*.[1] The outspoken Beatrice delights modern audiences, but Victorians thought her a bit of a 'hoyden' and infinitely preferred Rosalind, a rose without a thorn. But the Lyceum production surprised and delighted the public. After the initial run of 212 performances the comedy remained in the repertory until 1895 and was twice revived (1884 and 1891): Irving's tours made it as popular in America and the provinces as it was in London.[2] The rehabilitation of *Much Ado* as a popular comedy has been complete and enduring.

Text

Helena Faucit, who played Beatrice with Charles Kemble, wrote: 'In this play the name of "God" occurs continually, and upon the most trivial occasions. It so happens that it rises to Beatrice's lips more often than to any other's. In the book which I studied, "Heaven" was everywhere substituted for it; and I confess the word sounds

173

pleasanter and softer to my ear, besides being in the circumstances less irreverent.'[3] Irving followed this precedent except where it would disturb the rhythm of an important line: 'But keep your way o' God's name; I have done.'[4] He was always sensitive and alert to speech rhythms. Victorian tastes demanded a certain amount of moral laundering, however; the jokes about cuckoldry, which even Shaw thought vulgar, were cut with the notable exception of Benedick's last quip, 'There's no staff more reverend than one tipped with horn.'

Irving's first arrangement of the text omits two scenes – Hero's preparations for the wedding, with its irredeemably ribald dialogue (III.iv), and Dogberry's unsuccessful attempt to interest Leonato in his prisoners (III.v) – but others were merged to produce a thirteen-scene version some 569 lines shorter than the received text. When it was found that Dogberry failed to interest the audience, his examination of Borachio and Conrade was omitted (IV.ii) from the touring version, which was 200 lines shorter and used only seven or eight sets.[5] The second act began with I.iii (Don John and his henchmen) in 1882; but Ellen Terry wrote in a study-book, 'This was found not to be a good place to stop the Play – therefore a Drop scene followed (for Don John's scene) in turn followed by open stage for Ball scene, & so ending the first act at – "I will tell you my drift".' In each version, I.iii preceded I.ii, which was amalgamated with II.i.[6] This was the only significant transposition, but there was one notorious interpolation. The church scene (IV.i) traditionally ended with a 'gag' designed to bring down the house. By reiterating Beatrice's dramatic 'Kill Claudio' it stimulated the audience to anticipate the challenge and hence 'increased the "tug" of the play', as Stoker puts it.[7]

Benedick Enough. I am engaged; I will challenge him.
Beatrice You will?
Benedick By those bright eyes I will. I will kiss your hand, and so leave you. By this hand, Claudio shall render me a dear account.
Beatrice My dear friend, kiss my hand again.
Benedick As you hear of me, so think of me. Go, comfort your cousin; I must say, she is dead.
Beatrice Benedick, kill him, kill him if you can.
Benedick As sure as he's alive, I will.   *Exit.*[8]

The gag is clumsy but effective. Ellen Terry protested but Irving was unmoved and in the event few critics noticed it, perhaps because it was not printed in the acting version sold in the theatre.

Contemporary criticism

Few of the major commentators found much to say about *Much Ado*, and those who did usually confined their remarks to moral assessment of the characters. To anyone who looks for believable motives, Claudio is a fool and a prig, and Hero a doormat. The main critical theme concerned Beatrice and Benedick. While the stage usually treated them as a 'terrible termagant' and a 'talkative misogynist' who are tricked into a marriage which promises to be explosive,[9] most commentators elaborated upon Schlegel's view: 'Their friends attribute the whole effect to their own device; but the exclusive direction of their raillery against each other is in itself a proof of a growing inclination.' The 'germ of love' is there already, but it cannot grow until Beatrice and Benedick learn the folly of self-love and intellectual pride.[10] The war of wits expresses these attitudes, which are only tenable because unbroken prosperity has offered no tests of character. Their education begins with the trick, which wounds their vanity and forces them to see their pride. The crisis of Hero's wedding offers a sterner test in which both abandon frivolity and find in themselves a mature generosity which opens the way for sincere love.[11]

While critics were prepared to pardon Benedick's 'giddiness' as the inevitable mood of young manhood, the same characteristics in Beatrice were regarded as unladylike. Thomas Campbell thought her 'an odious woman', but the majority were less severe, finding like Mrs Jameson that the 'independence and gay indifference of temper . . . the satirical freedom of expression common to both are more becoming to the masculine than to the feminine character'.[12] This attitude impeded serious examination of her character and hence of the play. Helena Faucit admitted, 'Of Beatrice I cannot write with the same full heart, or with the same glow of sympathy, with which I write of Rosalind. Her character is not to me so engaging.' In performance, however, she presented Beatrice as 'a creature overflowing with joyousness, – raillery itself being in her nothing more than an excess of animal spirits, tempered by passing through a soul of goodness'. There can be little doubt that Faucit influenced Terry and Irving, who modified and developed her views into a coherent interpretation which even made sense of the Hero/Claudio plot.[13] Here they succeeded where criticism failed. The several plots of *Much Ado about Nothing* are quite distinct in stylistic treatment: whereas Beatrice and Benedick are naturalistically drawn, Claudio, Hero and Don John are conventional figures of romance. Critics who measured both groups by the same naturalistic standards found Claudio repulsive and rejected him and his story as a huge flaw in the comedy. Since Shakespeare had bungled the main plot, the play could have no unity. Claudio was condemned and swept under the rug, and criticism returned to the more congenial job of discussing Beatrice and Benedick.

Actors cannot dismiss what they dislike: Hero and Claudio must be played. Shakespeare's dexterous plotting ties them irrevocably to Beatrice and Benedick in a single compact narrative, but plot alone cannot create unity. Irving and Terry saw that they must find and develop common themes in the major plots. Only thus could *Much Ado* escape triviality and dislocation.

Performance

The Lyceum production emphasized a theme of seeing and blindness. Each of the principal characters had to learn how to penetrate deception. It was obvious from the beginning that the apparent conflict between Beatrice and Benedick was a deceptive combat between assumed characters. They posed as antagonists because neither was willing to let the other glimpse a growing love which might be rejected. Only the lovers were deceived, however: to everyone else their disguises were transparent.[14] Ellen Terry thought the wit of Beatrice 'should be spoken as the lightest raillery, with mirth in the voice and charm in the manner'. In performance all traces of the shrew and the guttersnipe were obliterated: 'the natural sweetness and wholesomeness, so to speak, of her manner, guided by the actress's excellent taste, relieve even her sharpest utterances of all harshness, while the brightness of the whole performance wins the spectator to her side'.[15] Benedick's sardonic humour never wholly disguised his solid virtues: Irving 'gave full due both to the soldier and gentleman of the Court and showed Benedick as a man one could imagine successful and honoured in both capacities'. The actor summed him up: 'The wit – the humourist – the gentleman – & the *soldier*'.[16]

From the start it was clear that Beatrice cared more for Benedick than she pretended. Lightly descending the steps of a marble villa, she listened for news of him while Leonato talked with the Messenger;[17] she enquired after him because she looked forward to his return, and their meeting was the reunion of sparring partners who delighted in each other as much as in the contest.[18] Benedick's gallantry and distinction rescued his opening quips from vulgarity: 'There was something of the greyhound about his bearing.' His response to Beatrice's rebuke, 'What, my dear Lady Disdain! Are you yet living?' (I.i.114–15) was a 'caress', and, in the banter that followed, even flat or dated epigrams like 'A bird of my tongue is better than a beast of yours' seemed witty and genial. She did not win this round; he generously allowed her to have the last word. Their wit was never meant to wound: it was an habitual pose for both of them, gladly put on, like party clothes, for the occasion.[19]

Benedick's pose was probably the longer established and it was certainly so entrenched that he believed it himself; Beatrice assumed her own role in response to his. Ellen Terry was able to convey the impression of youth even in late middle age, but at forty-four Irving played a mature Benedick using a 'rather finicky, deliberate method' which suggested the confirmed bachelor. His cynicism towards women concealed a vulnerability which Beatrice could not detect, but it spurred her to adopt the role of tease. In the Masked Ball scene she was at her merriest; spotting a pretty child, she kissed him and caught him up in her arms. Benedick was clearly in for the same kind of affectionate rough-stuff.[20] His mask and disguised voice were futile. Beatrice relentlessly pursued him amongst the dancers until she cornered him behind a table downstage; Signior Benedick, she told him, was only 'the Prince's jester, a very dull fool' (II.i.136–7). Routed, he made his escape, but she persecuted him until the music stopped and the couples left the stage two-by-two.[21] Ironically, while each had easily penetrated the other's masquerade, their false characters were becoming rigid and impenetrable, a trap which neither had the insight to escape. After the Ball, Benedick's thoughts returned to his fair adversary without understanding why: somehow he had got hold of one of her gloves and studied it without realizing that it was a conventional love-token.[22] There was a touch of pathos in the way Beatrice brushed away a tear when Hero became engaged to Claudio: 'Thus goes everyone in the world but I, and I am sunburnt. I may sit in a corner and cry "Heigh-ho for a husband"' (II.i.314–16). The moment was brief, however, and Don Pedro recalled her to her role. In her next speech an actress can give us a glimpse of another Beatrice. 'Lady Beatrice, I will get you one,' the Prince says, and she replies, 'I would rather have one of your father's getting . . .' After this, his refusal to take her seriously can send her away in tears. Significantly, Ellen Terry cut these lines, so that Pedro's 'Will you have me, lady?' was a simple gallantry. There was no pathetic subtext when she said, 'There was a star danced, and under that I was born', and 'with her right hand she made a sudden vertical dart upward, and with a pointed forefinger gave a swift little flourish as if she would shake rays of light from its tip'.[23]

To their friends the liking of Beatrice and Benedick was obvious, and the stratagem was a kindly intended device to show each the other's heart. Benedick hid in the arbour behind the marble bench where the conspirators sat to hear Balthazar sing 'Sigh no more, ladies.' Very well he sang, too; he was a young tenor accomplished enough to sing leads at the Savoy, and he was backed up by an offstage chorus.[24] Irving was at his best in this scene: 'His face, peering through the shrubbery . . . is a wonderful mirror, reflecting the swift-ly-chasing thoughts of the mind within. It seemed as though he were speaking all the time, though he had scarcely any share in the lines.' In fact, several exclamations clarified his mood; for instance, when Leonato said Hero was afraid Beatrice might 'do a desperate outrage to herself' (III.i.155), Irving murmured 'Poor thing, poor thing'.[25] At first, it seemed, he was amazed; then he suspected a trick. The 'quizzical and sceptical' look gradually faded and 'conviction settles on his features'. He was not a man swallowing an imposture, but one who saw the truth he had long been too blind to recognize; now, it was observed, 'he ceases to think of Beatrice as a young lady with a formidable tongue, and begins to be conscious of her as a beautiful and fascinating woman'. He saw the real Beatrice behind the pose, and was glad. That was the important point. He was glad because, if she loved him, he could safely acknowledge his own feelings: he was vulnerable no longer, and could abandon his own pose.[26] All of this became clearer still in his soliloquy: 'the glance of the eye, the peculiar quiver of the lip, the uncertain turn of the head prior to his exclaiming "This can be no trick", tell of themselves a little history before a word is uttered'. Beatrice came to invite him to dinner 'with a good-natured coquettishness' qualified by a 'little smothered yawn' which was part of her assumed character. For the first time Benedick used his eyes: 'he earnestly scans her face', and with his new insight he was not absurdly wrong to 'spy some marks of love in her'.[27]

Beatrice learned the truth in the 'bluish light of early morning'. Running exactly like the lapwing, 'close to the ground', she took her place in the arbour where Benedick had stood. She was much more easily persuaded than he, perhaps because she had been less frightened of rejection. The news was welcome to her, too; in the soliloquy, one critic noticed, 'she drops all flippancy and glows into tender and loving womanhood'. She cast aside her role with the image of Benedick which had demanded it, and emerged 'radiant'.[28]

The themes of seeing, blindness and imposture were repeated in the other plot. Here the potential consequences of deception were worse because the blindness which permitted it to flourish was more severe. Victorians were very hard on Claudio. He seemed everything a romantic hero ought not to be: too quick to believe Don John's calumnies, vindictive in publicly repudiating Hero, shallow in his repentance, and too easily compensated for her loss: in short, a cad. But in Irving's production, Claudio was merely blind. He was perceptive enough to understand the true feelings of Beatrice and Benedick, but he was blind to good and evil, a weakness which he shared with Leonato and Don Pedro. Had Claudio's blindness been wilful it would have been repulsive, but Irving avoided conveying any such impression by always giving the part to young romantic actors like Johnston Forbes-Robertson, George Alexander and William Terriss. They emphasized Claudio's callow youth and ardour in love. He was easily deluded because he was inexperienced, and the repudiation was played as an outburst of 'insanely suspicious jealousy' which was easier to forgive because it arose from his genuine passion for Hero: Forbes-Robertson's performance anticipated his Leontes.[29]

Claudio was further excused by the subtlety of his enemy. In the first scene a gimcrack Don John can show the audience that he is a villain by dressing in sombre colours and upstaging furiously. Irving kept him well in the background where his gay court dress blended with the rest of the royal party, and gave the part to Charles Glenney, a young man of twenty-five whom he was later able to cast as Don Pedro without incongruity (see plate 23).[30] His taciturnity and the hint of a

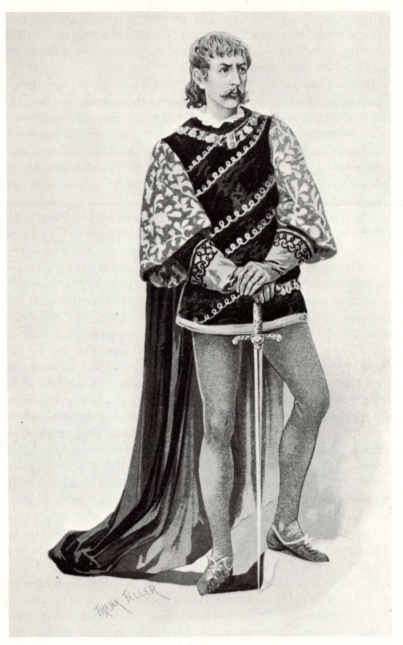

180

quarrel with his brother (I.i.150–3) may have sounded a sour note, but it was quickly covered by the general exit. Glenney presented John as a 'plausible and possible man' whose motives were revealed when he spoke to Conrade of Don Pedro: 'I had rather be a canker in a hedge than a rose in his grace' (I.iii.25ff). He was neither obvious nor melodramatic, and only Beatrice correctly interpreted his melancholy as bitterness: 'How tartly that gentleman looks! I never can see him but I am heartburned an hour after' (II.i.3–4). Blind to Benedick's true feelings, she is an astute observer of others.[31] Don John's characterization largely excused Claudio's credulity at the masked ball. At this festival of deception, nobody is deceived by false faces: ironically, Claudio is only deceived by John's false words because he believes his own incognito to be impenetrable. Every successful deception in the play is carried out by 'practicers' (in Bertrand Evans's term) who pretend to be unaware of the identity or presence of their victims.

When Claudio won his Hero he was gay and joyous again, helping to trick Benedick and joining in the horseplay in the 'toothache scene' (III.ii); Benedick entered with his goatee shaved off, Don Pedro snatched Beatrice's scented handkerchief and threw it to Claudio, and they tossed it back and forth to torment the neophyte lover.[32] It was not so much that experience had taught Claudio nothing: he was merely too happy to learn from experience. No critic found it incredible that he should believe another of Don John's calumnies, which was perhaps a tribute to the bastard's plausible 'guise of regret and forbearance' in the cedar walk scene. Once, Claudio made to draw on John when he promised 'you shall see her chamber window entered' (III.ii.109), but in belief he became 'sad and solemn'.[33] Here Claudio was at his blindest, permitting false words to distort his vision so grievously that he would see what Don John told him to see rather than what was before his eyes.

The scene of the wedding was a side-chapel in a great Sicilian cathedral. Three-dimensional columns, a roof canopied in crimson plush, and sunlight slanting through a stained-glass window, contributed to an illusion made perfect by the sight and smell of incense. 'Henry had the art of making ceremonies very real,' Ellen Terry

23 Charles Glenney as Don John, 1882 (Crown Copyright, Victoria and Albert Museum)

remembered: small acolytes glided about, lighting candles and genu-
flecting; vergers with halberds crowded the nave outside wrought-iron
gates. Leonato had hired a band for the occasion, and its secular music
contrasted significantly with the 'plaintive wail of the organ' while he
tenderly escorted his daughter to her humiliation. The scene was so
splendid that Irving had to cut Leonato's first line, 'Come, Friar
Francis, be brief. Only to the plain form of marriage'; Hero was
obviously in for the *de luxe* treatment.[34] Realistic spectacle on this
scale ruled out any possibility that the spectators' emotions would be
'distanced' enough to help them disbelieve in the shocking events they
were about to witness.[35]

Claudio can be cold and priggish or hot and outraged at the
wedding. Forbes-Robertson chose the more generous interpretation;
his outburst was sudden: 'There!' he cried, literally throwing Hero
away, 'Leonato, take her back again.'[36] By their reactions to this crisis
the other members of the wedding party show how clearly they can
see. Claudio and Don Pedro see only through the distorting spectacles
provided for them by Don John. They are honest men; if they will only
learn the wisdom of trusting their own senses rather than another's, to
look at the girl in the window, the man who talks to her, and the girl
weeping before their eyes, they will see their folly. Hero is exactly what
she appears to be: they are only deluded because they do not look at
her. Irving's Benedick had learned to use his eyes; 'a quick, covert
look' showed that he suspected Don John, and the actor wrote in his
study-book, 'Watch Hero'. Shakespeare allows Benedick two quips in
his old manner (IV.i.20–1, 68), which Irving cut. The effect was to
make him more serious and watchful. Don John was silent and
watchful too;[37] he had no illusions, of course, except the great one,
that evil can thrive unchecked. The Friar too kept silent and used his
eyes:

> Hear me a little,
> For I have only silent been so long,
> And given way unto this cross of fortune
> By noting of the lady.

> (IV.i.154–7)

Hearing this, Beatrice knelt to kiss his hand. She never doubted for a
moment that her cousin was belied. Blinded by tears – Terry could
shed real tears at moments like this – she trusted her judgement of

Hero against all the false words which fools and villains could speak, and she would demand the same act of faith from Benedick.[38]

Beatrice thought herself alone after the insensible Hero had been carried away. Benedick gently touched her hand, and asked, 'Lady Beatrice, have you wept all this while?' His declaration of love was the irrevocable abandonment of his accustomed protective pose; when Beatrice said, 'Ah, how much might the man deserve of me, that would right her' (260–1), he answered emphatically, 'Is there any way to show such friendship?' Then, suddenly, he kissed her hand. 'I do love nothing in the world so well as you,' he admitted, looking awkwardly at the hat he carried in his hand. 'Is not that strange?' For a moment their talk was playful. At length, when she too admitted her love, they embraced. 'Come,' said Benedick. 'Bid me do anything for thee.'[39]

'Kill Claudio.' The effect was sensational. Here, if anywhere, the elaborately sanctified setting justified itself. The sudden ferocity, the 'terrible resonance' and the 'gesture like that of thrusting a lance' shocked Benedick and the audience. When he refused, he had to hold her hand to prevent her from leaving him on the spot; she was disappointed in him. The passion with which Beatrice answered his question, 'Is Claudio thine enemy?' swept him to her side. Weeping and raging, she paced the stage, irresistible in her indignation.[40] 'O! God, that I were a man!' There was no substitution of 'Heaven' here. 'I would . . .' – a long pause, then 'with rage expressed in the scarcely suppressed tears' – 'I would eat his heart in the market place.' Here Ellen Terry 'attained a force that was perhaps not expected by some of her hearers'.[41] It was enough for Benedick. When he could get a word in edgeways, he consented; she responded with a 'burst of mingled gratitude and passion'. She prevailed because of her irresistible unselfishness. 'Women less noble than Beatrice might have forgotten Hero's tragedy, in her [sic] own joy,' Terry wrote.[42]

It is unrealistic to suppose that an audience can maintain a moderate awareness of the absurdities and ironies which contemplation in tranquillity reveals in these dramatic speeches.[43] On the stage this is a ticklish moment; if the tension breaks for an instant, the audience will see the whole scene as preposterous, and laugh.[44] That is the choice: tragic tension or a roar of laughter. There is no middle way. There was time enough for release when Benedick was persuaded to challenge Claudio. Then Irving used the 'gag' and got his laugh.

24   Ellen Terry as Beatrice, V.iv (Crown copyright, Victoria and Albert Museum)

184

The challenge scene (V.i) took place in the garden where Don Pedro and Claudio had opened Benedick's eyes to the love which now sent him upon this grim errand. His pose abandoned, he was a changed man, a 'fine-spirited and noble-hearted gentleman'. There was nothing laughable in the challenge. He turned aside the jests of the younger men without loss of dignity, and there was 'a tone of dangerous menace' in his challenge. In some performances he slapped Claudio with his glove. 'In the speech beginning "Fare you well, *boy*," [183–90] there was a wondrous courtesy and gentleness of voice and manner, from which all levity had gone out. It was the other side of Benedick, the manly, graver, sweeter side.'[45]

Claudio's self-righteousness is at its objectionable height when he jeers at Leonato and Benedick. But it is founded upon ignorance, and Benedick's challenge is the first painful stage in a process of enlightenment which is so rapid and violent that we can pity Claudio if he gives us half a chance. The second, sledgehammer blow is Borachio's confession, which Frank Tyars made 'exceptionally quiet and telling'. He 'commands our sympathies,' said *Punch*, 'and, when he is walked off in custody, we sincerely hope that he will only be reprimanded, warned against keeping bad company, and let off after giving something to the poor-box'.[46] Claudio's reaction attracted no comment, but his penance at the monument (V.iii) was played in full, sumptuously mounted for emphasis. Appropriately, it took place inside the church and Claudio confessed his error before the monks and vergers who had witnessed Hero's humiliation.

Meanwhile, Benedick and Beatrice had begun to restore the comic atmosphere in their garden scene (V.ii). Benedick sang his little song about the god of love in a high voice 'that breaks and fails him most lamentably', a deliberate effect, of course, designed to show that he is not such a fool as to become the complete lover in anything but jest. When Beatrice resumed her old habit of chattering, he accepted it with a 'comical shrug of the shoulders and air of martyred resignation'.[47] Ellen Terry wrote in 1891, 'Beatrice has *confessed* her love, and is now *softer*. Her voice should be beautiful now, breaking out into playful defiance now and again, as of old.'[48] Each had learned the inner worth of the other, and their gaiety no longer obscured their true feelings. In the last scene, all of the ladies entered with veils over their heads (see plate 24). Hero unveiled and Claudio was forced to believe his eyes at last. 'Which is Beatrice?' asked Benedick, but he needed nobody to tell him; 'he makes his quest among them, till at last, believing truly that the eyes of love have penetrated her mask, she replies, "I answer to that name"'.[49] Irving and Terry led the saraband which played its proper part as a symbol of the new harmony between what seems and what is. The scene was again the ballroom in Leonato's house, but the masks were gone.

Style and criticism

I have not yet mentioned Dogberry and the Watch because they seem to have played no significant part in the Lyceum *Much Ado* (see plate 25). They fulfilled their mechanical function in the plot, of course, overhearing the villains and running them in; but if Irving meant them to contribute to the development of the major theme, his audience utterly missed the point. Modern criticism often assigns to Dogberry and his crew a corrective role which would have harmonized well with Irving's interpretation: when they trust words they get everything ludicrously muddled, but when they use their eyes and ears they see what the clever people in the play cannot. Borachio says, 'What your wisdoms could not discover, these shallow fools have brought to light' (V.i.231–3).[50] Reviews which were otherwise extravagant in their praise invariably pummelled Dogberry. Irving made running repairs, cutting the clown's scenes to a bare minimum after the bad reviews of 1882 and restoring many passages in 1891, in the vain belief that he had found a more effective low comedian.[51] It was hopeless. The critics condemned both Sam Johnson (1882) and William Mackintosh (1891) for self-consciousness: 'Dogberry gave just that emphasis to his mispronunciation which showed that he was conscious of his own absurdity.'[52]

Irving surely would not have allowed such 'coarse acting' to pass if he had known what to do with Dogberry. But in his production both the old constable and the world he lived in were irremediably incongruous. Sets and costumes accurately represented Sicily early in the sixteenth century, but 'the audience, whose eyes had been filled by the

25 Arrest of Borachio and Conrade, III.iii (Shakespeare Centre Library, Stratford-upon-Avon)

WE CHARGE YOU IN THE PRINCES NAME.

ARREST OF BORACHIO & CONRADE.

radiance of a succession of sumptuous Sicilian scenes, failed to sympathize with the sudden and ungenial contrast presented by a troop of Elizabethan municipals'. The problem was one of style. 'Shakespeare himself had probably not a thought for costume or accessories,' said *The Times*, 'otherwise he would never have committed the solecism of throwing Dogberry and his companions, in their Elizabethan cloaks and slouched hats . . . into the midst of a brilliant throng of Italian and Spanish nobles. A faithful adherence to the spirit of the text has saved Mr. Irving from what would have been the still greater solecism of attiring Dogberry as a Sicilian commissary.'[53] In *Much Ado about Nothing* Irving made his first attempt to adapt the romantic world of Shakespeare's comedies to the theatre of illusion. He was wise to ignore the advice of those who urged him to begin with *As You Like It*. An audience which was disturbed to find an English constable in Messina would have had a difficult time indeed with the cosmopolitan menagerie of characters who wander in Arden forest. Subsequent chapters will show how Irving dealt with the even more difficult task of fitting *Twelfth Night* and *Cymbeline* into the conventions of his theatrical style.

It is universally acknowledged that the two main plots of *Much Ado* are stylistically distinct. Beatrice and Benedick are the relatively naturalistic creations of Shakespeare's imagination, while Claudio and Hero are drawn from Italian romance and behave accordingly. Placed beside the natural characters, the romantic figures look like puppets. Victorian commentators and actors were usually ready to suggest that Shakespeare had assimilated his materials imperfectly. Modern criticism finds in the dramatist's apparent ineptitude yet another example of his superlative subtlety. We are a people who value sublety and complexity for themselves: in Shakespeare we find the reflection of our own ingenuity. Modern solutions to the stylistic problem have taken several ingenious forms. According to E. C. Pettet, it does not matter that the romantic figures are made out of cardboard. 'They merely act out their tale of love-adventure. The tale is the thing, and Shakespeare never intended us to worry ourselves with their personalities and motives. In the main – though there are certain important exceptions – he was not much interested in the comedy of character.' Ralph Berry disagrees: 'My assumption is that the behaviour of the dramatis personae is, or ought to be, explicable in terms of naturalistic psychology. I take it to be axiomatic that Shakespeare's intuitive grasp of psychology is the foundation of his drama.' Alexander Leggatt attempts a compromise. He argues that *Much Ado* has a unity which is actually based upon the 'interplay of formality and naturalism'. Claudio behaves mechanically because he has not yet grown up enough to become an individual like Benedick: 'he is at once a figure in a conventional action, and a character with a conventional mind'. The most common modern approach, however, is to seek unity in common themes which bind together the stylistically disparate elements of the comedy.[54]

Irving's solution was thoroughly modern. As I have shown, he used a theme of blindness and seeing to establish a vital link between the two love-plots. In the theatre of illusion, however, the theme could be suggested but not insisted upon. He may have understood that the same theme was present in the Dogberry plot, and he may have directed his low comedians to emphasize it as much as possible. If the attempt was made, it failed. The theatre of illusion requires that the dramatic style of a scene or character be given an appropriate visual context. Dogberry and the Watch belong to Elizabethan Warwickshire;[55] dress them up as Sicilian commissaries and they become even more incongruous. In Irving's convention, no other choices were available: they were condemned to an exoticism which no merely suggested theme could overcome.

Irving knew that the same fate would befall Claudio and Hero if they remained romance-figures. Beatrice and Benedick are overwhelming characters and the prose which is their natural idiom makes up three-quarters of the dialogue. Terry and Irving played in the naturalistic style of contemporary comedy. For Claudio and Hero the choice was to adapt or perish. Their emotions were made as real as possible. Claudio's behaviour seemed partly excusable because his pain was sympathetically and realistically portrayed: to understand is to forgive, in the theatre if not in life. Played thus, Claudio and Hero could live without incongruity in the same Messina inhabited by Beatrice and Benedick. Only then could the common theme become effective as a unifying force.

7

Twelfth Night

8 July 1884

Theatrical context

Everything went wrong with *Twelfth Night*. Produced for a short off-season run between two overseas tours, it opened on 8 July 1884 at the height of a heat-wave that made audiences scarce and cantankerous. Competition from concerts in the illuminated gardens of the new Health Exhibition hurt all the theatres, and Irving lost more than £3,000 on the season.[1] On opening night, Ellen Terry was suffering from a painful infection in the thumb which took her permanently out of the bill after sixteen performances. Her sister Marion replaced her for the remainder of the thirty-nine scheduled performances, and Ellen played Viola only four more times, in New York.[2] Irving compounded his troubles by miscasting. Perhaps the failure of his resident comedians in *Much Ado* urged him to look outside the Lyceum, but the results were unfortunate. 'The cast was a quite remarkable example of square pegs in round holes,' recalled Martin-Harvey. 'David Fisher, who was then almost inarticulate, for Sir Toby, Frank Wyatt, a particularly charming dancer, for the ungainly Aguecheek, Stanislaus Calhaem [Clown], whose dental accoutrement rendered him almost unintelligible, and Rose Leclercq, long past the meridian of her charms, as Olivia.' Reviews agreed that she, too, was inaudible.[3] At sixty-eight, Fisher was too old for his part, and he annoyed the audience by playing Sir Toby as a senile, 'dull, offensive sot'. Wyatt was ineffectively foppish, and nothing Calhaem could do in such company would convince the critics that the Shakespearean clown was anything but a 'stupendous nuisance'. Irving later admitted that he ought never to have attempted the play without three great comedians. Even the loyally Irvingite critic Clement Scott could only say that it might have been worse.[4]

The first performance met hisses and hoots from a 'determined minority'. Irving rebuked the dissidents in his curtain speech and the conservative Press attacked 'the blatant vulgarity of a disreputable gang of foul first-nighters' as though they had hooted the sermon at St Martin-in-the-Fields.[5]

In his long provincial apprenticeship Irving played 600 parts, but none in *Twelfth Night*: it was little known in the theatre. The only London run it had sustained since his arrival in the capital was a poorly received vehicle for Adelaide Neilson in 1878. In living memory, only Phelps had made Malvolio a star part, and Irving was certainly aware of his interpretation. It is quite likely that he saw one of the old star's matinées at the Gaiety in 1876.[6] Phelps presented a Malvolio who was truly 'sick of self-love', deadpan, humourless and superior. His heavily lidded eyes saw nothing worthy of his notice: it was 'enough for him to contemplate the excellence within'. Olivia's love he accepted as evidence of her good sense, and he rewarded her with a wintry smile. He endured imprisonment calmly because he did not realize he had been tricked. In the early productions at Sadler's Wells, his discovery of the truth merely turned Malvolio's gaze contentedly inward again, but in late revivals his anguish was so bitter that the audience pitied him; gathering his dignity about him, he left the stage with a valedictory threat reminiscent of Shylock's last exit.[7]

Contemporary criticism

In 1765 Dr Johnson wrote: 'The marriage of Olivia, and the succeeding perplexity, though well enough contrived to divert on the stage, wants credibility.'[8] Shakespeare's plot abounds in improbabilities and downright absurdities; they are a convention of romantic comedy. But Victorian character criticism and the theatre of illusion both assumed that we cannot believe in illogically conceived characters or situations. While the theatre begged the question by leaving *Twelfth Night* alone, some critics assumed the unpromising task of showing that the improbabilities really did not exist. Shakespeare's Illyria, they argued, could be firmly anchored in time and space: it was the Adriatic coast early in the seventeenth century. With spectacular innocence, one editor accounted for the conjunction in this Balkan setting of Italian and homely English characters: 'Duke Orsino is a Venetian governor of that portion of Dalmatia . . . Olivia, Malvolio and Maria are also Venetians; . . . Sir Toby and Sir Andrew are English residents; the former a maternal uncle to Olivia – her father, a Venetian Count, having married Sir Toby's sister.'[9] Why not a paternal uncle? We could then have rejoiced in contemplating 'Olivia Belch'.

The romantic convention of love at first sight is difficult to rationalize. Viola's case is made easier to explain by the time which elapses between her decision to serve Orsino and our next glimpse of her, as the favoured servant who 'would be his wife'. Nevertheless, many critics preferred to believe that she loved Orsino before the play began, and was shipwrecked on her way to woo him in disguise. This is indeed what happens in Shakespeare's source, but by omitting it, the dramatist transforms the stormy sea from an accidental hazard into a providential agent which propels Viola and Sebastian towards their unexpected destiny.[10] The major commentators, however, mostly recognized with Hazlitt that in Illyria logic is irrelevant: 'Folly is indigenous to the soil, and shoots out with native, happy, unchecked luxuriance. Absurdity has every encouragement afforded it; and nonsense has room to flourish in.' Recalling that Twelfth Night is a feast of misrule, one scholar said, 'We are here in fairyland; why should we try to discover the real nature of these personages? They are children of the imagination.'[11]

In the theatre, airy fantasies have a way of coming heavily to earth. *Much Ado* had taught Irving that Shakespeare's mature comedies demanded a mixture of styles which could not be reconciled in the theatre of illusion. The thoroughly English Dogberry had been incongruous in the streets of Messina, but heavy cutting reduced the problem to nuisance proportions. The discordant characters in *Twelfth Night*, however, could not be suppressed; Sir Toby Belch and the 'lighter people' are half the play. Irving should have abandoned his convention and called upon his designers to create a fanciful visual style in which Toby, Olivia, Malvolio and Viola would be equally at home. Neither he nor his audience were ready to take such a radical step, so he compromised. A separate visual metaphor was provided for each of the incongruous groups of characters, but each metaphor was naturalistically expressed in terms of time and place. Thus Toby and his crew held their midnight revel in an obviously English servants' hall where a fire blazed to keep the winter's chill at bay; but Olivia inhabited the sunny terrace and formal garden of an Italian villa, Orsino languished in the marble bosom of his Renaissance palace, Viola and Sebastian were dressed in Balkan costume (see plate 27*a*). Only lighting was freed from the naturalistic convention, to show that Illyria was the realm of the imagination and not a Cook's tour: 'There is ... in some scenes, such as that in Orsino's palace, an apparently intentional effect to indicate a semi-magic light, neither that of common day nor of any visible lamp, torch or candle, but a suffused rich radiance contrasting exquisitely with the blue moonlight in the background.'[12] But this alone was not enough to break the trammels of convention. There was a good deal of grumbling to the effect that the servants' hall was 'scarcely in harmony with the external style of Olivia's mansion' and that 'it is well-nigh outside the limits of possibility to yield up the mind to the fantastic and unreal amidst surroundings that are realistic and commonplace to a fault'.[13]

Text

Twelfth Night is a short play, and Irving cut comparatively little.[14] No entire scenes were omitted, and dialogue was pared down without the disproportion that follows when one character or group is regarded as tiresome. Irving's acting version began, like John Philip Kemble's, with Viola on a rocky coast (I.ii), gazing sorrowfully into the red sunset that follows a storm (see plate 26).[15] Sir Toby and Sir Andrew (I.iii) were introduced before Orsino, whose lovesick scenes (I.i and iv) were amalgamated. Shakespeare stresses his languor by contrasting it with Viola's vigour in the sharp transition of pace and language between the first two scenes. This effect was lost in Irving's text, and the 'manly' acting of William Terriss ensured that the audience would perceive Orsino as 'a very ordinary good-looking young man'.[16] William Archer complained that music played too small a part in this production: 'The play begins with a symphony, and ends with a song, and should, on the stage, be steeped in music.' When Orsino's postponed symphony was at last played by four 'oriental creatures', it was so authentically Dalmatian as to seem rather indigestible as the 'food of love'. The Clown's songs, 'O mistress mine' (II.iii) and 'Come away, come away death' (II.iv) were both cut, as they were in Kemble's text; the song about the wind and the rain, which the Clown has in common

193

with Lear's Fool, became 'a jovial melody taken up by the Chorus', used as accompaniment to 'a species of procession and dance'.[17] Thus Irving hushed the dissenting note of sadness which Frye calls the 'minority mood' in comedy,[18] and the whole burden of alienation fell on Malvolio.

Two of Sebastian's scenes were transposed. Bertrand Evans notes that his first appearance is 'conspicuously early in the action, and the more conspicuous for its rather awkward interruption of the expected sequence of events'. Irving noticed this, too, and postponed it until after Viola's melancholy scene with Orsino,

> I am all the daughters of my father's house,
> And all the brothers too.

> (II.iv.121–2)

Up to this point, the naive spectator had nothing to assure him 'that all is and will be well'.[19] I suspect that Irving needed a 'carpenter's scene' here to facilitate a major scene change.

Performance

Ellen Terry believed that Viola should be very young. At the Lyceum, she was a convincing twin to her twenty-year-old brother, Fred, who played Sebastian delightfully, carefully imitating her gait. Saddened in her first two scenes by his supposed drowning, she nevertheless retained enough of her native sense of fun to enjoy the idea of assuming disguise. This was a modest and romanticized adaptation of Balkan dress, cream with plenty of gold embroidery and a blue cap. With its knee-length skirt and 'bodice of dubiously masculine cut', it was male only in a conventional sense (see plate 27*a*). Fred Terry must have looked rather foolish in his identical costume.[20] Archer said

This is a Viola . . . delicately carved in alabaster. It seems as though Patience had come down from her monument, and, still smiling at grief with distant wistful eyes, mingled for a season in the motley doings of men. Shakespeare's Viola has certainly a greater store of healthy animal spirits than this delicate, sylph-like creature; but she cannot have a lighter, airier grace, or, on occasion, a more refined and yet incisive humour.[21]

26 *Top*, Viola on the coast of Illyria, I.ii (the opening scene in Irving's version); *middle*, Malvolio interrupts Sir Toby's revels, I.iii; *bottom*, Orsino enjoys the food of love, I.iii in Irving's version (Crown Copyright, Victoria and Albert Museum)

27a   Ellen Terry as 'Cesario' (Crown Copyright, Victoria and Albert Museum)

This delicate characterization was misplaced in a ponderous production; she 'seemed to have wandered into it by mistake, her cry of "What shall I do in Illyria?" held a plaintive note of sincerity'. Her daughter Edith said the interpretation was too simple; people expected these romantic heroines in male disguise to be acted with the brash vivacity of the 'principal boy' in pantomime.[22]

Similar terms could be used to describe a modern Viola, but they would assume a different meaning. Today's actress wears her Cesario costume with assurance because she wears Levis to parties. Ellen Terry was acutely aware that Viola thinks first of serving Olivia but, finding that impossible, dons disguise to cover the *impropriety* of a woman serving a bachelor like Orsino. In his presence she was embarrassed by her garb, but with Olivia she could relax and enjoy the joke. She asked for the 'honourable lady of the house' with boyish cockiness (I.v.169). Examining her rival's face, she admitted it was 'Excellently done'; then added as a saucy afterthought, 'if God did all' (I.v.239). This was a bit hard on Rose Leclercq, who was thirty-nine and looked it. The effect must have been to make Orsino seem a man who is not only taken in by appearances, but by art as well.[23]

Terry knew that too much melancholy would kill the comic tone of the play. Her love was sincere and selfless. Pleading Orsino's cause, she spoke with real passion, and when she mentioned her supposed sister, 'She feels the pathos of the story. Her frame quivers as she tells it to Orsino with lowered head, and his head presses upon hers in mere brotherly sympathy.' Passing behind his couch, she dashed away a tear and looked down at him sorrowfully. But natural good sense and youthful high spirits prevented Viola from taking herself too seriously. Thus in the duel (III.iv) her fear would be tempered by awareness of the absurdity of the situation, and when she realized that Sir Andrew was the bigger coward, she fetched him a thwack across the bottom with the flat of her sword.[24]

When Malvolio cast Olivia's ring at Viola's feet, her bewilderment gave way to sudden understanding: 'She loves me, sure' (II.ii.21). Enjoying the humour of the situation, she exclaimed, 'I am the man', and for the moment 'assumed a manly gait' which reminded *Punch* of a Masher Prince and brought down the house.[25] This trumpery business offended the *Saturday Review*: 'That this is the right interpretation we cannot believe. Viola, lighthearted and brave as she was in

27*b* Malvolio, first dress (University of Victoria)

the midst of trouble, was not the person to be unfeeling towards the
trouble of another woman.' Terry was disturbed by this hint of cruelty
and she modified her reading: 'she now gives to the subsequent words
"poor lady, she were better love a dream", precisely the touch of
pathos which on the first night we missed,' said the same journal a
week later.[26] We cannot dismiss this as foolish sentiment. The sensi-

tive spectator constantly experiences responses which he suppresses because he is sure they are inappropriate. To me, there is a whiff of selfishness, for instance, in Sebastian's insistent tourism:

> I am not weary, and 'tis long to night.
> I pray you, let us satisfy our eyes
> With the memorials and things of fame
> That do renown this city.
>
> (III.iii.21–4)

I know I should not be irritated at his failure to apologize and proceed to the Elephant when Antonio explains his danger, but I am. My reaction derives from a real-life code of courtesy which would be tedious and irrelevant in romantic comedy, particularly in a verse scene. In the same way, the *Saturday Review* responded to Ellen Terry's business as though she and Olivia were real people: it is a moral judgement, not an artistic one. When an age like Irving's, or for that matter like ours, begins to apply its moral and social codes to an Elizabethan romantic comedy, the result will inevitably be distortion. We must accept the standards which operate in the ephemeral world of the play. It is probable that Terry invited this judgement because she momentarily emerged from what Northrop Frye calls the 'green world' of comedy. Irving's Malvolio went awry because he never entered it.

There was never anyone like Malvolio; but if there were, his public humiliation by a pack of fools would be an outrage. If we are to enjoy *Twelfth Night* in the proper spirit, two conditions must be satisfied. In the first place, we must be shown that Illyria is not to be mistaken for the real world; and in the second, Malvolio and the rest must retain that touch of the fantastic which makes them true citizens of Illyria. In the world of romantic comedy, anyone who bears himself as Malvolio does subscribes himself an ass; if Coriolanus were to turn up in the next shipwreck, his lofty bearing would mark him down as a legitimate target for practical jokes. Irving's Illyria was so naturalistic that it was almost indistinguishable from the world of the tragedies, and in the first performances his Malvolio also belonged to the real world, because there was nothing fantastic about him. The characterization was influenced by Charles Lamb's famous reminiscence of Robert Bensley's Malvolio: 'His quality is at the best unlovely, but neither buffoon nor contemptible. His bearing is lofty, a little above his station, but probably not much above his deserts.'[27] This is all wrong. Malvolio's deserts are a moral question. As soon as they are considered, we shall conclude that he is most notoriously abused. It follows that it is cruel to laugh at him, and that his tormentors are vicious. We shall begin to examine Toby's character, and condemn him for drinking, and gulling Sir Andrew. Next, we may apply moral judgements to Orsino's idleness and Olivia's violation of her oath to mourn her brother seven years. In short, we shall lose our sense of humour and spoil the comedy.

Irving's first costume was a Renaissance Venetian livery of black silk vertically striped with double gold braids. Its extremely high and tight collar and pointed waistline stressed Malvolio's stiff dignity; later he changed into a similar dress which permitted more freedom of movement. The initial effect was enhanced by the scanty hair, a goatee and 'an emaciated, oddly-lined and wrinkled visage'; like Phelps, he was scarcely recognizable in his make-up. He wore a seal of office and diamond earrings, and carried a long, slender staff whose lightness suggested a 'fantastic symbolism' (see plate 27b).[28] He was every inch a gentleman, but excessively conscious of the fact, contemptuous of his inferiors, amongst whom he sometimes seemed to number Olivia, who spoiled him with her indulgence. His gravity was slightly fatuous, and quite without humour. 'By virtue of the inalienable prerogative of birth and education', he presumed courteously to reprove Olivia for allowing herself to be drawn by the Clown (I.v), in whom he could see nothing 'either amusingly foolish or wittily wise'.[29]

When Malvolio interrupted the midnight revel (II.iii) the force of his humourless character saved him from absurdity. Sir Toby and his friends were caterwauling before a fire in a panelled alcove, a 'snug' set apart by light and warmth from the dark emptiness of the servants' hall. Malvolio entered from above stairs, a ghostly white figure carrying a candle, gliding down the steps in the shadows behind an ornamental screen. He wore a nightcap and gown that should have made him ridiculous (see plate 26). 'We see that Malvolio is a man who, even for his bedchamber, arrays himself with solemn propriety, and into whose head such an idea as looking absurd in any guise is not likely to come.'[30] His humourlessness preserved his dignity, but it infuriated the 'lighter people', who were able to use it to bring him down because it blinded Malvolio to the absurdity of a match between himself and Olivia. His enemies used this limitation to feed his pride until it became foolish.[31]

The soliloquy in the garden scene (II.v) was the sort of thing in which Irving excelled. He stood still and acted with his face, its rapid play of expression clearly revealing his daydreams. He toyed with a flower, throwing it away when he spoke of that mysterious lady of the Strachy who married the yeoman of the wardrobe. Reading the letter, he was 'more gratified than astonished' to learn of Olivia's love: why should she not share his affection for himself? His lack of humour prevented him from suspecting for a moment that this could be a practical joke. 'M,' he said, paused, and smiled: 'M, – why, that *begins* my name.' He ended with 'measureless content', his eyes shut with rapture, while the conspirators raged behind the box-hedge.[32] There was no clowning when he appeared before Olivia cross-gartered and wearing a smile that was false and frosty, rather than the self-congratulating smirk of a man who is conscious of having got more than he deserves.[33]

So far Irving's interpretation had been richly comic, but in the 'dark room' scene (IV.ii) Malvolio became too human. His dignity was broken. Instead of playing from the customary window, he grovelled abjectly on the straw of 'a dungeon worthy of *Fidelio*'. Where Phelps had maintained an unshakeable self-esteem, Irving evidently reasoned that a real person in Malvolio's shoes would be 'desperately wounded in his self-love'. Chained to a pillar like a maniac and trying to prove his sanity to the disguised Clown with 'sage, conscientious words', he was pathetic, and the pathos killed amusement.[34] This was aggravated by the deficiencies of the low comedians, who seemed such a contemptible gang that, preposterous as Malvolio was, their prank had gone much too far and seriously harmed a man who was worth more than all of them. The audience was forced to make moral judgements, and even Malvolio's enemies seemed aware that they had exceeded decent limits.[35] This mistaken emphasis was carried over into the last scene. Coming before Orsino and Olivia amongst a great assembly of nobility and soldiers, Malvolio had recovered his old dignity; but stung by the Clown's taunts, he gave way to a paroxysm of 'air-clawing rage'. His exit, 'I'll be revenged on the whole pack of you', was so vindictive that Olivia was frightened. He seemed quite capable of employing 'the poignard or the poison-bowl'. It was almost tragic.

The *World* summed up the universal reaction: 'I sat next to a gentleman, a total stranger to me, in the stalls; at Mr. Irving's last exit we turned to each other and, as if by one impulse, whispered the single word "Shylock".'[36] Irving subsequently acknowledged his mistake by softening the exit and eliminating the humiliation. 'Now Malvolio bears himself like a man,' said the *Saturday Review*, 'and the humour of the scene is no longer obscured by a disagreeable scene of his ill-usage. He stands up to answer the questions of the false Sir Topas, and he delivers the reply about the soul with a kind of fantastic grandeur.' Even the make-up was changed. W. H. Pollock wrote to Irving: 'The alteration in the colour of the hair and complexion had some share in lightening the character since opening – as it represented him as a less saturnine temperament than he had at first – & all the business in the dark room and afterwards, is now removed from the domain of tragedy to that of serious comedy.'[37]

Modern criticism

Nothing in the reviews of Irving's production seems stranger to a modern reader than the ubiquitous remark that *Twelfth Night* is a bad play, a little tiresome on the stage for want of unity and 'interest'.[38] Since Granville-Barker's revolutionary production in 1912 it has been a popular favourite, and the critical literature is both extensive and incisive. More than Shakespeare's other comedies, it has reflected the image of modern minds. It seems to us the subtle perfection of the dramatist's control over an infinitely complex medium. But *Twelfth Night* is not really intricate at all: it is diffuse, and the intricacy is imposed by our descriptions of its diffuseness. Before the stake and woodpile are prepared for me, I hasten to add that it is diffuse in the best sense. In this comedy, the mixture of conventions, styles, themes, images and techniques which is the true Elizabethan vintage attains its mellow, muddled best. But to interpret it as a cunningly contrived unity in which every detail contributes to the expression of a central theme is to impose upon it our own opinion of what is important. The play is so open that it will support our interpretations up to a point; but in the end, the overconfident actor or critic is betrayed by his own single-mindedness, and joins the Feast of Fools.

We often see *Twelfth Night* as a 'right way – wrong way' comedy in which Viola alone, like Beatrice or Rosalind, understands what love is all about in the real world. The educable characters are taught that love must endure the rain that raineth every day. Orsino and Olivia are isolated and mistaken: he is deluded, lethargic, in love with love (Gervinus was the first to say that, and it has been remorselessly repeated ever since); and she is wasting her youth, first in grief which is an enemy to life, and then in illusion. There is much truth in this, but nagging doubts remain; what does Viola see in Orsino? If she loves this man, must she not be blind, too? And the subplot, where so much labour is expended in an effort to educate Malvolio, who is sick of self-love, must seem a little futile when he learns nothing.

To interpret *Twelfth Night*, we must understand that it requires an exquisite balance between enthusiasms. We must apply fine tuning in order to allow for the temper of the times; then the play emerges as a richly ambiguous exploration of the conflicting claims of life and morality, love and responsibility, frivolity and seriousness. I repeat, it is an exploration, not an answer. When this balance is lost it becomes a redundant metaphor of contemporary attitudes, made trivial by simplification and marred by an unacceptable number of loose ends. *Twelfth Night* is not a thesis play about the right way to love, but love is one of its important themes. All of the main characters are lovers, save the Clown. Love is the constant factor; it moves them all equally, according to their several capacities and natures, even when it is only self-love. In the power of love we are all fools; nobody is exempt except the Clown, the professional Fool who sees the folly of others clearly, but only at the price of remaining a spectator of life. In his wise folly he outsmarts himself, and is left alone, singing about the weather.

The subplot offers us a choice of mistaken emphases, depending upon our attitudes to cakes and ale. The frankly self-indulgent mood of our times often leads us to see Malvolio as the embodied spirit of denial, justly exorcized by a life-celebrating, rubicund Toby who is a jolly good fellow. In a Vancouver Playhouse production in 1978, for example, the steward was played as a prim proto-Nazi, complete with German accent and *lederhosen*. It is well to remember that Sir Toby leaves the stage with a broken head before the festivities begin.

Irving's mistake was not merely his excessive emphasis on Malvolio. He went wrong because he forced the audience to see a comic situation through the eyes of one character, instead of from an impartial vantage point. Whether that character was suffering or triumphant at the time is secondary: the point is that the sympathies of the audience were illegitimately enlisted for the attitudes which Malvolio represented and alienated from the attitudes of his antagonists. Moral questions which should never have been asked destroyed the healthy diffuseness of the play, and left no room for humour.

8

Cymbeline

22 September 1896

There is still no critical consensus on the interpretation of *Cymbeline*, or even on its merit. The best authorities find it either a subtle masterpiece of Shakespearean mythography and symbolism, or an experiment in form which means nothing in particular; an exploration of major themes foiled by the dramatist's failure to master his materials, or his greatest technical achievement.[1] The perceptions of the cool and solitary reader differ markedly from those of the spectator in the theatre: one of the play's chief detractors admits that 'It is extremely agreeable and diverting to watch.'[2] *Cymbeline* is a highly theatrical play, fanciful and spectacular; many of its effects are achieved visually, and in the heat of performance its atmosphere commands belief. Irving had a fighting chance to do it justice because its stylistic demands can be met – or bungled – more effectively in the theatre of illusion than those of the mature comedies. Accordingly, his reading may carry an authority which we badly need in the present state of criticism.

Theatrical context

Garrick made *Cymbeline* popular in 1761 when he first appeared as Posthumus, which remained the male star's part until Irving chose to play Iachimo instead. Since the days of Siddons, however, *Cymbeline* had been considered Imogen's play, and the most famous Imogen was Helena Faucit, who last appeared in the part in 1865. Irving's production in 1896 was the first of any significance for thirty-one years.[3] Thus, there was no tradition at all for Iachimo, and Ellen Terry challenged only the greybeards' memories of Faucit, kept fresh by her essay on Imogen.[4] The popular verdict was that Irving had made a

dull play serviceable. It was performed eighty-eight times, a respectable run and a record for the play, but not enough to bring it back into
the popular Shakespearean repertory.[5]

Contemporary criticism

Ellen Terry's most difficult task was to live up to the extravagant praise
which Victorians heaped upon Imogen. Swinburne's encomium is
notorious: 'Imogen is the most adorable woman ever created by God
or man.' But Schlegel, Hazlitt, Mrs Jameson, Ulrici and Dowden are
not far behind, while Gervinus thought that 'Imogen is, next to
Hamlet, the most fully drawn character in Shakespeare's poetry.'[6] We
must remember that to many Victorians the idea of truth was bound
up with the 'ideal'; melodrama was thrillingly 'true' when it imitated
life *as it ought to be*, a mode which Aristotle recommends. In Imogen's
fidelity and obedience to Posthumus, her joy at the very thought of
him, Victorians of both sexes saw their ideal of womanhood. It is not
surprising, then, that Bernard Shaw sang a discord in the chorus of
praise. When he came to 'refinish' *Cymbeline* in 1931 he gave Imogen
the gumption to rebuke Posthumus for his male arrogance. 'He is not
even sorry,' she complains, before she goes home 'to make the best of
it / As other women must'.[7] Shaw's dissent must be related to his
famous feminism, of course, but it also signifies his belief that the
theatre ought to depict life *as it is*. Real young women simply do not
play Griselda. Writing to Ellen Terry while she was in rehearsal, Shaw
argued that there were two Imogens, a *real* woman and 'an idiotic
paragon of virtue produced by Shakespeare's *views* of what a woman
ought to be'.[8] Thus Terry rehearsed under pressure from advocates of
conflicting theatrical conventions, who urged her that Imogen should
belong entirely and consistently to one of them. But Shakespeare's
Imogen is both a paragon and a human being who sometimes leaps
prematurely to the conclusion that her husband 'has forgot Britain' or
fallen under the influence of 'some Roman courtezan'.[9]

Modern criticism

Shaw rebukes Shakespeare for mixing convention with naturalism,
but some modern critics think he added too much nature to conven-

tion. According to the New Arden editor, J. M. Nosworthy, Iachimo is a stock character who gets out of hand because 'In practice . . . he goes beyond convention. He carries an air of psychological probability at times, and admits touches of individualizing detail which are at odds with type portrayal.' Imogen is 'a superb accident, a Perdita or Miranda who defeated Shakespeare's intentions by coming to life'.[10] In other plays Shakespeare frequently violates the integrity of naturalistic characters by making them accept solutions which are dictated by his plots: Isabella's silent acquiescence in the Duke's announcement that she is to become his wife, for example, is psychologically absurd. But even in a play like *Cymbeline*, where the incongruity is extreme, it is rash to assume that the dramatist has blundered. We shall be wiser to assume that he mixes his conventions as a deliberate technique.

Several similar techniques, some of which have often been criticized as weaknesses, are present to a marked degree in *Cymbeline*. Dr Johnson observed, 'To remark the folly of the fiction, the absurdity of the conduct, the confusion of the names and manners of different times, and the impossibility of events in any system of life, were to waste criticism upon unresisting imbecility, upon faults too evident for detection, and too gross for exaggeration.'[11] Few real generals avenge disgrace by stealing their king's infant sons and bringing them up in a cave. It is unlikely that a crown princess would ever be found roaming the Welsh mountains disguised as a boy, or that, if she were, she would find her long-lost brothers there. An exhaustive list of improbabilities would be endless because the plot is largely composed of fantastic folk-motives in that impossible mixture we call Romance. There is no need to labour the point, but it should be noted that certain themes are insisted upon to the point of absurdity. The instinctive nobility of the nobly born is Belarius's favourite tune; he repeats it no fewer than four times when his boys 'prince it much / Beyond the trick of others'. Ellen Terry rightly calls him 'silly old potty'.[12] In comedy, to clap eyes upon the heroine is to admire her, but an unusual number of Imogen's beholders seem to become positively unbalanced at a glance: Iachimo, Lucius, the troglodyte brethren and the king all offer extravagant praise.[13]

The celebrated incongruities and anachronisms of *Cymbeline* go far beyond the presence of English figures in an Italian setting, as in *Much*

Ado and *Twelfth Night*. Ancient Romans and Renaissance Italians simultaneously visit an entirely mythical Britain. Johnson comments upon the magnificent Babel of names: Cymbeline and Cloten are British, but Guiderius and Arviragus are Romano-British and their assumed names are Welsh and Greek (Cadwal and Polydore); Philario and Iachimo are Italian, but Lucius is Roman and Imogen tells him she is mourning a Norman master, Richard du Champ. Shakespeare may not have expected his audience to cavil at Valentine's sea voyage from Verona to Milan, but they must have thought Milford Haven an odd port for London, and Lucius deserved defeat if he landed there instead of at Hastings.

In *Cymbeline* Shakespeare deliberately draws attention to these absurdities. The most incredible information is presented boldly, with no attempt at verisimilitude. Belarius steps right out of the dramatic frame to explain the history of his foster-sons (III.iii.79–107) and the first instalment is delivered by two blatantly informative gentlemen; the 'straight man's' response to his friend's wildly improbably tale, 'I do well believe you' (I.i.67), simply begs for a laugh. The dénouement, with its twenty-three separate revelations,[14] cannot fail to draw attention to itself as a technical achievement: the machinery shows, and is meant to show. In short, Shakespeare collects in *Cymbeline* all of the devices which he has repeatedly used in earlier comedies, and exaggerates them to the point of self-parody. Nowhere is this so clear as in the treatment of appearance and reality. He has used this theme often before. It underlies the clothes-imagery in *King Lear* and the disguisings of Julia, Portia, Viola and Rosalind. But in *Cymbeline* Imogen disguises herself twice and Cloten – on the flimsiest of pretexts – puts on Posthumus's clothes. Belarius is disguised and his 'sons' are ignorant of their own identity, while Posthumus fights disguised to 'make men know / More valour in me than my habits show' (V.i.29–30). All of Imogen that is 'out of door' is most rich, and the dissembling Iachimo sets out to prove whether reality matches appearance. Posthumus departing on shipboard seems small, Imogen at a distance seems guilty, Milford from a mountain-top seems close, it all depends upon your point of view. Everyone is in a state of multiple misconception all the time, and the number of situations or images which exploit the theme of appearance and reality almost defy computation.[15]

The sheer multiplicity and nakedness of these familiar devices transforms them into ironies. As the play proceeds, errors or illusions accumulate prodigiously, while a matching body of incredible reality keeps pace. Between falsehoods and alleged facts an increasingly ironical gap grows, and it culminates in a dénouement which systematically recapitulates the whole tangle. Shakespeare is inexorable: in this inventory of confusion, every audience must reach a point where irony overcomes the will to believe and reality merges with appearance. At Stratford, Ontario, in 1970 the audience 'believed' until Cornelius explained that Imogen had not really been dead at all and Belarius said, 'My boys, there was our error': then they laughed.[16] It is a phlegmatic audience indeed that can accept with a straight face the recognition of Guiderius by the mole on his neck. There must be laughter in the last scene.[17] It allows the vision of the mature Shakespeare to break through the dramatic illusion: all our certainties about what is true depend upon our point of view. If there is objective truth at all, it is beyond human knowing and the grasp of art, and exists only in the sight of the Providence that guides us through life's muddles without requiring us to understand.[18]

Text

'In a true republic of art Sir Henry Irving would ere this have expiated his acting versions on the scaffold.'[19] Shaw did not condemn Irving for cutting *Cymbeline*, which he regarded as 'for the most part stagey trash of the lowest melodramatic order'. His difference with the actor was rooted in the fundamental opposition of their theories of art. Shaw believed that the theatre should strive for 'a direct illusion of reality';[20] in their correspondence he urged Ellen Terry to cut every line which seemed false by naturalistic standards. But Irving, who had always modified nature in the direction of the ideal, was busy stretching his convention to its utmost limits to accommodate a play which he recognized as unrealistic Romance.

The last scene holds no surprises for an audience; we always know the truth. Our response to the 'headless man' scene (IV.ii.291ff) is complicated by this ironic awareness: Imogen's genuine grief may move us almost to tears, but we also want to laugh because we know the corpse is Cloten's. 'The apparent reality . . . is so absurd that few actresses have dared to use all the words provided.' Shaw wanted to distract attention from absurdity by focussing it on Imogen's *reactions* to the situation, which he thought should occur in a natural sequence.[21] 'A headless man' interrupted the sequence, so it must be cut. Also, it might get a laugh. The set and lighting should reinforce Imogen's mood: 'if I were a scene painter I'd have painted such an endless valley of desolation for you that at your appearance in its awful solitudes, lost and encompassed by terrors, everyone would have caught their breath with a sob before you opened your mouth'.[22] The audience would quite forget whose corpse lay there; total empathy would altogether eradicate any ironic awareness.

Irving angered Shaw by staging the scene in such a way as to allow the audience to adopt a more detached view.[23] Indeed, the whole production abandoned historical verisimilitude in favour of a temporally unlocated, romantic archaism which was as far as the Lyceum style could be bent without giving up the idea of illusion altogether. But the play had to be abbreviated and while Irving's acting version shows little concern for naturalism, it nevertheless suggests that he was unwilling to risk mixed responses, to allow Shakespeare's ironies to stand undisguised.

Shaw influenced the text through his advice to Ellen Terry, but not as much as he liked to think. A fortnight before the opening she sent him her rehearsal script, which he returned, commenting separately by post.[24] Some of his textual suggestions were incorporated in the printed acting version, but Shaw's major contribution was his influence on Terry's interpretation of her part.[25] Irving sought the aid of William Winter in the early stages of preparation, but the critic's suggestions probably had little permanent effect.[26] Only the stage tradition that went back to Garrick significantly influenced Irving's final arrangement.

Kemble and Phelps both adopted Garrick's arrangement. They cut two minor scenes (I.iii, III.viii) and the entire gaol sequence, with the dream-vision of Jupiter (V.iv). The act-divisions were rearranged, so that Act II began with the temptation scene (I.vii) and Act V with the mountaineers' decision to fight the Romans (IV.iv).[27] Thus far Irving followed them, but he cut three more scenes. Nobody missed Cymbeline's scene with Pisanio (IV.iii), but some critics regretted the loss of Lucius's embassy (III.i) with its patriotic speeches and of Imogen's little scene with Pisanio after Posthumus's departure (I.iv).[28] Irving's

Act III began with Cloten's serenade (II.iii) and Act IV with the first scene in Wales (III.iii); thus each act contained a separate and coherent movement of the narrative, which may have had the effect of emphasizing the action, suspense and illusion. Irving cut much more than his predecessors, nearly half the play. While he sometimes followed traditional cutting, he was usually quite independent, not infrequently restoring lines omitted by the mighty dead.[29] But Mrs Grundy influenced his text excessively; the exact terms of the wager (I.vii) and the nature of Iachimo's pretended success (II.iv) were expressed in the coyest of obliquities. The last scene was much abridged: the Soothsayer was entirely omitted, but none of the revelations except the Queen's death was left out. Guiderius's mole was cut, together with numerous explanations of things the audience already knew, with the inevitable effect that laughter was avoided and illusion preserved.

Performance

Laurence Alma-Tadema, R.A., was the perfect design consultant for *Cymbeline*. His unequalled scholarly knowledge of the physical realities of life in the ancient world made the much-postponed production of *Coriolanus* archaeologically correct, but his paintings show a regard for the ideal which was much to Irving's taste. When accuracy and beauty clashed, both artists agreed that the latter must prevail. The programme gives the period of *Cymbeline* as the first century A.D., but if period had been too strictly observed, incongruities would have embarrassed Irving far more than they had in *Much Ado*. The problem was to find a visual style in which Britons, Romans, the Italian Renaissance figure of Iachimo and assorted minor anachronisms could comfortably mingle.

Irving's Britons were improbably civilized. Cymbeline's soldiers were picturesquely turned out in horned helmets, skins and soup-strainer moustaches, but their appearance suggested none of the rough barbarism of King Lear's retainers (see plate 32). Imogen had grown up amongst these people. Their costumes were made of silk and satin, decorated with 'coloured plaques, discs, Runic and Druidic symbols'. Imogen's court gowns were exquisite: Ellen Terry thought one of them amongst the loveliest dresses she had ever worn. *Punch* doubted

28 Cymbeline's garden, I.i. Posthumus and Imogen at right (Shakespeare Centre Library, Stratford-upon-Avon)

29 Iachimo tempts Imogen in a cloister, I.vi (Shakespeare Centre Library, Stratford-upon-Avon)

30 The cave of Belarius (University of Victoria)
31 Gordon Craig as Arviragus: 'the wild freedom of Bedford Park' (Crown Copyright, Victoria and Albert Museum)

'whether ancient Britons were quite such gorgeous swells' but it was generally allowed that Irving was right 'to give us a beautiful picture and let archaeology go hang'.[30] The garden of Cymbeline's palace (I.i) had just the sort of tastefully ordered informality one would expect such Britons to go in for: decorated obelisks stood around a lawn bordered by natural vegetation, and a low parapet framed a view of white cliffs and the sea (see plate 28). British architecture was delicate and fanciful: the temptation scene took place in a curved cloister with exquisitely tapered columns (see plate 29).[31] Shaw wanted the Welsh mountains represented realistically, but while Irving used built-up rocks for the cave, the effect produced was picturesquely Arcadian (see plate 30). The mountaineers were noble savages in a dream; they wore spotless fleshings beneath their picturesque kilts, and Gordon Craig (Arviragus) sported a leopard skin that belonged to Romance more than to historical Wales (see plate 31). A literal-minded critic grum-

213

bled about 'amiable savage boys who never come downstairs less than two steps at a time, and generally pause half way with one leg elegantly thrown back – who spy deer on the back scene the moment the word is given to hunt, and come bounding home again carrying a 250 lb. carcase as if it were a feather'. Shaw sneered at this from the depths of his outraged naturalism: 'every pose, every flirt of their elfin locks, proclaims the wild freedom of Bedford Park'.[32] The battle evidently took place on Salisbury Plain, an appropriately unlikely location, for a skyline of standing stones was silhouetted against the setting sun. Irving knew how to make a stage combat real, but in *Cymbeline* he avoided doing so; the battle was 'as merry a game as the rest'. The whole engagement was choreographed with spirit but, significantly, not one man fell, and in the midst the King gyrated with raised sceptre, his presence more symbolic than real.[33]

Alma-Tadema saw to it that Rome was authentic – there is a whiff of pedantry in the programme notes that identify the two scenes as the *triclinium* and *atrium* of Philario's house (I.v, II.iv) – but he selected details that would seem slightly bizarre. The wager took place at a banquet. The guests lounged on couches to watch 'dancing girls in diaphanous *coae*' while outlandish guards stood along the walls. The cosmopolitan company were dressed in gorgeous robes instead of classical white, and garlanded with roses. Iachimo wore 'a wonderful robe of crimson and purple'.[34] This was a Roman feast at which a visitor from the Renaissance did not look like a stray, and talk of courtly love was not out of place.

'The Britons are figures on a tapestry, the Romans are figures on a mock triumphal arch,' wrote Henry James, 'and as the play never leaves us for many minutes in one place, the place is indulgently impressionistic.' Those critics who were not committed to historical authenticity agreed that Irving and Tadema had tastefully used poetic licence to create a consistent scenic style which complemented the poetic fancy of a Romance like *Cymbeline*.[35]

Even in Romance, the theatre must develop character, and it was through the characters of Imogen and Iachimo that Irving compelled the audience to believe in the *Cymbeline* world.[36] Posthumus was played by Frank Cooper, a young man advanced beyond deserving by Ellen Terry, whose innocent partiality the audience did not share. Beside Irving he seemed 'a very "slight thing" indeed', and the play would obviously have profited had one of the juvenile leads of former years been available: Forbes-Robertson, Alexander or Terriss.[37] Belarius and the Queen fell to players of the old school. Frederick Robinson had been with Phelps at Sadler's Wells and was warmly welcomed, but his proud pot-belly made him funnier than he meant to be: 'one critic I know will discover that *at last* an actor has arrived in our midst who can deliver Blank Verse,' Terry predicted. 'Looks as if he were going to deliver something else.' The critic – Clement Scott – came through with the expected praise, but the 'breezy 'fore-the-mast vein' of Robinson's playing and his energetic attempts to keep up with the noble savages rendered him too comic.[38] Genevieve Ward had begun her career in opera, and subsequently won a respect-able reputation as a 'heavy woman'. Her Queen was a melodramatic villainess 'like some vivified portrait-bust of the Vatican or Capitol, some hard, high-frizzled Agrippina or Faustina'. Amongst the sup-porting characters only Cloten (Frank Tyars) really came to life, but he was such a fool that the audience pitied his death.[39] To an unusual degree at the Lyceum the play depended upon the two stars. Imogen must dominate in any case, but some critics thought that a Iachimo who overwhelmed Posthumus upset the balance of the play. The idea of balance in *Cymbeline*, however, is based upon the preconception that it is mainly about the conflict between Posthumus and Iachimo. Irving redirected the focus upon the relationship between Imogen and Iachimo, a legitimate emphasis which made the heroine a less passive figure.

Irving's Iachimo was an original characterization, but probably not quite so startling as two critics believed. Victorian actor-managers frequently 'realized' paintings on the stage; one scene in Irving's *Richard III* was copied from a current Royal Academy canvas, and his make-up as Charles I was taken from a triptych by Vandyke. Clement Scott and the critic of the *Queen* were thus following theatrical tradition, if not common sense, when they concluded that when Iachimo was brought before the King for judgement, he was intended to recall Christ. 'Made up after a sacred picture by Guido, calm, serene, a "man of sorrows and acquainted with grief"', the repentant villain suggested to Scott 'the most pathetic figure in the world's history'. He was no doubt thinking of the *Head of Christ Crowned with Thorns*, which was then considered the best example of Guido Reni's

32　*Cymbeline* V.v. Iachimo, Posthumus, Cymbeline, Imogen, Arviragus, Guiderius, Belarius (Shakespeare Centre Library, Stratford-upon-Avon)

work in the National Gallery; but in fact it bears little resemblance to Irving's make-up.[40] According to the *Queen*, Iachimo's 'dignified . . . white-robed and manacled' figure in this scene suggested 'the central figure in one of Munkacsy's best-known paintings'. In Michael Munkacsy's *Christ before Pilate* a saccharine Jesus faces Pilate with wrists crossed and tightly bound with rope. Irving stood before Cymbeline with wrists joined only by a three-foot chain; his cloak may have been white, but it did not disguise his Roman armour, an odd costume for a Christ figure (see plate 32). Scott evidently realized that his idea was blasphemous, if not downright stupid, and his subsequent notices left the man of sorrows respectfully alone.[41]

　　Like Shaw, Helena Faucit 'refinished' *Cymbeline* in her own way. Of course, she was too romantic to question the probability of Imo-

216

gen's character. This ideal woman is 'too noble to know she is noble', and 'a grand and patient faithfulness is at the root of her character'. But while Iachimo could not shake her faith in her husband, Posthumus's letter 'sufficed to blight, to blacken, and to wither her whole life'. The facile reconciliation made her smile again but nothing could heal her; she would fade away and die.[42] This reading gave the last scene a painful subtext which made it much easier to believe, but its tragic ironies sprang from the alienation between Imogen, with her broken heart, and the shallow joy all around her. Ellen Terry sought to preserve the comedy without sacrificing probability. Her Imogen was a person who could not only survive Posthumus's doubt but wholeheartedly forgive him in the end, and bring about Iachimo's salvation at the same time.

She had the resiliency of youth. In 1896 Terry was nearly fifty years old, but she seemed so young that at her entrance 'the audience gasped – there was a silence, then thunders of applause'. Here was the actress 'with twenty years and more off her merry shoulders' and the public simply lay down at her feet. Innocent and high-spirited despite the melancholy circumstances, she was youthfully in love. Shaw persuaded her that the key to her character was impulsiveness, but no shallowness was implied: 'Her impulses are always wholehearted.' When Posthumus gave her the bracelet, she kissed it, and then him. Her answer to her father's rebuke was spirited; Terry reminded herself to give it 'more ginger'.[43]

The wager was not the result of too much wine but of clashing values and temperaments. In the suave luxury of Philario's banquet, the genuine feelings of Posthumus seemed a trifle ill-bred. Iachimo personified the society he inhabited. Aristocratic, urbane and coldly cynical, he believed in nothing, least of all a woman's honour, and he treated the Briton with contempt. Every inch the 'patrician cad', he insolently manipulated this loud-mouthed provincial 'with an outrageous self-confidence and disgusting callousness subtly underlying it'. Of course, his victim's style offended him, but his deeper motive lay in a sceptical refusal to believe in virtue; experience had taught him that it was invariably hypocritical. Thus the wager became a confrontation between sophisticated cynicism and naive goodness, redeemed from the melodramatic by Iachimo's complex character and a sense of inevitability; this conflict had been ordained the moment Posthumus left his native land. The party broke up acrimoniously: 'Of *course he won't take his hand*? I hope not,' Ellen Terry wrote.[44]

In the temptation scene Iachimo seemed so sincere that William Archer confessed himself almost taken in. 'Ravishingly sweet in her slowness to think ill of Posthumus', Imogen was slowly brought to distrust him by the same smooth guile which had led her husband into the wager. The villain took a false step when he said, 'Some men are much to blame', but seeing her quick, defensive anger he applied more oil. His 'low musical method' of persuasion lent conviction to the description of Posthumus's supposed misdemeanours (I.vi.99–112). 'Let me hear no more,' Imogen whispered at last, covering her face with her hands and dropping into a chair. Faucit had spoken this line as an unbelieving rebuke, but Terry was convinced. When she asked, 'How shall I be revenged?' Iachimo sat beside her and whispered in her ear. His proposition came to her as a revelation, and the suddenness of her anger gave the audience a vivid glimpse of Iachimo's chagrin before he adopted a new pose of mingled 'courtesy, friendliness and deep respect'. Terry had originally meant to 'come round very slowly', but when Shaw persuaded her that Imogen should be impulsive, she altered her approach: 'Her indignation with him for traducing her husband and trying to undermine her loyalty is intense, but it passes quickly when Iachimo, seeing he has made a mistake, begins to praise him.' She eagerly agreed to his praises, interjecting 'Yes! Yes!' here and there, although one critic detected a trace of reserve in 'You make amends' and the subsequent words of welcome.[45]

Irving produced the maximum of effect with the greatest economy of means in the bedroom scene. Designed for atmosphere rather than accuracy, this set may have been achieved entirely with hangings. The room was a gloomy cavern lit by a single lamp. Imogen lay under a protective 'cloud-canopy' and tapestries matching Iachimo's descriptions covered the walls. Since she was already abed when the curtain rose, it is difficult to believe that the chest was carried on by porters, and the bit of red cloth which supposedly hung out to show that Iachimo was inside seems unlikely in view of the fact that he was entirely dressed in green brocade.[46] The chest was small and *Punch* wondered what Jackimo in the Boximo did with his legs; it probably had no bottom and stood over an open trap. Before Imogen composed

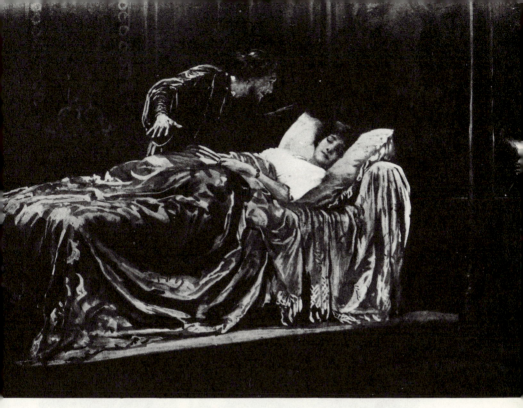

33 Iachimo gestures hypnotically, II.ii (State Library of New South Wales)

herself for sleep, she kissed the bracelet. The trunk opened 'like a great mouth of a shark' and Iachimo emerged to 'a shudder almost pantomimic'. A pure, soft light shone on the sleeping Imogen, but a shadow fell across her face when Iachimo took the lamp away to inspect the chamber.[47] Then, bending over the sleeper, Irving made a series of hypnotic gestures which observers unanimously described as spectral or ghoulish, but were at a loss to explain (see plate 33). To some they denoted lust, but the majority saw Iachimo as a cold seducer who believed that Imogen was a hypocrite and who meant to discredit her. When he took the bracelet, she stirred in her sleep and he glimpsed the 'mole cinque-spotted'.[48]

Terry's Imogen was too human to pretend to the kind of perfection Faucit aimed at. The next morning (II.iii) her anxiety over the lost bracelet made her squabble with Cloten 'like Baby when she's pestered'. But she was impulsive and mercurial; she received Posthumus's summons to Milford with 'girlish abandon'. Her exuberance

219

34   Ellen Terry as 'Fidele' (Crown Copyright, Victoria and Albert Museum)

sounds ridiculous: 'She bounds about the stage like a young fawn, she kisses her hand, she kisses her dear lord's letter, she is a wilful madcap and a romp.'[49] It is the measure of Terry's genius that she could carry off this sort of thing at fifty. When Pisanio gave her the other letter – Posthumus's order for her death (III.iv) – she reacted with almost tragic power. She read it quietly, not to Pisanio but as a soliloquy. Tearing Leonatus's letters from her bosom was an impulsive gesture of rejection: 'Mighty. The Ocean. *Electrical* – or – nothing at all,' Terry wrote. But her spirit was unbroken, and Pisanio's suggestion that she don boyish disguise met a ready response: 'She wants ONLY *to get* to him – for she loves him.' The impulse of denial had passed as suddenly as it had come.[50]

The scene before the cave was played for comedy. Terry could not copy Faucit, who had fled from the echo of her own voice, but she retreated once, and then made the most of Imogen's fear of the sword. Terry's natural anxiety about wearing boy's dress was relieved by the costume designer, who gave her an exceedingly conservative attire such as no proper boy would be caught dead in (see plate 34). When she awoke beside Cloten's corpse her grief was harrowing in its intensity despite the pastoral surroundings and Bank-holiday sunshine to which Shaw objected so bitterly. But Imogen's indomitable spirit carried her through this ordeal, too, and in the last scene the unclouded joy of her reunion with husband, brothers and father vindicated both her fidelity and her impulsive optimism.[51]

We cannot be sure what Irving was trying to do with Iachimo; he left no study-book or notes, and most critics are uncertain. It is true that Shaw praised him for creating 'a true impersonation, unbroken in its life-current from end to end', but he did not explain. The last scene offers a significant clue, however. While the critics who saw the defeated Iachimo as a Christ figure were misguided, they were responding to a new dignity and nobility in his bearing which many others noticed. As he leaned against a heap of spoils or stood shackled awaiting judgement, his face wore 'a sad expression of nobility' which won universal sympathy.[52] His schemes had all come to nothing, of course; but when it is recalled that Irving's Iachimo forced the wager on Posthumus because he disbelieved his boasts, it seems likely that the really devastating discovery he made in the last scene was that the simple Briton had been telling nothing less than the truth. Iachimo's sophisticated cynicism was founded on the conviction that all men – and women – are hypocrites, and his stratagems on the belief that the biggest hypocrite wins. His temporary success seemed to prove him right, but defeat in battle revealed his error. The values by which he had lived were wrong, and acting on them, he had wrought much harm. A man cannot become a cynic unless he begins with a strong moral sense. Iachimo became a villain because he longed for virtue but despaired so much of finding it that he almost destroyed it when it came his way. When he learned that he had harmed people who were honestly as good as they seemed, his life became evil in his own eyes. Few passages in the play are so full of terms contrasting villainy and virtue as is his confession. He became a villain, then, because he had a soul to save; and Imogen saved it with her steadfast goodness.[53]

Irving's clear and sometimes original interpretation of the chief characters in *Cymbeline* interested and satisfied his contemporaries, but for us the Romances present problems which the most perceptive character-criticism cannot solve. Why is the fable so fantastic? What does Shakespeare mean? I have suggested answers, and it remains to be seen whether Irving's experience with the play helps to confirm or deny them.

If he was concerned with a theme at all, Irving probably understood it in terms of character. Imogen's goodness and faith save the soul of cynical Iachimo: faith, one might say, is the right arm of Providence. Perhaps Irving was trying to suggest the presence of spiritual supervision when he brought Iachimo to judgement and redemption under the spreading branches of a symbolic 'fate tree' (see plate 32). The question of style and convention, however, may have occurred to Irving as a separate problem: historical illusion had failed him in two earlier comedies, so his style had to be modified. But his actor's need to develop comprehensible relationships between natural characters was incongruous with his director's need to use an impressionistic visual style. This is exactly the incongruity of Shakespeare's play. Instead of abusing the poor Bard for letting some of his puppets come to life, as modern critics have sometimes done, or for wasting an exquisite and 'real' heroine in a ridiculous play, as Victorians were wont to do, Irving simply accepted the incongruity.

He would not have played for irony, of course, but he left Shakespeare's irony to speak for itself, albeit in muted tones. His cut-down acting text inevitably weakened the sense of absurdity which is created by the too frequent repetition of conventional themes. And working in a theatrical convention which uses every device to create illusion, actors of the calibre of Terry and Irving will inevitably compel belief most of the time. But the essential honesty of the production, with its faithful response to the apparently contradictory demands of the play, kept the sense of irony alive in the audience, which waited only for some extra touch of absurdity to nudge it into laughter.

9

The Merchant of Venice

1 November 1879

'I think we must plainly recognize,' says Ralph Berry, 'that ambivalence is central to our experience of *The Merchant of Venice*. I do not
seek to explain away this ambivalence, to find a solution that smoothes
away the difficulties.'[1] Commentators ignore this ambivalence at their
peril. Procrustean efforts to rack the play until it fits a logical scheme of
Shakespearean comedy have usually either begun with a similar dis-
claimer or come to grief. Tempted by Shakespeare's lifelike characterization, Victorian critics tried and failed to make naturalistic sense of
the romantic plot, while moderns who take too seriously Granville-
Barker's assurance that the play is a 'fairy tale' containing no more
reality than Jack and the Beanstalk,[2] become divorced from the
common experience of audience and reader, and forget that *The
Merchant* is a successful and popular *play*.

Contemporary criticism

For the character-critic, everything in the play takes its colour from
our attitude to Shylock. Schlegel and his followers believed that 'his
morality is founded on the disbelief in goodness and magnanimity'.
His chief motive is avarice rather than revenge for the wrongs, real or
imaginary, suffered by himself or his people; he invokes the letter of
the law, which recoils with ironic justice on his own villainous head.
Accordingly, his enemies are accepted at their romantic face-value.
Portia and Antonio are the real centres of interest because they have
the right answers – love and friendship – which are the reverse of
Shylock's self-interest. Intrinsic worth is more valuable than commo-
dity.[3]

In Hazlitt's view, Shylock has been treated shabbily in the past, and

224

the appeal to his mercy is 'the rankest hypocrisy'. He is 'a good hater' who burns to avenge the woes of Israel. In his undoubted malevolence, many critics saw 'the remains of a great and noble nature, out of which all the genial sap has been pressed by accumulated injuries'.[4]

Irving's production provoked a controversy in which members of both schools took up extreme positions. The voices of those who remembered the play's ambivalence were drowned in the uproar, and when drama critics joined the battle, objective assessments of the performance grew scarce. But the production, and his modest contribution to the controversy, show that Irving leaned towards Hazlitt's side of the question.[5]

Modern criticism

Scholars who trace the development of Shakespeare's comic art or seek common themes in the comedies find *The Merchant of Venice* recalcitrant material. H. B. Charlton admits that it is 'hard to fit into a progressive series of Shakespeare's comedies' and argues that Shylock got out of hand and defeated the dramatist's purpose. In a scheme which John Russell Brown applies convincingly to the other comedies, *The Merchant* resists interpretation as 'a play about Shakespeare's ideal of love's wealth'. Character is too ambiguous, and our sympathies partly oppose the apparent theme. Northrop Frye finds Shylock the 'chief exception' to the rule that 'the greater the emphasis on reconciliation in comedy, the more the defeated forces of the comedy tend to become states of mind rather than individuals'.[6] In short, aside from those who impose a spurious unity by ignoring ordinary human responses to the characters,[7] the only commentators who are happy with the play are those who treat it as a unique work of art and accept its ambivalence.[8]

Other comedies mix naturalistic characterization and romantic plots: I have discussed Irving's difficulties on that score with *Much Ado*, *Twelfth Night* and *Cymbeline*. But Alexander Leggatt shows that while the stories of the bond and the caskets are as fantastic as anything in Shakespeare, and some of the characters are naturalistically drawn, *The Merchant of Venice* is the earliest play in which 'the different idioms are *superimposed* on each other throughout the play, and we are asked to respond to them simultaneously'.[9] This is the source of its ambivalence. While the stylized plots seem to suggest one kind of thematic statement, the characters are capable of supporting a subtext which may pull in an entirely different direction. We may legitimately speculate about them because they can bear more than one interpretation.

Theatrical context

If *The Merchant of Venice* is a romantic comedy, Shylock is plainly the villain, a subordinate figure. As such, he conveniently takes his place in several conventional thematic patterns. But stage history has shown that the Jew is the chief personage, the star part.[10] As soon as that was recognized by Charles Macklin (1741), the play emerged from obscurity and took its place in the popular Shakespearean repertory. It is no coincidence that Macklin was a comparatively naturalistic actor. His method revealed a subtext in which Shylock could be read as a malevolent but impressive figure, and Edmund Kean's similar technique (1814) added a sense of suffering from Christian persecution which had made him the villain that he was. Like his two great predecessors, Irving was more concerned with individual complexities of motive and character than with generalized types of humanity. He dug still deeper into the subtext and emerged as something very like a tragic hero. Against all arguments that he was wrong we must set the fact that in his hands *The Merchant of Venice* realized its potential as a play for the theatre. His personal popularity cannot account for this phenomenon: Irving was unable to make *Twelfth Night* or *Coriolanus* really popular.

Between Kean and Irving, nobody made *The Merchant* his own. Phelps was a good Shylock, and Faucit a celebrated Portia, but they never played together. America's greatest Shylock, Edwin Booth, was well received in London in 1861, but after Irving his villainous reading seemed old-fashioned and wrong.[11] When Irving's production opened, Kean's reputation was unchallenged: I am afraid we shall have to discount the claims of one M. C. Rice, whose performance in a two-act version which preceded the Drury Lane pantomime in 1876 was puffed as 'the greatest since the Elder Kean'. Ellen Terry was already the reigning Portia when she came to the Lyceum: her success in the Bancrofts' picturesque production in 1875 was marred only by an inadequate Shylock.[12]

Irving's production ran for 250 performances. He revived it in nearly every season, took it on every tour, played it perhaps a thousand times, and was still playing it the week he died, more than twenty-five years after the first night.

Text

Like anyone who studies *The Merchant of Venice* closely, Irving was aware of its ambivalence. His interpretation of Shylock was naturalistic; therefore the romantic improbabilities of the plot and the lyrical passages of verse gave him trouble. Since the play had to be shortened, these were the elements he tended to cut. His acting version was based on Charles Kean's published text (1858).[13] In I.ii, for example, Irving's cuts in Portia's descriptions of her suitors correspond exactly with Kean's, which in turn correspond with those in Bell's Shakespeare (1773). Three scenes were omitted because they were impracticably short or failed to advance the action significantly (II.iii, III.v, IV.ii) and a fourth, the Prince of Arragon's scene (II.ix), was deleted because it was of the stuff of folklore rather than of life. Similar considerations probably prompted Irving to combine and compress the Morocco scenes, and to apply the blue pencil more liberally to Bassanio's casket scene and Jessica's moonlit idyll with Lorenzo than to any other part of the play, apart from bawdy passages. Portia's dialogue, of course, was mercilessly cleaned up.

The text is neither heavily cut nor extensively rearranged. The popular myth that Irving usually played *The Merchant* without Act V is a calumny: for two months in 1880 a one-act trinket entitled *Iolanthe* was substituted, but the play was usually presented intact.

Performance

Irving described the origin of his interpretation of Shylock. In the summer of 1879 he was a guest on a yacht, cruising the Mediterranean:

I saw a Jew once, in Tunis, tear his hair and raiment, fling himself in the sand, and writhe in a rage, about a question of money, – beside himself with passion. I saw him again, self-possessed and fawning; and again, expressing real gratitude for a trifling money courtesy. He was never undignified until he tore at his hair and flung himself

35   Portia and her Page, III.ii (University of Victoria)

down, and then he was picturesque; he was old, but erect, even stately, and full of resource. As he walked beside his team of mules he carried himself with the lofty air of a king.[14]

Dignity, fawning, transports of rage: satisfied by observation that the same man could display all of these moods in real life, Irving did not hesitate to combine them on the stage, where some critics thought them inconsistent.[15] The play was interpreted from Shylock's point of view: he never saw himself as a villain, and audiences usually accepted his opinion.

The first scene was full of local colour. The 'Public Place in Venice' was a canal-side quay in deep perspective, with a ship moored at Right (see diagram above, p. 19).

As the Curtain Rises – 2 Boys, (Fruit vendors) discov'd, lying down, basking in the sun, – One up RC, – the other up LC – Two Gondoliers (talking) up C – and a Water carrier asleep, by his water jars – against wing L3E. The two Gondoliers come down to the Water carrier, wake him, get a drink, for which they give him a coin, and *Exeunt L3E* – The boy up LC – rises and joins the other – The Water carrier slings his jars on his shoulders, and xes up RC – the boys have a drink. He then goes on board the vessel R2E. Three Arab Coolies (with heavy bales) then come from Vessel R2E x and *Exeunt L4E*.[16]

It was all most economically done, with painted flats and only eight 'supers'. The boys, who were 'idle as only Italians and stage supernumeraries know how to be', turned up again as black Pages in Morocco's casket scene (see plate 35).[17]

Antonio entered with Salanio and Salarino, played by Pinero and Elwood as 'skipping, feather-brained fops'.[18] Irving acted with many Antonios, but the first was Forrester, who had played Iago and Claudius as smiling villains. Here he was melancholy, middle-aged and dull; it was hard to see why Shylock hated him so much. Bassanio was always entrusted to a popular young leading man like 'handsome Jack' Barnes, Terriss or Alexander (Terry's favourite in the part), but his 'business chat' with Antonio was heard impatiently; the audience wanted to see Irving.[19] Belmont (I.ii) was a painted drop in the first grooves (see plate 36). Ellen Terry played Portia with elegance and spirit; in a gold brocade gown, she lounged on a couch and laughed as she described her absurd suitors.[20]

The third scene took place on the same quay as the first. Shylock entered upstage, followed by Bassanio: he was 'a man between fifty

36 Belmont, I.ii: watercolour by Hawes Craven (Ludwig Berger Archiv, Akademie der Künste, Berlin)

and sixty years of age, infirm enough to need the support of a stick, with an iron-grey wisp of a beard'. Photographs show his sombre, fur-trimmed gaberdine and gown, relieved by a multi-coloured sash (see plate 39). He leans on a cane and wears a round cap with a yellow stripe that suggested the identifying 'badge' Venetian Jews were compelled to wear. Pictures cannot show his disdainful dignity: 'He towers head and shoulders above the coxcombs and poltroons who surround him.'[21]

'Three thousand ducats – well,' he began. To one alert listener at an early performance, he spoke 'with the reflective air of a man to whom money means very little'. This was not Irving's meaning, and he changed the reading: money was very important to Shylock as a shield against persecution. He knew Antonio for a Jew-hater, and hated him heartily in return. Galled by the man's arrogance, he recalled past offences with angry sarcasm:

> What should I say to you? Should I not say
> Hath a DOG *money?* Is it possible
> A CUR can lend *three thousand ducats?*
>
> (I.iii.115–18)[22]

Irving said, 'My view is, that from the moment Antonio turns on him, declaring he is "like to spit upon him again" . . . I imagine Shylock resolving to propose his pound of flesh, perhaps without any hope of getting it. Then he puts on that hypocritical show of pleasantry which so far deceives them as to elicit from Antonio the remark that "The Hebrew will turn Christian; he grows kind." [23] He puts on a pleasant business manner, jocular and teasing at 'Why look you how you storm'. As though carried away with good will, he touched Antonio on the breast when he agreed to lend the money:

> This kindness will I show,
> Go with me to a notary, seal me there
> Your single bond.
>
> (139–41)

Antonio shrank from his touch, and Shylock bowed low 'with a polished courtesy, tinged with subtle sarcasm'.[24] The Christian's instinctive reaction showed that the Jew had not exaggerated his prejudice.

We must make no mistake about Irving's Shylock. He was an accomplished bounder, eaten up with hate. But his first scene showed how a steady diet of racial contumely had made him that way, and his dignity suggested the noble nature that he might have had.

The two Gobbos used the ancient traditional business, a circumstance that suggests that Irving took little interest in them; neither did the audience. Launcelot knelt for his blessing with his back to his blind father, who felt his back hair and mistook it for a beard (I.ii.81, 89). Later, seeking employment with Bassanio, he repeatedly thrust Old Gobbo forward to plead his case, and back behind him when the pleas seemed inadequate (113–44).[25] Lorenzo's front-scene was received with equal apathy, but in the meantime the carpenters had built a full set representing Shylock's house beside a practicable bridge (see plate 37). Through the darkness that covered the set-change a 'Noise of Bolts etc.' was heard. Shylock gave Launcelot his instructions and warned Jessica against the revellers; then he set out to dine with his enemies. In later years he wore a heavily jewelled headscarf in order to 'flaunt his wealth in the Christian dogs' faces'. After Shylock's exit the supers appeared again:

A Gondola (With a Lady seated in it. A Noble reclining on the prow, playing a Zither, and a Gondolier) *Comes on from L3E xes and goes off, under bridge RUE.* At the same time 2 Ladies & a Noble arm-in-arm, follow'd by another Lady and Noble, all masked,

& laughing, *Enter LI E* x over & go up steps R look over at Gondola passing. *Then enter Gra etc.* They step on one side to allow the party to pass, bowing to them. The others, returning the Salute, & *Exeunt LUE.*

Gratiano, Salanio and Salarino conversed for thirteen lines, omitting the wisecracks about the 'strumpet wind'. Then 'A Gondola (with a lot of serenaders, bearing colour'd Lanthorns) *Comes on slowly from RUE.* Stops in front of Jes^cas window.' A Serenade was sung before Lorenzo entered, the gondola gliding off again as he approached. At the end of the scene Jessica eloped with him amid a whirl of masquers with tabors and pipes.[26]

The use of the masquers, the bridge and the practicable gondola was nothing new; Charles Kean had managed the scene in very similar fashion. But Irving ended it with a piece of business which was perfectly original. There was a 'Very Quick' act drop, which rose again immediately with the applause. 'When it went up again the stage was empty, desolate, with no light but the pale moon, and all sounds of life at a great distance – and then over the bridge came the wearied figure of the Jew.' The drop fell as he was about to enter the house. It was a most effective stroke. 'For absolute pathos, achieved by absolute simplicity of means,' writes Ellen Terry, 'I never saw anything in the theatre to compare with . . . Shylock's return home over the bridge to his deserted house after Jessica's flight.' The contrast between the elegant, gregarious Christians and their lonely victim won a good deal of sympathy for the latter, 'the father of a daughter,' said the *Spectator*, 'who amply justifies his plain distrust of her, an odious, immodest, dishonest creature, than whom Shakespeare drew no more unpleasant character, and to whom one always grudges the loveliest love-lines ever spoken, especially when it is borne in mind that the speaker, Lorenzo, was at best the receiver of stolen goods'.[27]

Portia's house in Act III was another full-stage set. The orchestra played a 'Moorish Flourish' to take up the curtain. Portia was attended by three ladies, behind whom stood three Nobles, and a little black Page. The grouping was formal, perhaps as a reflection of the ritual quality of the casket ceremony. The Prince of Morocco entered with three Moors (see plate 38). While he praised himself a 'tremolo' was played; as he debated which casket to choose, Terry registered her feelings in by-play which most critics found enchanting. By adding a

37 Shylock's house by a bridge, by Hawes Craven (Crown Copyright, Victoria and
    Albert Museum)

subtext to a formal scene she helped to reconcile it with the naturalistic
style of the rest of the production.[28]

Shylock's fury at Jessica's flight (III.i) taxed Irving's skill to the
utmost. In the scene with the fops, and with Tubal, he used the wild
passions he had observed in his Tunisian Jew. He left no doubt that it
was the abduction of his daughter and not the loss of the ducats which
excited him, but he most certainly did *not* undercut the text by
contradicting his wish to see her dead at his feet with an interpolated
'No, no, no' as Kean had done.[29] Robbed of the only person he loved,
his Jewish sense of family outraged by his worst enemies, Shylock
decided to enforce his bond if ever the opportunity should arise. His
determination mounted with his anger as he repeated 'let him look to
his bond' and through the great speech which ended, 'This villainy *you*

233

teach me I will execute, and it shall go hard but I will BETTER THE INSTRUCTION.' Exhausted with rage, the old man solemnly, slowly beat his breast when he told Tubal, 'the curse never fell upon our nation till now, I never *felt* it till now'.[30] There was pathos in 'no sighs but o' my breathing, no tears but o' my shedding' (87–8) but it was eclipsed by Irving's reaction to the news that Jessica had given his ring for a monkey: 'it was my turquoise, I had it of Leah when I was a bachelor: I would not have given it for a wilderness of monkeys' (110–13). The *Spectator* thought this 'as beautiful a touch as ever has been laid on the many-stringed lyre of human feeling', and a host of other critics agreed. Booth had played it for laughs.[31]

Shylock was ferocious and pathetic by turns, but with the news that Antonio's ship was lost his desire for vengeance transcended personal

38   Morocco takes his leave, II.vii: sketch by E. Webling (Ellen Terry Memorial Museum, Smallhythe)

234

motives. An American paper compared Irving's business with Booth's:

Booth . . . flings his arms over his head, he comes staggering down in mighty strides to the footlights, and, sobbing in a delirium of revengeful joy, he flings himself into Tubal's arms, crying all the while, 'I thank God, I thank God – Is it true? is it true?' When Irving in the part of Shylock hears the same news he is standing beside his friend. There is an inarticulate moan as if speech had failed him; then the slow, awful words, 'I thank God,' thrilling in their terrible intensity: then a horrible suspicion and a hungry, gasping inquiry, 'Is it true? Is it true?' All is the work of a second.

Booth had mentioned God as a mere figure of speech, but Irving spoke as a devout man giving thanks to a real divinity. The first 'I thank God' was furious; he paused, and spoke the second 'with uplifted hands in lofty accents of religious doom'. From this point onwards, Shylock seemed to believe that he had been given the task of redressing the sufferings of his people. He was still a spiteful old man, but he was also 'a Jew already conscious of the Spinozas, the Sidonias, the Disraelis, who were to issue from his loins', the chosen scourge of the Lord God of Israel.[32]

Ellen Terry's manuscript notes on Bassanio and Portia differ in several important respects from the published text of her lecture, edited by 'Christopher St John'. In the lecture she cannot understand why the man who wins Portia should be considered 'a poor specimen of manhood'; she commends his loyalty to Antonio, and his charm. But the notes tell another story: 'Shakespeare suggested that Bassanio is a bit of a loafer, a well-dressed handsome youth of good birth who lives on his charm.'[33] Irving probably agreed. When the Venetian suitors arrived in Belmont their dandified costumes attracted particular comment, and the atmosphere of fashion and music stood in strong contrast to the sombre, prosaic world of Shylock and Tubal.[34]

In her opening speech Terry displeased *Blackwood's Magazine* by holding Bassanio 'caressingly by the hand, almost in an embrace' when she urged him to tarry awhile before choosing; when he had chosen correctly and could 'claim her with a loving kiss' (III.ii.138) he merely kissed her hand. The suggestion of indelicacy wounded the actress and made her self-conscious in the scene for years. She defends herself by pointing out that the woman who can tell Bassanio,

> One half of me is yours, the other half yours,
> Mine own I would say: but if mine then yours,
> And so all yours (III.ii.16–18)

surely 'was not concealing her fondness like a Victorian maiden'. Again Terry acted the subtext of Portia's silence. While Bassanio was choosing, her 'eager surging love . . . ever and anon would vent itself in ejaculations more eloquent than words'; she was tempted to break her vow; her anxiety 'was seen in her face, in her eyes, and in her twitching fingers'. When he touched the leaden casket 'her smile came back; she did not fly to him, she let him open the casket, find the picture, read the legend, and sat there looking at him, smiling and quoting the legend ahead of his reading'.[35]

Shylock's scene with Antonio and the Gaoler, and the 'merry interview' in which Portia and Nerissa planned their stratagem of disguise (III.iii, iv), aroused little interest. During the interval a box set was erected for the trial scene. Irving achieved a rich effect by the simplest means: portraits of Doges, a Verrio ceiling, gilt carvings and crimson tapestries were all the work of Hawes Craven's paintbrush.[36] The crowd of spectators upstage included peasants, old men and monks, and among but not of them stood Tubal and a group of Jews. The reactions of the spectators underlined the conflicts of the trial. Eight Magnificoes in black preceded the scarlet-robed Doge to the high rostrum at Left.[37]

Ellen Terry says Irving played the trial scene quietly, and as an 'heroic saint'. If misconceptions are to be avoided, these points need explanation. Shylock entered without truculence or bravado, and all critics praised his quiet bearing during the proceedings (see plate 39). His fury had resolved itself into a terrible, cold vengefulness. He stated his case with the dignity of a man who believes that vengeance is his sacred duty; violence would have implied that he was conscious of wrongdoing, and that his motive was personal revenge. This man was religious – every time God was named 'his wicked head bows with unaffected reverence' – a strict Jew who spoke from conviction when he said, 'I stand here for law.'[38] It was futile to appeal to him for mercy, a Christian notion alien to the Law by which he lived. To offer him twice the sum owing was a pitiful attempt at bribery: he tapped the bags of gold three times with his dagger before rejecting them, as though to demonstrate how little money meant to him when compared with his just revenge. But fanatical rectitude is not an amiable quality, and Shylock was a hateful fanatic. Practically every observer commented upon his cruelty, his 'infernal malignancy', his rattlesnake

39 Shylock at the Trial, V.i:
    sketch by E. Webling
    (Ellen Terry Memorial Museum,
    Smallhythe)

fascination. 'Malignity almost inhuman marks every utterance, his eyes softening a little when they turn toward the court, and blaze [*sic*] in the intensity of their hatred when they alight upon Antonio.'[39]

When Portia entered he eyed her suspiciously. Terry gave the 'mercy speech' all her charm:

> The quality of mercy is not *strain'd*,
> It *droppeth* as the gentle rain from heaven
> Upon the place beneath.

Her elocution was universally admired, but a few critics sensed a studied insincerity in its perfection.[40] Terry called the speech 'a noble kinsman to the Lord's Prayer', but her manuscript shows that she did not admire Portia for using it to bait a trap. When she declared that the law would uphold his claim, Shylock appeared at his most loathsome: he fawned and wheedled, crouched, grinned and sneered. He pretended to search the bond for a clause that required him to provide a surgeon: 'I cannot find it: 'tis not in the bond,' he said with hypocritical helplessness. But his 'hellish cruelty' suddenly surfaced when he advanced with 'greedy ferocity', his eyes fixed on his victim, at the words 'A sentence: come, prepare' (IV.i.300).[41]

Then Portia struck: 'This bond doth give thee here no jot of blood.' The news smote Shylock like a thunderbolt. He turned pale, dropped his scales and asked, 'Is – *that* – the – *law?*'[42] But then, in defeat, he began to win back the sympathy of the audience. He was on the run, and the pack was in full cry. He tried to take his principal, and when he was prevented he lost his temper for the first time in the scene and tore the bond to shreds, crying, 'Why then the devil give him good of it' (341).[43] Utterly beaten down by the confiscation of his goods, he heard the decree that he accept the faith of his enemies like a man in a dream. Shylock's exit was Irving's supreme moment. From his anguished expression and dejected gait the audience sensed that he would soon die. 'What a pitiful cur is Gratiano to yelp at his heels!' said a typical critic. The dignity with which he shrugged off the touch of the 'exulting booby', and his look of bottomless contempt, seemed to condemn the whole court and its proceedings. It was a tragic exit, and many of the audience actually wept.[44]

After Shylock crept the Jews in the crowd: '*A Pause. Then a general movement. The Jews up in the R. corner leave the court crestfallen. – the others shrink from them as they pass, then follow in a body. *3 Yells are heard outside the court.*' Evidently a mob was following him, and perhaps a *pogrom* had begun.[45]

Portia left the court with a comic masculine swagger which must have seemed to partake of the spirit of Gratiano. Irving condemned her conduct in the trial: 'The Duke and Portia preach to Shylock of mercy, but when the day goes against him they do not practise what they preach – nay, even insist upon him changing his faith.'[46] The audience thought the technicality she had invoked to save Antonio a 'miserable quibble', and 'bloodthirsty as it may sound,' said one spectator, 'I confess that I was distinctly disappointed when, by means of a miserable legal quibble, Shylock was cheated of his pound of Antonio's flesh'.[47] Terry wrote, 'However one looks at it one cannot admire it. It has an unattractive element of moral deceit – of the dangerous doctrine that the means is justified by the end.'[48] Irving, Terry and the audience all saw Shylock as an oppressed man, but few critics were disturbed to find his oppressors led by a charming Portia. In the trial, said a representative review, 'the memory of his cruelty, meanness, and smallness of heart, all vanish in sympathy with the strong man in his utter discomfiture'. Two sentences later comes a panegyric on Portia, 'the girl of noble, generous and courageous impulses, yet full of gay, tender mischief'. Only a few noticed any incongruity: 'Before a persecuted Hebrew prophet for hero, a dull, ill-mannered Christian for villain, and an incomparable Portia flinging in her lot with the might-is-right party, Shakespeare retired discomfited.'[49]

The last act did nothing to resolve this apparent problem. The moonlit garden was exquisitely beautiful, and the lovers' chaff was played in a light key. There are several potential ironies, but they were muted. Lorenzo and Jessica talked of faithless Cressida and tragic Thisbe, but unhappy Dido and the terrible Medea were left out.[50] Bassanio and Gratiano cannot have been much troubled by their ladies' teasing, for all the threats and mock-confessions of cuckoldry were laundered away. The groupings ensured that there was no sense that Antonio was left out or dejected at the end. One critic suggested lamely that this act accentuated our feelings about Shylock by showing the rejoicings of his foes,[51] but if these pleasant young people were supposed to be taken for triumphant villains, Irving failed to put his point across and persisted in failure for twenty-five years.

Unless we are willing to propose that Irving and Terry were dunces who did not know whether a play held together or not, we must assume that *The Merchant of Venice* had some sort of unity. Even in later years, when Irving played a nastier Shylock, he was accepted as a tragic figure; and while that forbids us to conclude that he meant the piece to be taken for a romantic comedy, the treatment of Portia and the last act did not fit a Tragedy of Shylock: tragedy does not benefit from an ironic post-mortem in which charming villains or Erinyes dance upon the hero's grave.

Commenting on an article by Frederick Hawkins, Irving wrote: 'He points out that the enemies of Shylock are scarcely permitted to gain even our respect, but this is not enough. In *The Merchant of Venice* the Jew appears to less disadvantage that the Christian. *Both are animated by the spirit of intolerance*, the latter especially.'[52] If we look at the production in that light, a number of hints emerge and form a pattern. The opulence and gaiety of the Belmont scenes and the masque in which Jessica was abducted contrasted boldly with Shylock's sombre and solitary drabness. The Jew was vicious but wronged. Terry thought Bassanio a loafer, and Portia immoral in the trial. The 'mercy speech' was beautiful, but insincere and part of a trap. The lady of Belmont was callous enough to let Morocco see her satisfaction when he chose the wrong casket, and although she was a dutiful daughter herself, she welcomed the runaway Jessica because *her* father was a Jew.[53] Yet she was charming and kind to everyone else: she simply did not consider the feelings of Moors or Jews.

The worlds of Christians and Jews were separated by hatred and suspicion, like the houses of Capulet and Montague. There were no villains, and it was not the tragedy of Shylock alone; he was not the only one who failed to know himself or his world. Portia and her friends were pleasant young people who behaved as though they were living in a comedy, but they ignorantly defended their way of life by denying Shylock his humanity. Thus in a sense they denied that part of their own humanity which was akin to his.

Was Irving right? That depends upon what we mean by right. Shakespeare probably did not intend to write a tragedy of intolerance, and an Elizabethan audience would hardly have accepted it if he had. But we were speaking of what *The Merchant of Venice* is, not what it was meant to be; and the experience of a Victorian audience, or a modern one, for that matter, is as valid as that of those inspired 'stinkards' at the Theatre. Irving and his audience found one of the true interpretations.

Not long after this play was written, John Donne said, 'No man is an *Iland*, intire of it selfe; every man is a peece of the *Continent*, a part of the *maine* . . . any mans *death* diminishes *me*, because I am involved in *Mankinde*; And therefore never send to know for whom the *bell* tolls; it tolls for *thee*' (*Devotions*, XVII). This is what the young folk in *The Merchant of Venice* fail to understand about their world; as they rejoice in the last, apparently comic act, the bell of Shakespeare's irony tolls for them. It is their tragedy, too, but they do not know it. The 'beautiful people' cannot see the emptiness of a beauty which can only live by destroying those who are not beautiful, and by driving the outsider farther out.

IO

Conclusion

It is easy to think of Henry Irving as the apotheosis of the Victorian actor-manager. There is a sense in which he was just that, of course – to the extent that he was the greatest of those who 'stage-managed for one actor's sake'.[1] In this respect he merely perfected the techniques of his predecessors. His unique acting style owed something to Phelps; he exercised more control over a better company than anyone before him had been able to do; and with this excellent instrument he brought the historical illusion and dramatic unity pursued by Macready and Charles Kean to its most tasteful and balanced expression. One of his friends quotes Irving as saying, 'whatever is best in my work at the Lyceum – not only in playing but also in production – you and I both know, d—d well, that is *all* Phelps'.[2] After Irving, the theatre of illusion could go no further. His imitator, Tree, and his disciple, Martin-Harvey, ruled the metropolitan, provincial and colonial stages by the power of his dead hand, and impeded theatrical evolution for a generation.

But Irving could be imitated in the theatre no more satisfactorily than in the drawing room, where caricature of his alleged mannerisms long remained a favourite social accomplishment. Remember the Russian gallant in the ballad:

> He could imitate Irving, play euchre or pool
> And perform on the Spanish guitar;
> In fact quite the cream of the Muscovite team
> Was Ivan Skivinski Skivar.

Tree and Martin-Harvey could duplicate the form but not the substance. While they belonged to the past, Irving, who grew out of the past, belonged equally to the future. His tribute to Phelps, if indeed his friend was not a d—d liar, was 'a fantastic, generous exaggeration'.[3]

The essential Irving was unlike any predecessor; as an actor, his real successors were Konstantin Stanislavsky and even Vsevolod Meyerhold, and as a stage-manager his true disciple was Gordon Craig.

Poetics

Irving's uniqueness is the key to his romantic conception of the Shakespearean drama. His personal distinction pervaded the protagonists he played, conferring upon them an air of intrinsic significance that was independent of their rank or influence. Paradoxically, the uncommon man in exceptional circumstances can easily become tragic in a universal sense because he confronts the ultimate forces which have always governed our world, while the common man makes an inadequate hero because he merely fails to cope with conditions peculiar to his place and time, and with which the spectator may successfully grapple every day.

Bradley said that the action of Shakespearean tragedy consists primarily of 'characteristic deeds'. Irving said exactly the same thing: drama is 'human nature in . . . characteristic action'.[4] But while both thought conflict was the result of evil deeds and hence of evil in human character, they differed concerning its ultimate source. For Bradley, evil originates within the moral order which 'poisons itself' by producing Iago as well as Desdemona, and even the best tragic heroes have moral defects which contribute to their fall. Irving's view was almost Manichaean: evil is an intruder in a moral order that is both just and distinguished by perfect harmony between appearance and reality, particularly in terms of love. The agents of evil freely choose their allegiance. Macbeth, Claudius, Richard, Iago and Edmund could be villain-heroes or antagonists according to emphasis, but they were independent sources of the chaos that invaded the world, hiding lovelessness and isolation behind a mask of fair-seeming. Hamlet, Lear, Romeo and Othello were innocent protagonists; the cause of their fall was not a moral flaw, but the disintegration of the order to which they were committed. This was marked by the betrayal and failure of love. In *Romeo and Juliet*, it was the city of Verona which had chosen evil; Coriolanus carried his own antagonist within him in the loveless aridity of his character; but in both cases the essential pattern was the same.

There was tremendous pathos in the suffering of the innocent heroes, but the catastrophe restored them to a love which was crystallized imperishably in death. Even Othello crawled to Desdemona's side to die, surely not without hope of a reunion in Heaven where all misunderstandings would be forgiven, and Lady Macbeth found salvation through repentance and her selfless love for an unworthy husband. The hand of divine Providence was usually discernible, guiding the conflict towards an inevitable resolution in which evil would be expelled and order restored. Only in his conflict with this infinite force could the agent of evil, the villain-hero, truly express his personality; and in his inevitable defeat he attained his full significance as an individual. Whether he or the innocent hero restored to love was the centre of interest, the realization of human potential in catastrophe called for exultation.

Irving's romanticism excluded him from the world of Romance. In the theatre of illusion, tragic and comic states of being could not differ significantly because both were supposed to be 'true' imitations of essential nature. The point of view might shift but there was no way, for example, in which evil could be quite shut out. Thus, the possibility that any action might have tragic consequences was never absolutely ruled out. Given the right circumstances, the characters were potentially tragic in proportion to the realism with which they were conceived and the personal distinction they possessed. Thus, *Much Ado* and *Twelfth Night* were comic by accident, not because they were different in kind from tragedy. Experience taught Irving that he must break with illusion before he could fully realize Shakespeare's comic world: *Cymbeline* was a tentative step in that direction.

In comedy, evil was not very profound and suffering was never prolonged. If Malvolio's anguish reached almost tragic proportions, it was because he was too naturalistically and nobly conceived, but his pain was his own fault. Like Claudio, he lacked the wholesome capacity to see through impostures which were transparent to the wise eyes of Beatrice or Imogen. Don John was an evil fair-seemer, but he puzzled only fools, while his henchman Borachio was a sketch for Iachimo, repentant when he recognized that he had wronged real innocence. Cloten's wickedness was rendered impotent by his own folly, while Iachimo's motive was cynicism born of thwarted idealism rather than of a commitment to evil. Irving learned to safeguard comedy by letting the fantastic bones of its mechanism show instead of clothing them in illusion. The absurdly contrived plots of Shakespeare's comedies relieve any anxiety we might be inclined to feel for his more lifelike characters. We are shown that there is no real danger; rescue has been prepared, and is held back only that it may be released at the most dramatic and delightful moment.

Irving's early failure to distinguish between tragic and comic worlds served him well when it gave him the key to *The Merchant of Venice*. He wisely avoided any attempt to make this play conform to the pattern in which he habitually interpreted Shakespearean tragedy, but recognizing that Shylock is a genuinely tragic character, he gave him the fulfilment of a tragic death, offstage.[5] The conventions of illusion did the rest by suppressing the comic improbability of the plot and giving the romantic lovers a naturalistic subtext which made them subject to moral judgement. In a truly comic world Shylock would become a wraith, but his enemies took on flesh and blood when they entered the realm of tragedy.

Illusion and the deadly audience

One of man's most successful characteristics is his capacity for learning from experience. The theatre today is in danger of losing much of its experience because it has lost its memory. We are as foolish to forget the work of great actors of the past as we should be to copy them slavishly. No doubt a Victorian low comedian perpetrated what Peter Brook calls 'deadly theatre' when he observed hallowed tradition by removing a dozen waistcoats while he talked to Hamlet in the graveyard;[6] a modern actor who thinks he has invented the business would give it more life. But the real danger is that he may never discover what kind of business is available to him. History and criticism can lay before us a rich fund of the choices offered by a Shakespearean text.

As an actor and commentator, a practical critic like Irving can teach us what some of these choices are. His interpretations of a dozen major parts, the readings of Ellen Terry and some of their colleagues will not always command imitation, but they must often suggest directions in which unimagined solutions can be sought. His interpretations of certain plays – *Hamlet, Much Ado, Macbeth, Cymbeline, The Merchant of Venice* – are original and coherent enough to be added to the catalogue of defensible readings, and even his simple conception of love as the chief talisman of order in Shakespearean tragedy must impress us as a novel emphasis. Something can be learned from Irving's failures as well as his successes, if we exercise a little discretion: an interpretation which failed to impress a Victorian audience might seem full of meaning today. And finally, we may be assured that whatever else his commentaries may be, right or wrong, profound or foolish, they were designed to be serviceable in the theatre.

The theatre of illusion had severe limitations which frequently restrained Irving's choices when he produced plays written for Elizabethan conventions. But we should remember that all theatrical styles are conventional: we voluntarily accept restrictions as a necessary condition of theatrical art. While the Victorian theatre was often rigid where the Elizabethans were free, it is important to recognize that the converse is also true. Irving's convention presented unique opportunities. Historical costume was not always a liability; it could make a statement clearly and economically. Shylock's return to his empty house could not have been achieved effectively without a drop-curtain. If the need to locate each scene in time and place muted the poetry of Duncan's arrival at Inverness or led to absurd wrangles over Osric's hat, it also allowed Irving to project a vivid impression of Verona's heat and 'the mad blood stirring', to stress Polonius's betrayal of his family, or to provide subtle visual metaphors for Lear's mental decay and his growing emotional nakedness.[7]

We are accustomed to this kind of visual reinforcement on the modern stage: in fact, we get far too much of it. The contempory unit set, for example, permits us to realize the fluid movement of Shakespeare; but unlike the visually neutral space of the Elizabethan stage, it is frequently designed as a dominant metaphor. There it stands, authoritative, explicit, unequivocally selecting one theme and suppressing the rest. The convention of illusion ruled out excesses of this kind. Since a symbol like Irving's 'fate tree' had to pass muster as a real tree in a believable setting, its effect could only be subconscious and ambiguous. Not one critic I have read recognized it as a symbol in any of the plays in which it was used, but many felt its powerful effect.

Interpretation was primarily left in the hands of the actor, who was subject to the same convention. Everything he did had to agree with the illusion of psychological truth, so he could use none of the devices by which modern directors often make an explicit statement of theme, explaining the whole concept in a little essay in the programme. Irving had to concentrate upon character, which is where the focus ought to be. Character is the central metaphor of a Shakespearean play, the richest image by which the dramatist expresses his meaning in all its ambiguous complexity. Interpretation remains honest commentary only so long as we remember this. The splendid tools which the modern theatre and contemporary criticism have fashioned for us are excellent servants but tyrannical masters – set and costume design, sophisticated lighting, creative directing techniques, discoveries about history, imagery, theme and structure – all must ultimately be subordinate to the actor's encounter with his character.

There is no such thing as progress in the theatre: there is only change. Irving was never so narrow as when he patronized the Elizabethan theatre for its simplicity, and assumed that Shakespeare was better served in the theatre of illusion; but we shall be equally mistaken if we imagine that we are so much closer to the spirit of Shakespeare that the nineteenth century can teach us nothing. If most of our theatres have broken down the barrier of the proscenium arch, we still sit benighted while action proceeds in a pool of light. A modern audience seldom contributes significantly to the creative process: nobody addresses us, seeks our applause, shuns our disapproval, forces us to become involved or self-aware. How many of us have ever been part of an audience which was simply compelled to leap to its feet and cheer for twenty minutes, as sometimes happened at the Lyceum? If we allow ourselves to become a deadly audience, we shall get the Shakespeare we deserve: safe, and fatally dull.

Appendix 1: Texts

There is a story that James Quin, hearing of Garrick's plan to restore Shakespeare's *Macbeth* to the stage, exclaimed in amazement, 'Have I not all this time been acting Shakespeare's play?' He had been acting Davenant's version, of course; and Cibber's *Richard III*, Tate's *King Lear*, and the anonymously doctored texts that adorn the pages of Bell's *Shakespeare*. Similar stories have been told of many stars of the eighteenth and nineteenth centuries, but never of Irving. He combined a scholarly temperament with a passion for originality. He knew the precise authority for every word he played; and instead of accepting established acting versions like most of his predecessors and contemporaries, he made his own. He too abridged and rearranged: he cut nearly half of *Cymbeline* and *King Lear*, and combined and transposed scenes in all of his Shakespeare productions. But his textual knowledge ensured that the surgery was performed sympathetically and wisely, and the play usually survived the operation. Nevertheless, we must never make the mistake of assuming that he or any actor played Shakespeare intact and in sequence. These tables show the structure of some of his acting versions, and the extent of the cuts. I have included details of a few draft texts to show how they evolved. Irving's texts are numbered chronologically in each table; the preliminary list indentifies them. Identification includes the numbers assigned to each by Charles H. Shattuck in *The Shakespeare Promptbooks* (Urbana, Illinois, and London, 1965), where detailed bibliographical information is supplied. Each text is compared with a modern standard edition: the New Arden wherever it is available, and the Signet where it is not. I have also compared Irving's *Cymbeline* with the arrangements of earlier actors, to give some impression of the extent of his originality.

Hamlet	1	1874 draft and study-book, Shattuck 91, Harvard Theatre Collection. Based on Clark and Wright edition, 1873
	2	1877 souvenir prompt-book, Shattuck 90, Harvard Theatre Collection. A late stage of the 1874 acting text.
	3	1878 prompt-book, Shattuck 93, Shakespeare Centre. Based on Irving's printed text.
	4	MS alterations in 3.
Macbeth	1	1875 draft and study-book, Shattuck 81, Furness Collection, University of Pennsylvania. Based on Clark and Wright edition, 1874.
	2	1875 late draft, Shattuck 91, Smallhythe. Based on Clark and Wright.

	3	1888 proof of Irving's printed text with MS alterations, Shattuck 92, Harvard Theatre Collection.
	4	1889 edition of Irving's printed text, Shattuck 93, Harvard Theatre Collection. Probably the closest text to the version used on opening night.
King Lear	1	draft and study-book, Shattuck 95, Folger Shakespeare Library. Based on a nineteenth-century Works.
	2	Irving's printed text with MS revisions, Shattuck 95a (supplement). Probably the closest text to the actual acting version.
Much Ado	1	1882 edition of Irving's printed text, Shattuck 45, Folger Shakespeare Library.
	2	1883 [?] MS alterations in 1, probably for touring.
Twelfth Night		1884, Irving's printed text.
Cymbeline	1	John Philip Kemble's prompt-book, ed. Shattuck (Charlottesville, Virginia, 1974).
	2	Samuel Phelps's Sadler's Wells prompt-book, Shattuck 18, British Theatre Museum.
	3	1896, Irving's printed text.
Merchant of Venice		1879, Irving's prompt-book, Shattuck 56a (supplement), collated with souvenir prompt-book based on 1887 edition of his printed text, Ludwig-Berger-Archiv, Akademie der Künste, Berlin.

HAMLET

Signet	1	2	3	4	
I.i	I.i	I.i	I.i	I.i	
I.ii	I.ii	I.ii	I.ii	I.ii	
I.iii	I.iii	I.iii	I.iii	I.iii	
I.iv	I.iv	I.iv	I.iv	I.iv	
I.v	I.v	I.v	I.v	I.v	
II.i	II.i	—	II.i	—	
II.ii	II.ii	II.i	II.ii	II.i	
III.i } III.ii	III.i	III.i	III.i	III.i	
III.iii	III.ii	III.ii	III.ii	III.ii	
III.iv	III.iii	III.iii	III.iii	III.iii	
IV.ii	—	—ᵃ	—ᵃ	—ᵃ	
IV.i } IV.iii	IV.i	—	—	—	
IV.iv	—	—	—	—	
IV.vi	—	—	—	—	
IV.v } IV.vii	IV.ii	IV.i	IV.i	IV.i	
V.i	V.i	V.i	V.i	V.i	
V.ii { V.ii / V.iii	V.ii / V.iii	V.ii / V.iii	V.ii / V.iii	V.ii / V.iii	

		1	2	3	4	
Cut		1,216	1,297½	1,400	1,643½	lines
Cut since previous text			383	78	243½	,,
Restored since previous text			101½	175½	0	,,
Length	3,861	2,645	2,362½	2,461	2,217½	,,

ᵃ 13 lines transposed to III.ii, see above pp. 32 and 63.

MACBETH

New Arden	1	2	3	4
I.i	I.i	I.i	I.i	I.i
I.ii	—	—	I.ii	I.ii
I.iii	I.ii	I.ii	I.iii	I.iii
I.iv	I.iii	I.iii	I.iv	I.iv
I.v	I.iv	I.iv	I.v	I.v
I.vi	I.v	I.v	I.vi	I.vi
I.vii	I.vi	I.vi	I.vii	I.vii
II.i ⎫				
II.ii ⎬	II.i	II.i	II.i	II.i
II.iii ⎭				
II.iv	—	—	—	—
III.i ⎫			III.i	III.i
III.ii ⎬	III.i	III.i	III.ii	III.ii
III.iii	III.ii	III.ii	—	—
III.iv	III.iii	III.iii	III.iii	III.iii
III.v	—	—	—	—
III.vi	—	—	—	—
IV.i	IV.i	IV.i	IV.i	IV.i
—	—	—	—	IV.ii[b]
IV.ii	—	—	—	—
IV.iii	IV.ii	IV.ii	V.i	V.i
V.i	IV.iii	IV.iii	V.ii	V.ii
V.ii	V.i	V.i	VI.i	—
V.iii	V.ii	V.ii	VI.ii	VI.i
V.iv	V.iii	V.iii	VI.iii	VI.ii
V.v	V.iv	V.iv	VI.iv	VI.iii
V.vi	V.v	V.v	VI.v	VI.iv
V.vii ⎫				
V.viii ⎬	V.vi	V.vi	VI.vi	VI.v
V.ix	—	—	—	—

Cut		476	510½	557½	574	lines
Length	2,092	1,616	1,581½	1,534½	1,518	,,

[b] Interpolated Witch scene, see above pp. 91 and 110–11.

KING LEAR

1	New Arden	2
I.i	I.i	I.i
I.ii	I.ii	I.ii
I.iii	{ I.iii / I.iv }	I.iii
—	I.v[c]	—
II.i	{ II.i / II.ii }	II.i
II.ii	II.iii	II.ii
II.iii	II.iv	II.iii
III.i	III.iii	—
III.ii	{ III.i / III.ii / III.iv }	III.i / III.ii
III.iii	III.vi	III.iii
IV.i	{ III.v / III.vii }	— / —
IV.ii	IV.i	IV.ii
IV.iii	IV.ii	IV.i
IV.iv	{ IV.iii / IV.iv / IV.vi }	IV.iv / — / IV.iii
—	IV.v	—
IV.v	IV.vii	IV.v
V.i	V.i	V.i
—	V.ii	—
V.ii	V.iii	V.ii

Cut	1,126½		1,507	lines
Length	2,148½	3,275	1,768	,,

[c] Lines 14–48 transposed to II.iv.

252

MUCH ADO

Signet	1	2
I.i	I.i	I.i
I.iii	II.i	I.ii
I.ii II.i }	II.ii	I.iii
II.ii	III.i	II.i
II.iii	III.ii	II.ii
III.i III.iia }	III.iii	III.i
III.iib	III.iv	III.ii
III.iii	III.v	III.iii
III.iv	—	—
III.v	—	—
IV.i	IV.i	IV.i
IV.ii	V.i	—
V.i V.ii }	V.ii	V.i
V.iii	V.iii	V.ii
V.iv	V.iv	V.iii

	Signet	1	2	
Cut		569	792½	lines
Length	2,718	2,149	1,925½	,,

TWELFTH NIGHT

New Arden	Irving
I.ii	I.i
I.iii	I.ii
I.iv ⎫ I.i ⎭	I.iii
I.v	II.i
II.ii	II.ii
II.iii	II.iii
II.iv	III.i
II.i	III.ii
II.v ⎫ III.i ⎭	III.iii
III.iii	IV.i
III.ii	IV.ii
III.iva	IV.iii
III.ivb ⎫ IV.i ⎭	IV.iv
IV.ii	IV.v
IV.iii	V.i
V.i	V.ii

Cut		537	lines
Length	2,550	2,013	,,

CYMBELINE

New Arden	1	2	3
I.i ⎫		I.i ⎫	I.i
I.ii ⎬	I.i	I.ii ⎬	
I.iv ⎪		I.iii	—
I.vi ⎭		I.iv	I.i cont'd
I.iii	—	—	—
I.v	I.ii	I.v	I.ii
I.vii	II.i	II.i	II.i
II.i	II.ii	II.ii	II.ii
II.ii	II.iii	II.iii	II.iii
II.iii	{ II.iv / II.v	II.iv	III.i
II.iv	III.i	III.i	III.ii
III.i	III.ii	III.ii	—
III.ii	III.iii	III.iii	III.iii
III.iii	III.iv	III.iv	IV.i
III.iv	III.iv	III.iv	IV.ii
III.v	{ III.v / IV.i	III.v / IV.i }	IV.iii
III.vi	IV.ii	IV.ii	IV.iv
III.vii ⎫			
III.viii ⎭	—	—	—
IV.i	IV.iii	IV.iii	IV.v
IV.ii	{ IV.iv / IV.vi	IV.iv / IV.v }	IV.vi
IV.iii	IV.v	IV.vi	—
IV.iv	V.i	V.i }	V.i
V.i	V.ii	V.ii }	
V.ii	V.iii	V.iii	V.ii
V.iii	{ V.iv / V.v }	V.iv	V.iii
V.iv	—	—	—
V.v	V.vi	V.v	V.iv

Cut			1568½	lines
Length	3,297		1,728½	,,

MERCHANT OF VENICE

New Arden	Irving
I.i	I.i
I.ii	I.ii
I.iii	I.iii
II.ii	II.i
II.iii	—
II.iv	II.ii
II.v } II.vi }	II.iii
II.i } II.vii }	III.i
II.ix	—
II.viii } III.i }	III.ii
III.ii	III.iii
III.iii	III.iv
III.iv	III.v
III.v	—
IV.i	IV.i
IV.ii	—
V.i	V.i

Cut		587	lines
Length	2,578	1,991	,,

Appendix 2: Playbills

The Lyceum persisted longer than most London theatres in publishing only surnames in advertising and programmes. Wherever possible, I have supplied the missing names in the fullest form obtainable, but stage names using initials (e.g. the playwright R. C. Carton, whose real name was Richard Claude Critchett) are unchanged. Where identifications are less than absolutely certain the names are enclosed in brackets. Actors I have been unable to trace are of course identified only by the surname that appears in the programme; actresses are shown as Miss or Mrs.

I have included bills of all first productions of plays discussed in this book. Bills of subsequent productions, or revivals, of the same piece are given only when the play was mounted for an indefinite run; thus, for example, I have excluded the almost annual revivals, for a pre-arranged seven or twelve performances, of *The Merchant of Venice*.

HAMLET

31 October 1874

HAMLET   Henry Irving
CLAUDIUS   Thomas Swinbourne
POLONIUS   William Henry Chippendale
LAERTES   Edmund Leathes
HORATIO   George Neville
OSRIC   H. B. Conway
ROSENCRANTZ   Webber
GUILDENSTERN   Allen Beaumont
MARCELLUS   Frank Clements
BARNARDO   Alfred B. Tapping
FRANCISCO   James Harwood

FIRST PLAYER   James Beveridge
SECOND PLAYER   Norman
PRIEST   [John] Collett
FIRST GRAVEDIGGER   Henry Compton
SECOND GRAVEDIGGER   Chapman
MESSENGER   Branscombe
GHOST   Thomas Mead
GERTRUDE   Georgina Pauncefort
PLAYER QUEEN   Miss Hampden
OPHELIA   Isabel Bateman

MACBETH

25 September 1875

DUNCAN   Frank Huntley
MALCOLM   [E. H.] Brooke
DONALBAIN   Miss Clair
MACBETH   Henry Irving
BANQUO   Henry Forrester
MACDUFF   Thomas Swinbourne
LENNOX   A. Stuart
ROSS   George Neville
MENTEITH   Mordaunt
CAITHNESS   Seymour
FLEANCE   Willa Brown
SIWARD   Henry
YOUNG SIWARD   Sargent
SEYTON   Norman

DOCTOR   Allen Beaumont
PORTER   [John] Collett
ATTENDANT   Branscombe
MURDERERS { Butler / Alfred B. Tapping
APPARITIONS { James Harwood / [Willa] Brown / Kate Brown
LADY MACBETH   Kate Bateman
GENTLEWOMAN   Miss Marlborough
HECATE   Georgina Pauncefort
WITCHES { Thomas Mead / John Archer / Mrs [Frank] Huntley

OTHELLO

14 February 1876

OTHELLO   Henry Irving
DUKE   [John] Collett
BRABANTIO   Thomas Mead
RODERIGO   R. C. Carton
GRATIANO   [Frank] Huntley
LODOVICO   John Archer
CASSIO   [E. H.] Brooke
IAGO   Henry Forrester

MONTANO   Allen Beaumont
ANTONIO*   Sargent
JULIO*   Alfred B. Tapping
MARCO*   James Harwood
PAULO   Butler
DESDEMONA   Isabel Bateman
EMILIA   Kate Batemon

* John Philip Kemble named eight attendant gentlemen, of whom these three survived in Irving's text. There were more, unnamed, attendants, but these three appeared in the programme because they had a line or two to speak.

RICHARD III

29 January 1877

KING EDWARD IV   Allen Beaumont
EDWARD, PRINCE OF WALES   Willa Brown
RICHARD, DUKE OF YORK   Florence Harwood
GEORGE, DUKE OF CLARENCE   Walter Bentley
RICHARD, DUKE OF GLOUCESTER   Henry Irving
HENRY, EARL OF RICHMOND   [E. H.] Brooke
CARDINAL BOURCHIER   [John] Collett
DUKE OF BUCKINGHAM   Thomas Swinbourne
DUKE OF NORFOLK   James Harwood
LORD RIVERS   R. C. Carton
LORD HASTINGS   Robert Charles Lyons
LORD STANLEY   Arthur Wing Pinero
LORD LOVEL   Sargent
MARQUIS OF DORSET   Seymour

LORD GREY   Arthur Dillon
SIR RICHARD RATCLIFF   H[enry] Louther
SIR WILLIAM CATESBY   John Archer
SIR JAMES TYRREL   A. Stuart
SIR JAMES BLUNT   Branscombe
SIR ROBERT BRACKENBURY   H. Smyles
DR SHAW   Alfred B. Tapping
LORD MAYOR   James H. Allen
FIRST MURDERER   Thomas Mead
SECOND MURDERER   [Frank] Huntley
QUEEN MARGARET   Kate Bateman
QUEEN ELIZABETH   Georgina Pauncefort
DUCHESS OF YORK   Mrs [Frank] Huntley
LADY ANNE   Isabel Bateman

HAMLET

30 December 1878

HAMLET   Henry Irving
CLAUDIUS   Henry Forrester
POLONIUS   William Henry Chippendale
LAERTES   Frank Cooper
HORATIO   Thomas Swinbourne
OSRIC   Kyrle Bellew
ROSENCRANTZ   Arthur Elwood
GUILDENSTERN   Arthur Wing Pinero
MARCELLUS   Gibson
BARNARDO   Alfred B. Tapping
FRANCISCO   [Frederic] Robinson

REYNALDO   Charles Cartwright
FIRST PLAYER   Allen Beaumont
SECOND PLAYER   Everard
PRIEST   [John] Collett
FIRST GRAVEDIGGER   Samuel Johnson
SECOND GRAVEDIGGER   Albert Garcia
Andrews
MESSENGER   James Harwood
GHOST   Thomas Mead
GERTRUDE   Georgina Pauncefort
PLAYER QUEEN   Miss Sedley
OPHELIA   Ellen Terry

259

APPENDIX 2

THE MERCHANT OF VENICE
1 November 1879

SHYLOCK   Henry Irving
DUKE OF VENICE   Allen Beaumont
PRINCE OF MOROCCO   Frank Tyars
ANTONIO   Henry Forrester
BASSANIO   John H. Barnes
SALANIO   Arthur Elwood
SALARINO   Arthur Wing Pinero
GRATIANO   Frank Cooper
LORENZO   Norman Forbes
TUBAL   John Carter

LAUNCELOT GOBBO   Samuel Johnson
OLD GOBBO   [Thomas Clifford] Cooper
GAOLER   Charles Hudson
LEONARDO   Branscombe
BALTHAZAR   Alfred B. Tapping
STEPHANO   [Richard] Ganthony
CLERK OF THE COURT   [Walter] Calvert
NERISSA   Florence Terry
JESSICA   Alma Murray
PORTIA   Ellen Terry

OTHELLO
2 May 1881

OTHELLO   Edwin Booth/Henry Irving
DUKE   Allen Beaumont
BRABANTIO   Thomas Mead
RODERIGO   Arthur Wing Pinero
GRATIANO   John Carter
LODOVICO   Charles Hudson
CASSIO   William Terriss

IAGO   Henry Irving/Edwin Booth
MONTANO   Frank Tyars
ANTONIO*   [Edwin] Clifford
JULIO*   H[enry] Louther
MARCO*   James Harwood
DESDEMONA   Ellen Terry
EMILIA   Georgina Pauncefort

* John Philip Kemble named eight attendant gentlemen, of whom these three survived in Irving's text. There were more, unnamed, attendants, but these three appeared in the programme because they had a line or two to speak.

260

ROMEO AND JULIET

8 March 1882

ROMEO   Henry Irving
MERCUTIO   William Terriss
TYBALT   Charles Glenney
PARIS   George Alexander
CAPULET   Henry Howe
MONTAGUE   Charles Harbury
FRIAR LAURENCE   James Fernandez
PRINCE ESCALUS   Frank Tyars
BENVOLIO   John Child
GREGORY   John Carter
SAMPSON   John Archer
ABRAHAM   H[enry] Louther

BALTHASAR   Charles Hudson
PETER   Albert Garcia Andrews
FRIAR JOHN   G[eorge F.] Black
CITIZEN   James Harwood
APOTHECARY   Thomas Mead
CHORUS   Howard Russell
PAGE   Kate Brown
NURSE   Fanny Stirling
LADY MONTAGUE   Louisa Payne
LADY CAPULET   Georgina Pauncefort
JULIET   Ellen Terry

MUCH ADO ABOUT NOTHING

11 October 1882

BENEDICK   Henry Irving
DON PEDRO   William Terriss
DON JOHN   Charles Glenney
CLAUDIO   Johnston Forbes-Robertson
LEONATO   James Fernandez
ANTONIO   Henry Howe
BALTHAZAR   J. G. Robertson
BORACHIO   Frank Tyars
CONRADE   Charles Hudson
FRIAR FRANCIS   Thomas Mead
DOGBERRY   Samuel Johnson

VERGES   Stanislaus Calhaem
SEACOAL   John Archer
OATCAKE   Charles Harbury
SEXTON   John Carter
MESSENGER   William Haviland
BOY   Kate Brown
HERO   Jessie Millward
MARGARET   Lucia Harwood
URSULA   Louisa Payne
BEATRICE   Ellen Terry

TWELFTH NIGHT

8 July 1884

MALVOLIO   Henry Irving
ORSINO   William Terriss
SIR TOBY BELCH   David Fisher
SIR ANDREW AGUECHEEK   Francis Wyatt
FABIAN   Albert Garcia Andrews
CLOWN   Stanislaus Calhaem
SEBASTIAN   Fred Terry
ANTONIO   Henry Howe
SEA CAPTAIN   Frank Tyars

VALENTINE   William Haviland
CURIO   Fuller Mellish
FRIAR   Charles Harbury
FIRST OFFICER   John Archer
SECOND OFFICER   James Harwood
OLIVIA   Rose Leclercq
MARIA   Louisa Payne
VIOLA   Ellen Terry

MACBETH

29 December 1888

DUNCAN	William Haviland	SERGEANT	[Arthur] Raynor
MALCOLM	Ben Webster	PORTER	Samuel Johnson
DONALBAIN	John Martin Harvey	MESSENGER	[Walter] Coveney
MACBETH	Henry Irving	ATTENDANT	Roe
BANQUO	Thomas Edmund Wenman	MURDERERS	{ G[eorge F.] Black / John Carter }
MACDUFF	George Alexander		
LENNOX	Leonard Outram		{ Baird
ROSS	Frank Tyars	APPARITIONS	{ [Dorothy] Harwood
MENTEITH	John Archer		{ Mrs [M.] Holland }
ANGUS	S[idney] Lacy	LADY MACBETH	Ellen Terry
CAITHNESS	Leverton	GENTLEWOMAN	Amy Coleridge
FLEANCE	John Harwood	HECATE	Frances Ivor
SIWARD	Henry Howe	SERVANT	Miss M. Foster
SEYTON	[Charles] Fenton		{ Alice Marriott
OFFICERS	{ Hemstock / Cass }	WITCHES	{ [Juliet] Desborough
DOCTOR	A. Stuart		{ [Julia] Seaman }

MUCH ADO ABOUT NOTHING

5 January 1891

BENEDICK	Henry Irving	VERGES	Davis
DON PEDRO	Francis Henry Macklin	SEACOAL	John Archer
DON JOHN	William Haviland	OATCAKE	[Walter or T.] Reynolds
CLAUDIO	William Terriss	SEXTON	S[idney] Lacy
LEONATO	Thomas Edmund Wenman	MESSENGER	Edward Gordon Craig
ANTONIO	Henry Howe	BOY	John Harwood
BALTHAZAR	J. G. Robertson	HERO	Annie Irish
BORACHIO	Frank Tyars	MARGARET	Kate Phillips
CONRADE	John Martin Harvey	URSULA	Amy Coleridge
FRIAR FRANCIS	Alfred Bishop	BEATRICE	Ellen Terry
DOGBERRY	William Mackintosh		

KING LEAR

10 November 1892

LEAR   Henry Irving
EDGAR   William Terriss
EDMUND   Frank Cooper
EARL OF GLOSTER   Alfred Bishop
EARL OF KENT   William J. Holloway
DUKE OF CORNWALL   Clarence Hague
DUKE OF ALBANY   Frank Tyars
KING OF FRANCE   Percival
DUKE OF BURGUNDY   Acton Bond
CURAN   John Martin Harvey
OLD MAN   Henry Howe

FOOL   William Haviland
OSWALD   Edward Gordon Craig
PHYSICIAN   S[idney] Lacy
KNIGHT   R. P. Tabb
GENTLEMAN   Ian Robertson
OFFICER   W. J. Loriss
HERALD   Lionel Belmore
MESSENGER   Powell
GONERIL   Ada Dyas
REGAN   Maud Milton
CORDELIA   Ellen Terry

CYMBELINE

22 September 1896

CYMBELINE   Francis Henry Macklin
CLOTEN   Norman Forbes
POSTHUMUS LEONATUS   Frank Cooper
BELARIUS   Frederic Robinson
GUIDERIUS   Ben Webster
ARVIRAGUS   Edward Gordon Craig
PISANIO   Frank Tyars
CORNELIUS   S[idney] Lacy
BRITISH CAPTAINS { John Archer / Needham

BRITISH LORDS { Clarence Hague / Lionel Belmore
QUEEN   Genevieve Ward
HELEN   Mrs [Frank] Tyars
IMOGEN   Ellen Terry
IACHIMO   Henry Irving
PHILARIO   Fuller Mellish
CAIUS LUCIUS   H. Cooper Cliffe
ROMAN CAPTAIN   R. P. Tabb

263

RICHARD III

19 December 1896

KING EDWARD IV Edward Gordon Craig
EDWARD, PRINCE OF WALES Lena Ashwell
RICHARD, DUKE OF YORK Miss Norman
GEORGE, DUKE OF CLARENCE H. Cooper Cliffe
RICHARD, DUKE OF GLOUCESTER Henry Irving
HENRY, EARL OF RICHMOND Frank Cooper
CARDINAL BOURCHIER Cushing
DUKE OF BUCKINGHAM Francis Henry Macklin
DUKE OF NORFOLK S[idney] Lacy
LORD RIVERS Fuller Mellish
LORD HASTINGS Ben Webster
LORD STANLEY Frederic Robinson
LORD LOVEL John Archer
MARQUIS OF DORSET Howard

BISHOP OF ELY [Walter or T.] Reynolds
SIR RICHARD RATCLIFF Lionel Belmore
SIR WILLIAM CATESBY Frank Tyars
SIR JAMES TYRREL Clarence Hague
SIR ROBERT BRACKENBURY John Martin Harvey
LORD MAYOR R. P. Tabb
OFFICER Rivington
FIRST MURDERER Norman Forbes
SECOND MURDERER William Farren, Jun.
KING'S PAGE Edith Craig
QUEEN MARGARET Genevieve Ward
QUEEN ELIZABETH Maud Milton
DUCHESS OF YORK Mary Rorke
LADY ANNE Julia Arthur

CORIOLANUS

15 April 1901

CAIUS MARCIUS CORIOLANUS Henry Irving
TITUS LARTIUS William Lugg
COMINIUS Frank Tyars
MENENIUS AGRIPPA John H. Barnes
SICINIUS VELUTUS James Hearn
JUNIUS BRUTUS Laurence Irving
YOUNG MARCIUS Queenie Tarvin
SENATOR R. P. Tabb
HERALD Percy Nash
AEDILE Mark Paton
SOLDIER [Albert] Fisher
FIRST CITIZEN C. Dodsworth
SECOND CITIZEN Clifford Bown

THIRD CITIZEN C. H. Kenney
FOURTH CITIZEN [Walter or T.] Reynolds
VOLUMNIA Ellen Terry
VIRGILIA Mabel Hackney
VALERIA Maud Milton
GENTLEWOMAN Edith Thompson
TULLUS AUFIDIUS W. E. Ashcroft
LIEUTENANT TO AUFIDIUS Marsden
VOLSCIAN LORD Buller
SENTINEL Lionel Belmore
FIRST SERVINGMAN John Archer
SECOND SERVINGMAN W. L. Ablett
CITIZEN OF ANTIUM Lambert

Further reading

Numerous biographies and histories of Irving and his theatre were published in his lifetime and shortly after his death. By far the most useful and systematic of these is Austin Brereton, *The Life of Henry Irving*, 2 vols. (1908). Bram Stoker, *Personal Reminiscences of Henry Irving*, 2 vols. (1906), is anecdotal and overweighted with snobbery, but contains valuable fugitive information. The best collection of reviews is Clement Scott, *From 'The Bells' to 'King Arthur'* (1897). E. R. Russell's reviews are more precise and intelligent, but were never collected: amongst the most accessible are his treatment of Irving's *Hamlet* in *Arrested Fugitives* (1912); 'Mr. Irving's Interpretations of Shakespeare', *Fortnightly Review* xxxiv (October 1883), 466–81; 'Mr. Irving's Work', *Fortnightly Review* xxxvi (September 1884), 401–10; '*Romeo and Juliet* at the Lyceum', *Macmillan's Magazine* xlvi (1882), 325–36. Irving's best account of himself is to be found in *The Drama: Addresses* (1893). Ellen Terry, *The Story of My Life* (1908), is a great autobiography, and contains much that is useful about Irving, the Lyceum, and her own incomparable contribution to both.

The only serious modern biography is Laurence Irving, *Henry Irving: The Actor and His World* (1951), an adulatory but sound and sensitive piece of work. Edward Gordon Craig, *Henry Irving* (1930), is eccentric, but contains a brilliant evocation of Irving's acting style and an unparalleled description of his performance in *The Bells*. *We Saw Him Act* (1939), a collection of reminiscences edited by H. A. Saintsbury and Cecil Palmer, is comprehensive but uneven in quality. The best modern biography of Ellen Terry is Roger Manvell, *Ellen Terry* (1968).

Notes

Place of publication is London unless otherwise stated.

Introduction

1 The population of Greater London was 1,114,644 in the census of 1801, and 6,581,402 in 1901, an increase of 590 per cent; between 1871 and 1881 it grew from 3,885,641 to 4,766,661, or 22.67 per cent, the fastest rate in the century: based upon a definition of Greater London and figures in Karl Gustav Grytzell, *County of London: Population Changes 1801–1901* (Lund, 1969), p. 123.

2 T. C. Barker and Michael Robbins, *A History of London Transport* (1963), I, 250.

3 William Ashworth, *An Economic History of England, 1870–1939* (1960), p. 240.

4 The Bancrofts raised the price of Stalls to 10s in 1874, and abolished the Haymarket Pit in 1880. Irving raised Stalls from 6s to 10s in 1877, Dress Circle from 5s to 6s in 1878, and Upper Circle from 3s to 4s in 1880.

5 Michael R. Booth, 'Shakespeare as Spectacle and History: The Victorian Period', *Theatre Research International*, I, 2 (1976), 103.

6 At the Lyceum: 200 in 1874–5, 108 in 1878–9, of which 88 were consecutive.

7 *Daily News*, 11/3/82.

8 Michael R. Booth, 'The Metropolis on Stage' in H. J. Dyos and Michael Wolff (eds.), *The Victorian City: Images and Realities* (1973), I, 224.

9 For example, in August 1878 he read in aid of Hartwell Church, Northampton; laid the cornerstone of the Harborne and Edgbaston Institute, Birmingham; and read for the Samaritan Hospital in Belfast. On 16/9/93 he unveiled the Marlowe Memorial in Canterbury.

10 *Saturday Review*, 12/10/78; *The Theatre*, I, 2nd ser. (Nov. 1878), 255–9; New York *Herald*, 7/4/85.

11 Henry Irving, 'Acting: An Art', *Fortnightly Review*, LVII, N.S. (March 1895), 368.

12 *Touchstone: or The New Era*, 4/5/78.

13 *The Times*, 2/5/84.

14 Chicago, *The Morning News*, 27/12/87.

1 An actor's commentary

1   Bram Stoker, *Personal Reminiscences of Henry Irving* (1906), I, 27.

2   Ellen Terry, 'Shakespeare's Heroines: Some Reflections', *Windsor Magazine*, XXXIII (1911), 62.

3   L. C. Knights, 'How Many Children Had Lady Macbeth' in *Explorations* (1946), p. 16; G. G. Gervinus, *Shakespeare Commentaries*, trans. F. E. Bunnett (1875), p. 21.

4   Henry Irving, *The Drama: Addresses* (1893), p. 20.

5   S. T. Coleridge, *Lectures and Notes on Shakespeare and Other English Poets*, ed. T. Ashe (1893), pp. 98–9.

6   See Maurice Morgann, *Essay on the Dramatic Character of Sir John Falstaff* (1777); Mary Cowden Clarke, *The Girlhood of Shakespeare's Heroines* (1850–2) is often mentioned as an extreme example by people who have never read it, but it is pure fiction, and was never meant to be anything else.

7   Irving's productions of *Much Ado*, *Twelfth Night* and *Cymbeline* showed his growing awareness of this problem.

8   Herbert R. Coursen, 'In Deepest Consequence: *Macbeth*', *Shakespeare Quarterly*, XVIII (Autumn 1967), 382.

9   Irving, *Addresses*, pp. 21, 15, 25, 71, 151, 72; Irving, 'The Theatre in Its Relation to the State', *Fortnightly Review*, LXIV, N.S. (July 1898), 90.

10 Irving, *Addresses*, pp. 27, 151–2, 162; 'Relation to the State', pp. 90–1.

11 Irving, *Addresses*, pp. 162–3, 69; *The Art of Acting: A Discussion by Constant Coquelin, Henry Irving and Dion Boucicault* (New York, 1926), p. 50; 'Acting: An Art', *Fortnightly Review*, LVII, N.S. (March 1895), 375; 'Relation to the State', p. 90.

12 Irving, *Addresses*, pp. 24, 57, 159.

13 Coquelin *et al.*, *The Art of Acting*, pp. 13, 65.

14 Sir John Pollock, *Curtain Up* (n.d.), p. 206.

15 Louis Calvert, *Problems of the Actor* (n.d. [1919]), pp. 81–2; see below, p. 178; Ellen Terry, *The Story of My Life* (1908), p. 338.

16 Bram Stoker Collection, Shakespeare Centre, Stratford-upon-Avon: dated 25/9/98.

17 *Academy*, 4/8/77; E. R. Russell, 'Irving as Hamlet' in *Arrested Fugitives* (1912), p. 58; William Archer, Robert Lowe and George Halkett, *The Fashionable Tragedian* (Edinburgh and Glasgow, 1877), p. 7; Archer, *Henry Irving, Actor and Manager: A Critical Study*, 2nd edn (n.d. [1883]), p. 63.

18 See Dene Barnett, 'The Performance Practice of Acting: The Eighteenth Century', *Theatre Research International*, II, 3 (May 1977), 157–86; III, 1 (Oct. 1977), 1–19; III, 2 (Feb. 1978), 79–93.

19 Henry James, *The Scenic Art* (1949), pp. 122, 104.

20 H. A. Saintsbury and Cecil Palmer (eds.), *We Saw Him Act* (1939), p. 413. Speeches from *Richard III* and *Henry VIII* may be heard on Richard Bebb (ed.), *Great Actors of the Past* (1977), an Argo record.

21 Archer, *Henry Irving*, p. 69; Archer *et al.*, *Fashionable Tragedian*, p. 9; H. A. Clapp, 'Henry Irving', *Atlantic Monthly*, LIII (March 1884), 415, says he

pronounced 'face' as 'fããāce' and 'no' as 'nâo' or 'nawo'; Ellen Terry, *Story*, p. 155, says he pronounced 'God' as 'Gud', but this is not true in the recording.

22 Edwin Drew, *Henry Irving on and off the Stage* (n.d. [1889]), p. 5.

23 Irving, *Addresses*, pp. 58–9; Edward Gordon Craig, *Henry Irving* (1930), pp. 62–9; Drew, *Henry Irving*, pp. 32–53.

24 Craig, *Henry Irving*, pp. 32, 79–80, 74, 77, 62–7; *The Mask*, IV (1911–12), 80.

25 *Talma on the Actor's Art (Mémoires de Lekain, précédés de réflexion sur cet acteur et sur l'art théâtral)* (1883); Irving comments briefly in 'Does Punch Feel?', *The Era Almanack* (1881), 97–8; Stoker, *Personal Reminiscences*, II, 1; Terry, *Story*, p. 338; L. J. Claris, 'Henry Irving, Actor and Artist', *The Theatre*, V, 3rd ser. (March 1882), 158; J. Comyns Carr, 'English Actors: Yesterday and Today', *Fortnightly Review*, XXXIII, N.S. (Feb. 1883), 226–7.

26 Clapp, 'Henry Irving', p. 417.

27 Accounts of Irving's rehearsals are to be found in the following: Craig, *Henry Irving*, pp. 111–15; Terry, *Story*, pp. 152–3, 169–70, 172; *The Autobiography of Sir John Martin-Harvey* (n.d. [1933]), pp. 42, 74, 100; G. B. Burgin, 'The Lyceum Rehearsals', *The Idler*, III (1893), 123–41; Edwin Booth, *The Theatre*, II, 4th ser. (Oct. 1883), 223; *Madame*, 20/4/01; W. H. Pollock, *Century Magazine*, XXVI (1883), 953–4.

28 Alan Hughes, 'The Lyceum Staff: A Victorian Theatrical Organization', *Theatre Notebook*, XXVII (1974), 11–17; figures in this article are here corrected and augmented from several sources, particularly Irving's Christmas gratuity lists of 1886 and 1891 in the Enthoven Collection.

29 *The Sketch*, 16/1/95; *The West-End*, 12/4/99. For really big productions, Loveday says, 700 were engaged.

30 Electric footlights were installed in 1891. Up to 25 limelights could be used at once. At least four shades of blue were available, and a similar range of other colours. See Percy Fitzgerald, *The World behind the Scenes* (1881), and 'On Scenic Illusion and Stage Appliances', *Journal of the Society of Arts*, XXXV (18/3/87), 456–66, and 'The True Principles of Stage Scenery', *Journal of the Society of Arts*, XLIX (3/5/01), 445–53; Bram Stoker, 'Henry Irving and Stage Lighting', *The Nineteenth Century: And After*, LXIX (May 1911), 903–12. Much of my information comes from prompt-books, and from documents in the Enthoven and Stoker Collections.

31 See Fitzgerald, *World behind the Scenes*, pp. 43–6, and *Henry Irving: A Record of Twenty Years at the Lyceum* (1893), pp. 159–61 for detail of the Temple scene. There is an illustration in the *Illustrated London News*, 5/1/81.

32 The first documented use of this system was in *Romeo and Juliet* (1882). Intervals could be as short as four minutes.

33 M. H. Spielmann, 'A Shakespearean Revival: *Macbeth*', *The Magazine of Art* (1889), 98; Seymour Lucas, 'Art in the Theatre: The Art of Dressing an Historical Play', *The Magazine of Art* (1894), 276–81. Figures are from the Lyceum account books: see Alan Hughes, 'Henry Irving's Finances: The Lyceum Accounts, 1878–99', *Nineteenth Century Theatre Research*, I (Autumn 1973), 79–87.

34 Nevertheless, 'carpenter's scenes' were used extensively in the last act of *Macbeth* in 1888.

35 Musical directors were Hamilton Clarke, 1878–81, then Meredith Ball to 1899. Some of these pieces were published, e.g. Clarke's overtures to six plays, including *Hamlet* and *The Merchant of Venice*. Edward German's *Henry VIII* dances are still played.

36 Percy Fitzgerald, *Henry Irving: A Biography* (1906), pp. 114, 209; Craig, *Henry Irving*, p. 56. See *Saturday Review*, 4/3/93; *Athenaeum*, 21/10/05; *The Times*, 31/10/88, 6/1/92.

37 See below, p. 76.

38 The first figure is an educated guess; the latter comes from an auction catalogue dated 1903, in the Westminster Public Library. In 1884 the capacity was 1,455, and in 1899, 1,600.

39 Respectively, 1,500, 1,000, 1,280, and 3,500.

40 A border masked proscenium height to about 28 feet. The stage was $41\frac{1}{2}$ feet deep, extra depth being supplied by using a scene dock. The grid was 47 feet high until 1885, when it was raised to 68 feet. There were 60 sets of hemp lines and three of wire in 1904.

41 Galleries were 10 feet deep until 1881, when they were deepened to more than 17 feet by taking in corridors behind. There were 130 Stalls in 1875–8 and 351 in 1902.

42 Terry, *Story*, p. 184; *Building News*, 11/9/85.

43 1874–1901: one-act plays and pieces produced for special performances are omitted.

44 Michael R. Booth, 'The Metropolis on Stage' in H. J. Dyos and Michael Wolff (eds.), *The Victorian City: Images and Realities* (1973) I, 224.

45 *Charles I, Eugene Aram, Olivia, Vanderdecken*, and *Faust*.

46 Archer joined in 1875: he appeared in *Becket* on the night of Irving's death. Johnson, 1875–99; Mead 1874–89, when he died. There were others, like John Carter and a whole family of Harwoods.

47 *Two Can Play At That Game*, 18/5/79; *Daisy's Escape*, 20/9/79; *Bygones*, 18/9/80.

48 King Philip in Tennyson's *Queen Mary*, 1876; Synorix in *The Cup*, 1881; Mephistopheles in *Faust*, 1885.

49 A letter from Mrs Bateman to Irving dates the agreement 31/8/78; it asks for the agreed sum of £1,000: Enthoven Collection. *Builder*, 28/9/78.

50 Stoker, *Personal Reminiscences*, II, 65–71; time sequence corrected, C. E. Pascoe (ed.), *Dramatic Notes: 1879*, p. 15.

51 *The Theatre*, III, 2nd ser. (Oct. 1879), 176 and (Nov. 1879), 242; *The Theatre*, III, 3rd ser. (Feb. 1881), 248; Daniel J. Watermeir, *Between Actor and Critic: Selected Letters of Edwin Booth and William Winter* (Princeton, N.J., 1971), pp. 132–45, 156–79; [Theodore Martin], 'The Meiningen Company and the London Stage', *Blackwood's Magazine*, CXXX (Aug. 1881), 252; Terry, *Story*, p. 203.

52 Neilson was twenty-two when she played Juliet first, in 1868; she died in 1880. Her last Romeo, William Terriss (Haymarket, 1880) played Mercutio at the Lyceum. Forbes-Robertson and Modjeska played *Romeo and Juliet* at the Court in March, 1881, just before Irving's announcement.

53 Terry, *Story*, p. 224.

54 The profit was more than £15,700.

55 *The Theatre*, III, 4th ser. (April 1884), 217.

56 Terry, *Story*, p. 302.

57 *Ibid.*; W. H. Pollock, *Impressions of Henry Irving* (1908), pp. 91–3; Tree played Falstaff on 13/8/88; Dowden commended *Antony and Cleopatra* in a letter to Stoker, now in the Folger Shakespeare Library, 18/11/81: 'the two parts are so *predominant* in the play, and each so glorious'. Victorian morality would not have cared for it.

58 New York *World*, 5/12/93.

2 Hamlet

1 Bandmann, Princess's, 10/10/73; Creswick, Drury Lane, 15/12/74; *Saturday Review*, 19/12/74.

2 25/10/84. See Russell Jackson, 'Designer and Director: E. W. Godwin and Wilson Barrett's Hamlet of 1884', *Shakespeare Jahrbuch* (1974), 186–200.

3 Laurence Irving, *Henry Irving: The Actor and His World* (1951), pp. 114–15.

4 Edward Hubler (ed.), *Hamlet*, Signet Shakespeare (New York, 1963), II.ii.616–17. All references and figures are based on this edition.

5 *Examiner*, 11/10/35, quoted in Alan S. Downer, *The Eminent Tragedian: William Charles Macready* (Cambridge, Mass., and London, 1966), p. 279.

6 1 Irving's study-book, Harvard Theatre Collection: Shattuck No. 91.
   2 Souvenir prompt-book prepared by J. H. Allen in 1877, Harvard Theatre Collection: Shattuck No. 90.
   3 Prompt-book, 1878, Shakespeare Centre, Stratford-upon-Avon: Shattuck No. 93.
   4 Further pencilled cuts in 3, above.
   A table of cuts and scene arrangements in all versions is given in Appendix 1.

7 J. Dover Wilson, *The Manuscript of Shakespeare's 'Hamlet'* (Cambridge, 1963).

8 Based on Goethe's description. It would be instructive to survey the critics from Goethe to Wilson Knight who call Hamlet 'lovable', 'adorable' or even, according to Gervinus, 'womanly' (*Shakespeare Commentaries*, trans. F. E. Bunnett (1875), p. 565). Irving ascribed to Hamlet 'all the most lovable weaknesses of humanity' in 'Four Favourite Parts', *English Illustrated Magazine*, X (Sept. 1893), 926.

9 Walter Raleigh (ed.), *Johnson on Shakespeare* (1925), p. 195.

10 Traditional. The problem here is: why does Claudius sit through the pantomime enactment of his crime, only to rise and call for light in the play? Granville-Barker and Dover Wilson attempt solutions in *Prefaces to Shakespeare* (1958), I, 86–92 and *What Happens in 'Hamlet'*, 3rd edn (1951), pp. 146–53.

11 W. G. Clark and W. A. Wright (eds.), *Hamlet*, 2nd edn (Oxford, 1873).

12 In 1878 'incestuous' was substituted for 'enseamèd'.

13 The rest of the dialogue stayed out. Ophelia replied, 'You are merry, my lord.'

14 Goethe, *Wilhelm Meister's Apprenticeship* in *Works*, ed. N. H. Dole (n.d. [1839]), I, 268–9.

15 *Ibid.*, pp. 302–4.

16 S. T. Coleridge, *Lectures and Notes on Shakespeare and Other English Poets*, ed.
    T. Ashe (1893), pp. 164, 344, 531; A. W. Schlegel, *Lectures on Dramatic Art and
    Literature*, trans. John Black (1879), p. 405.

17 William Hazlitt, *Characters of Shakespeare's Plays* in *Works*, ed. P. P. Howe
    (1930), IV, 235, 237, 234; Gervinus, *Commentaries*, pp. 561–2.

18 Clark and Wright (eds.), *Hamlet*, p. xvi.

19 H. N. Hudson, *Shakespeare: His Life, Art and Characters* (Boston, Mass.,
    1872), II, 252.

20 Stanislavsky recommended something very like this to establish some of the
    'given circumstances' of a part.

21 E. R. Russell, *Arrested Fugitives* (1912), p. 66.

22 Dutton Cook, *Nights at the Play* (1883), p. 375.

23 J. Ranken Towse, 'Henry Irving', *Century Magazine*, XXVII (March 1884), 666;
    Chicago *Tribune*, 12/4/84.

24 Ellen Terry, *The Story of My Life* (1908), p. 170; Frederic Daly, *Henry Irving in
    England and America* (1884), pp. 193–4. Details in this section are drawn from
    115 descriptions and reviews, the prompt-books, and other sources. Since they
    are too numerous to mention in a footnote each time they are used, specific
    reference is usually made only to those directly quoted.

25 Horatio did not know that Barnardo had already mentioned him to Francisco,
    presumably.

26 *Leaves from the Autobiography of Tomaso Salvini* (1893), p. 165.

27 It was plausible, too, inasmuch as Hamlet has just said, " 'Tis now the very
    witching time of night' (III.ii.396).

28 *The Theatre*, II, 2nd ser. (Feb. 1879), 47. R. C. Lyons, Horatio in 1877, was only
    twenty-four. Swinbourne was recruited at the last moment to replace Henry
    Teesdale, aged thirty-seven, who proved unequal to the part. Henry Forrester
    was fifty-two when he succeeded Swinbourne.

29 Russell, *Fugitives*, p. 65.

30 *Ibid*.

31 W. H. Clemen, *Shakespeare's Dramatic Art* (1972), p. 175, calls it 'an expression
    of court ceremonial . . . a demonstration of regal responsibility and position'.

32 Swinbourne, *The Times*, 12/11/74; Forrester, *The Theatre*, II, 2nd ser. (Feb.
    1879), 47; Frank Tyars, *Saturday Review*, 2/7/81.

33 Russell, *Fugitives*, p. 74.

34 *The Autobiography of Sir John Martin-Harvey* (n.d. [1933]), p. 74. It is hard to
    believe that Rosencrantz and Guildenstern appeared in this scene. Irving may
    have borrowed the idea of the Fool from *Der bestrafte Brudermord*, where the
    Fool Phantasmo partly corresponds to Osric; he is a tool of the King.

35 Russell, *Fugitives*, pp. 74–6; C. L. Kenney, 'Mr. Irving in *Hamlet*', *Belgravia*, V,
    3rd ser. (Dec. 1874), 187; Clement Scott, *From 'The Bells' to 'King Arthur'*
    (1897), p. 61; *Illustrated Sporting and Dramatic News*, 7/11/74; *New York Times*,
    27/11/84. The different perceptions of his mood are found in illustrations as
    well: compare plates 5a and 5b. The pose depicted by the statue is confirmed by
    a sketch published in George Rowell, 'A Lyceum Sketchbook', *Nineteenth
    Century Theatre Research*, VI (Spring 1978), 8. The cartoon probably represents
    Irving's attitude after the room had cleared.

36   The only practicable column, in third grooves right.

37   Irving followed the F1 practice of softening oaths: Q2 gives 'God's love'.

38   Terry, *Story*, p. 131.

39   *Graphic*, 7/11/74.

40   Jan Kott, *Shakespeare Our Contemporary* (1964), p. 57.

41   *Standard*, 31/12/78; Montreal *Star*, 4/10/84. Chippendale played Polonius in the second production until 15/1/79, when Frederick Everill replaced him; he appeared once more at his retirement Benefit, 24/2/79.

42   Granville-Barker, *Prefaces*, I, 66.

43   Kenney, 'Mr. Irving in *Hamlet*', p. 187.

44   *Academy*, 7/11/74.

45   *Punch*, 11/1/79.

46   *Morning Post*, 31/12/78; F. A. Marshall, Preface, *'Hamlet'* . . . *arranged for the Stage by Henry Irving* (1879), p. vii; *Graphic*, 4/1/79.

47   Russell, *Fugitives*, p. 82.

48   In this change, Irving probably followed the suggestion of G. H. Lewes, *On Actors and the Art of Acting* (1875), pp. 122–4. This essay, first published in *Blackwood's Magazine* in 1861, may have escaped Irving's attention before it was reprinted.

49   Kenney, 'Mr. Irving in *Hamlet*', p. 183.

50   Arthur Elwood was twenty-eight and Arthur Wing Pinero twenty-three as Rosencrantz and Guildenstern respectively in 1878; Norman Forbes, brother of Forbes-Robertson, was twenty-six as Rosencrantz in 1885. Pinero and Forbes, like Lyndal, the Guildenstern of 1885, were actors in a comic line of business.

51   *Macmillan's Magazine*, XXXI (1874), 239.

52   Clement Scott, *The Drama of Yesterday and Today* (1899), II, 60.

53   Martin-Harvey, *Autobiography*, p. 29.

54   Irving, 'An Actor's Notes on Shakespeare, No. 2: Hamlet and Ophelia', *Nineteenth Century*, I (May 1877), 525.

55   *Blackwood's Magazine*, CXXIX (April 1879), 476.

56   Irving, 'Hamlet and Ophelia', pp. 527–8.

57   *Athenaeum*, 4/1/79; *The Theatre*, II, 2nd ser. (Feb. 1879), 20.

58   Irving, 'Hamlet and Ophelia', p. 527.

59   Russell, *Fugitives*, p. 90; Chicago *Times*, 14/2/84.

60   Hazlitt, *View of the English Stage* in Howe (ed.), *Works*, V, 188; *Saturday Review*, 9/5/85; Irving, 'Hamlet and Ophelia', p. 530.

61   Terry, *Story*, p. 128.

62   This was the traditional arrangement. The Maclise painting of Macready's production shows how it worked. In 1878 a dais of a different shape was used, but in the same position: see the sketch in Rowell, 'Lyceum Sketchbook'.

63   Irving emended the archaic 'pajock'.

64   Dover Wilson, *What Happens in 'Hamlet'*, p. 138. Thomas Abthorpe Cooper did the crawl as early as 1795; Macready, Charles Kemble, Booth, Benson and Tree followed suit: see A. C. Sprague, *Shakespeare and the Actors* (Cambridge, Mass., 1948), p. 159.

65   Russell, *Fugitives*, p. 99; Ellen Terry's study-book, Smallhythe, Shattuck No. 95; Chicago *Tribune*, 14/2/84. This of course was how he got hold of the fan. An

illustration in C. E. Pascoe (ed.), *Dramatic Notes: 1879*, p. 14, shows him holding it earlier, at 'Miching Mallecho'; either this is a mistake, or he obtained the fan in some other way in 1874.

66 Ellen Terry's study-book. 'The players cannot keep council' and the following speech (146–51), upon which Dover Wilson builds a case for the view that the dumbshow has almost given away the game, and that Hamlet fears that a Presenter may betray him, were cut.

67 *Morning Post*, 31/12/78.

68 Chicago *Morning News*, 15/2/84; Chicago *Tribune*, 14/2/84; *New York Times*, 27/11/84; William Winter, *Shakespeare on the Stage*, I (New York, 1911), 359.

69 *Academy*, 4/1/79.

70 The repetition was Irving's interpolation.

71 *The Times*, 12/11/74; Russell, *Fugitives*, pp. 69–70.

72 Irving, 'An Actor's Notes on Shakespeare, No. 3: "Look here, upon this picture, and on this"', *Nineteenth Century*, V (Feb. 1878), 260–3. There is an intriguing hint that this business was changed in the last revival; in a cutting from an unidentified paper dated 4/5/85, a reviewer says: 'After the killing of Polonius, Hamlet now catches sight of the King's "portrait in little" on a chain around [Gertrude's] neck, and tears it from her as she kneels to him. The idea tells well.'

73 Opened 30/11/74: *The Times*, 2/12/74. Some personal animosity may have been a factor here, since Irving had originally been engaged by Bateman to support Belmore.

74 *Blackwood's Magazine*, CXXIX, 477–8; Russell, *Fugitives*, p. 99; Irving's study-book, Shattuck No. 91.

75 *Academy, Athenaeum*, 7/11/74; *Liverpool Post*, 4/9/77; Chicago *Morning News*, 15/2/84.

76 *Macmillan's Magazine*, XXXI (1874), 241; *Graphic*, 7/11/74, 4/1/79; Marshall, Preface, *'Hamlet' arranged for the Stage*; illustration, *Illustrated Sporting and Dramatic News*, 1/11/74.

77 *The Times*, 12/11/74: Ellen Terry ascribes this review to Tom Taylor, *Story*, p. 124; Dover Wilson, *What Happens in 'Hamlet'*, p. 254; Terry's study-book. She always took a special interest in, and some responsibility for, the women's playing at the Lyceum.

78 Terry's study-book.

79 *Athenaeum*, 4/1/79. II.ii.86–105, 131–9, 190–2 were cut.

80 Terry, *Story*, p. 157; Scott, *Drama of Yesterday and Today*, II, 61; Charles Hiatt, *Ellen Terry and Her Impersonations: An Appreciation* (1898), p. 115; a photograph of Terry in this scene has been widely published: see Austin Brereton, *The Lyceum Theatre and Henry Irving* (1893), p. 213.

81 Montreal *Star*, 4/10/84.

82 Terry, *Story*, p. 154; Toronto *Globe*, 11/10/84; Richard Bebb (ed.), *Great Actors of the Past*, Argo record (1977): words are quoted as spoken.

83 Bebb, *Great Actors*; some of the tunes can be heard here. Terry, who was sixty-four at the time of recording, sings them remarkably well.

84 In the descriptions and reviews I have examined. The prompt-books and

study-books contain only the meagrest of stage directions and no significant marginalia referring to this scene.

85 Unidentified cutting, Smallhythe, 4/5/85; also *Standard*, 31/12/78. The *Eugene Aram* graveyard may be examined in an illustration in the *Illustrated London News*, 7/11/73; for a sketch of the 1878 set, see Rowell, 'Lyceum Sketchbook', p. 8.

86 Towse, 'Henry Irving', p. 666.

87 *Athenaeum*, 4/1/79. In 1874, in addition to the characters in the Q2 stage direction there were Barnardo, Marcellus, Francisco and 29 supernumeraries, almost exactly the same number (28) used in I.ii. In 1878, 38 supers were used here and 37 in I.ii. There was also a crowd of peasants.

88 Letter, 4/1/79, Enthoven Collection. The lines he mentions are probably part of Flecknoe's elegy on Burbage:

> Oft have I seen him leap into the grave,
> Suiting the person which he seemed to have
> Of a sad lover . . .

89 This 'picturesque and realistically exciting' business may have been added in 1885, when Irving knew immeasurably more about crowd-handling. It is mentioned only in an unidentified cutting at Smallhythe, 4/5/85.

90 Marshall, Preface, '*Hamlet*' *arranged for the Stage*, pp. xi–xii.

91 Russell, *Fugitives*, p. 102.

92 Dover Wilson, *What Happens in 'Hamlet'*, p. 286.

93 *Graphic*, 4/11/74; *The Times*, 18/1/75.

94 *Saturday Review*, 7/11/74; Marshall, *A Study of Hamlet* (1875), pp. 107 and 200, suggests that both should be accidentally disarmed; the exchange should occur when 'each snatches at the first weapon that comes to his hand'.

95 Russell, *Fugitives*, p. 102.

96 John Russell Brown, *Free Shakespeare* (1974), p. 28.

97 Cook, *Nights at the Play*, p. 374.

98 Clemen, *Shakespeare's Dramatic Art*, p. 150.

99 Marshall, Preface, '*Hamlet*' *arranged for the Stage*, p. ix.

100 'Double time' in Shakespeare was first discussed by John Wilson in a series of dialogues entitled 'Dies Boreales: Christopher under Canvass', *Blackwood's Magazine*, LXVI (Nov. 1849), 620–54 and LXVII (April 1850), 481–512. Selections were reprinted shortly before Irving's revival, as 'Double-Time-Analysis of *Macbeth* and *Othello*', *The New Shakespeare Society's Transactions*, II (1875–6), 351–87.

101 Several critics were still unsatisfied, complaining that there was no point in locking the doors of a hall with an open colonnade.

102 Morris Weitz, '*Hamlet*' *and the Philosophy of Criticism* (Chicago, 1964), p. 316.

103 Dover Wilson, *What Happens in 'Hamlet'*, pp. 103ff; New Cambridge *Hamlet*, pp. lvi–lix; Harry Levin, *The Question of 'Hamlet'* (New York, 1959), p. 117.

104 For example, G. B. Harrison, *Shakespeare's Tragedies* (1951), p. 109.

105 Ernest Jones, *Hamlet and Oedipus* (1949); Levin, *Question*; L. C. Knights, 'Prince Hamlet' in *Explorations* (1940); Lily B. Campbell, *Shakespeare's Tragic Heroes: Slaves of Passion* (Cambridge, 1930), pp. 109–47. But see Patrick

Cruttwell, 'The Morality of *Hamlet* – "Sweet Prince" or "Arrant Knave"' in John Russell Brown and Bernard Harris (eds.), *Hamlet* (1963), pp. 114–15.

106 Fredson Bowers, 'Hamlet as Minister and Scourge', *P.M.L.A.*, LXX (1955), 740–9.

107 T. S. Eliot, *The Sacred Wood*, 7th edn (1950), pp. 95–103; C. S. Lewis, *Hamlet: The Prince or the Poem?* (1942), p. 15.

108 Edward Dowden, *Shakespeare: A Critical Study of His Mind and Art* (1874), p. 125.

109 Programme note on *The Room* and *The Dumb Waiter*, in Ronald Hayman, *Harold Pinter* (1968), pp. 8–9.

110 Salvador de Madariaga, *On Hamlet* (1948). G. Wilson Knight says, 'Hamlet is an element of evil in the state of Denmark . . . the only hindrance to happiness, health and prosperity: a living death in the midst of life' (*The Wheel of Fire*, 4th edn (1949), pp. 38–40). Knights finds him spiteful, cruel, self-righteous and maladjusted ('Prince Hamlet', pp. 77–84).

111 Harrison, *Shakespeare's Tragedies*, p. 246. See for example Traversi, Knight and Knights.

112 Kenneth Muir, *Shakespeare the Professional* (1973), p. 20; Brown, *Free Shakespeare*, p. 9.

113 Francis Fergusson, *The Idea of a Theatre* (Princeton, N.J., 1949), p. 101.

114 Gareth Lloyd Evans, *Shakespeare*, IV (1972), 33.

115 Fergusson, *Idea of a Theatre*, p. 105. H. D. F. Kitto, *Form and Meaning in Drama* (1956), takes a similar view. Philip Edwards, *Shakespeare and the Confines of Art* (1968), pp. 83–6, sees *Hamlet* as a play about 'killing the king', a play 'not about *inaction*, but about action'.

116 Anne Righter, *Shakespeare and the Idea of the Play* (1962), pp. 154–64; Caroline Spurgeon, *Shakespeare's Imagery and What It Tells Us* (Cambridge, 1935), pp. 316–20; Maynard Mack, 'The World of Hamlet', *The Yale Review*, XLI (1952), 510–18.

117 Lloyd Evans, *Shakespeare*, IV, 38.

118 Irving Ribner, *Patterns in Shakespearian Tragedy* (1969), pp. 68, 80; his bibliography lists critics who take this view. See also Granville-Barker, *Prefaces*, I, 139; L. C. Knights, *An Approach to 'Hamlet'* (Stanford, California, 1961), p. 89, notes the change but finds it indecisive because the Ghost is evil. Cruttwell and Harrison see no need for a change. A. C. Bradley, *Shakespearean Tragedy* (1904), thought him merely indifferent.

119 E. M. W. Tillyard, *Shakespeare's Problem Plays* (1950), p. 23.

120 Ribner, *Patterns*, p. 62; Mack, 'World of Hamlet', pp. 521–2. Bowers, 'Hamlet as Minister', pp. 745–6, believes he is right to spare the king but wrong to kill Polonius.

121 Helen Gardner, *The Business of Criticism* (Oxford, 1959), p. 46; Peter Alexander, *Hamlet: Father and Son* (Oxford, 1955), pp. 144–7.

122 Ribner, *Patterns*, p. 66.

3 Macbeth

1 *The Times*, 18/9/75.

2   André Antoine, *Mes souvenirs sur le Théâtre-Libre* (Paris, 1921), p. 136.

3   Three performances in London and 21 in the U.S.A.

4   W. G. Clark and W. A. Wright (eds.), *Macbeth* (Oxford, 1874).

5   Irving, 'Shakespearean Notes No. 1: The Third Murderer in *Macbeth*', *Nineteenth Century*, 1 (April 1877), 327–30; Moy Thomas, *Athenaeum*, 14/4/77.

6   503½ lines were cut in the longest version, 617½ in the shortest. Kenneth Muir (ed.), *Macbeth*, New Arden Shakespeare (1966). All references and figures are based on this edition.

7   There are no prompt-books, but I have examined several study-books: Shattuck No. 81, in the University of Pennsylvania Library, and Shattuck No. 91 at Smallhythe, both based upon Clark and Wright, represent the 1875 text. Shattuck No. 92, in the Harvard Theatre Collection, is based on a proof copy of Irving's acting version, which exists in two published editions, dated 1888 and 1889. No. 93, at Harvard, is based on the latter, and No. 94, which contains a spectator's notes, on the former. Two books of Ellen Terry's, No. 97 and No. 98 are at Smallhythe.

8   Preface, *Macbeth: As Arranged for the Stage by Henry Irving* (1888).

9   He read '*May* of life' at V.iii.22, '*pall* in resolution' at V.v.42 (both Dr Johnson's emendations); and 'quail'd' for 'cool'd' at V.v.10 (Collier). Syntax was modernized, at I.vii.28 with the addition of 'side' to 'falls on the other', and the substitution of 'is' in 'their sense *are* shut'. Irving found all of these in Clark and Wright's notes, but had to look elsewhere to find 'silvered' for 'slivered' at IV.i.28 (Rowe).

10 Michael Mullin (ed.), '*Macbeth*' *Onstage: An Annotated Facsimile of Glen Byam Shaw's 1955 Promptbook* (Columbia, Missouri, 1976).

11 Bram Stoker, *Personal Reminiscences of Henry Irving* (1906), I, 23.

12 *St. James's Gazette*, quoted Charles Hiatt, *Ellen Terry and Her Impersonations: An Appreciation* (1898), p. 200.

13 *Ibid.*, p. 202.

14 See A. W. Schlegel, *Lectures on Dramatic Art and Literature*, trans. John Black (1879), pp. 408–9; G. G. Gervinus, *Shakespeare Commentaries*, trans. F. E. Bunnett (1875), pp. 591, 604; William Hazlitt, *Characters of Shakespeare's Plays* in *Works*, ed. P. P. Howe (1930), IV, 187, 192.

15 S. T. Coleridge, *Lectures and Notes on Shakespeare and Other English Poets*, ed. T. Ashe (1893), pp. 369, 372; H. N. Hudson, *Shakespeare: His Life, Art and Characters* (1872), II, 278, 304.

16 In both 1875 study-books Irving wrote 'con' in the margin at I.vii.25–8 and II.ii.49–51. This has been misread as 'cow' by Bertram Shuttleworth, 'Irving's Macbeth', *Theatre Notebook*, V (1951), 30. Laurence Irving refers to a text overwritten 'Liar, Traitor, Coward'; it is not listed by Shattuck, but probably dates from 1888.

17 George Fletcher, '*Macbeth*: Knight's Cabinet Edition of Shakespere', *The Westminster Review*, XLI (1843), 1–72. Terry's copy is in the British Theatre Museum. Faucit gave it to Irving, perhaps during the run of the 1875 production, but it did not then influence his performance: even at the end of the run, the *Academy* said, 'It is a great point in Mr. Irving's art . . . that he brings into high relief all that Macbeth had of noble or of the remains of noble' (23/12/76).

18 Irving address, 'The Character of Macbeth', in H. H. Furness (ed.), New Variorum *Macbeth*, 5th edn (Philadelphia, 1903), p. 470.

19 Gervinus, *Commentaries*, p. 598; Schlegel, *Lectures*, p. 409.

20 Thomas Campbell, *The Life of Mrs. Siddons* (1834), II, 11.

21 Hazlitt, *Characters*, p. 189.

22 Terry, *Four Lectures on Shakespeare*, ed. Christopher St John (1932), p. 163.

23 Shattuck No. 98.

24 5/1/89.

25 Shattuck No. 92; William Archer, 'Scenic Aspects of the Lyceum *Macbeth*', *Scottish Art Review* (Feb. 1889), 249; *The Times*, 31/12/88.

26 *Pall Mall Budget*, 3/1/89. Alice Marriott (First Witch) had been on the stage nearly thirty years and was no stranger to 'hag' parts. In 1895 the witches were played by men.

27 Archer, 'Scenic Aspects', pp. 249–50; Shattuck No. 92; Edwin Drew, *Henry Irving on and off the Stage* (n.d. [1889]), p. 39; *The Theatre*, XIII, 4th ser. (Feb. 1889), 102.

28 31/12/88.

29 Emphasis marked in Shattuck No. 92; *Saturday Review*, 5/1/89.

30 Shattuck No. 91.

31 *Saturday Review*, 5/1/89.

32 Shattuck No. 92; emphases, Drew, *Henry Irving*, p. 42.

33 Shattuck No. 97.

34 Fletcher, '*Macbeth*: Knight's Cabinet Edition', p. 4; *Saturday Review*, 15/1/89.

35 Stoker, *Personal Reminiscences*, I, 24; *The Autobiography of Sir John Martin-Harvey* (n.d. [1933]), p. 106; Archer, 'Scenic Aspects', pp. 250–1.

36 *Saturday Review*, 2/10/75.

37 W. Graham Robertson, *Time Was* (1931), pp. 150–1; *The Times*, 31/12/88; 'An Old Hand' [E. R. Russell], '*Macbeth*' at the Lyceum (Liverpool, 1889), p. 2.

38 Archer, 'Scenic Aspects', p. 255; Robertson, *Time Was*, p. 151.

39 Hiatt, *Impersonations*, p. 112; *The Times*, 31/12/88; *Illustrated Sporting and Dramatic News*, 5/1/89.

40 *Spectator*, 5/1/89.

41 *The Times*, 31/12/88; Clement Scott, *Ellen Terry: An Appreciation* (New York, 1900), p. 119; Shattuck No. 97.

42 Shattuck No. 97; Scott, *Ellen Terry*, p. 116.

43 Shattuck Nos. 92, 91, 97, 98; Roger Manvell, *Ellen Terry* (1968), pp. 357–66; Drew, *Henry Irving*, pp. 50–1; *The Times*, 31/12/88.

44 *Punch*, 9/10/75; *Saturday Review*, 2/10/75. By February 1889 the scene was sunlit, if we can believe *The Theatre*, Feb. 1889, p. 103.

45 Archer, 'Scenic Aspects', p. 251; Martin-Harvey, *Autobiography*, p. 106. This was the moment Sargent chose for his vigorous study preliminary to the famous portrait.

46 *Punch*, 12/1/89; Shattuck No. 97.

47 *The Times*, 31/12/88.

48 *Illustrated London News*, 15/12/75; *Punch*, 9/11/75.

49 Herbert R. Coursen, 'In Deepest Consequence: *Macbeth*', *Shakespeare Quar-*

terly, XVIII (1967), 375–88, is an admirable summary of the arguments as to Shakespeare's intention with respect to the faint/feint.

50 Irving, 'Character of Macbeth', pp. 470–1.

51 *Gentleman's Magazine*, 226 (April 1889), 208.

52 Coleridge, *Lectures*, p. 470; Manvell, *Terry*, p. 358; illustration in *Graphic*, 5/1/89; Russell, *'Macbeth' at the Lyceum*, p. 2.

53 *Pall Mall Budget*, 3/1/89.

54 Shattuck No. 92; Drew, *Henry Irving*, p. 57.

55 Shattuck No. 97; Russell, *'Macbeth' at the Lyceum*, p. 3; *Saturday Review*, 5/1/89.

56 *Saturday Review*, 5/1/89.

57 Russell, *'Macbeth' at the Lyceum*, p. 3; Manvell, *Terry*, p. 359; Archer, 'Scenic Aspects', p. 252.

58 Shattuck Nos. 92, 97.

59 *Athenaeum* 2/10/75; Russell, *'Macbeth' at the Lyceum*, p. 3; Shattuck No. 97.

60 The last couplet, cut in 1875, is underlined in all Irving's 1888 study-books; Irving, 'Character of Macbeth', p. 471.

61 Shattuck No. 92; in 1875 the set representing a hall at Forres, which had been used for I.iv, was used again.

62 Shattuck No. 91; Robertson, *Time Was*, pp. 165–6.

63 Manvell, *Terry*, p. 359; Shattuck No. 97.

64 *Daily Chronicle*, quoted Hiatt, *Impersonations*, p. 210; Shattuck No. 97; Manvell, *Terry*, p. 360; Shattuck Nos. 93, 92.

65 *The Times*, 27/9/75; *Saturday Review*, 2/10/75; Scott, *From 'The Bells' to 'King Arthur'*, (1897), p. 77; a cartoon in the *Illustrated Sporting and Dramatic News*, 2/10/75, shows a stagehand holding what seems to be a stooping, outsized cut-out. See George Speaight, 'Professor Pepper's Ghost', *Revue d'histoire du théâtre*, XV (1963), 48–56.

66 Archer, 'Scenic Aspects', p. 254; Russell, *'Macbeth' at the Lyceum*, p. 3; *Dramatic Notes*, 29/12/88; *Society Herald*, 31/12/88; T. N. Willan, *First-Night Impressions of Mr. Irving's 'Macbeth'* (Bath, 1889), p. 5; *Athenaeum*, 5/1/89; *Pall Mall Budget*, 3/1/89; *The Theatre*, XXVI, 4th ser. (Oct. 1895), 243.

67 M. H. Spielmann, 'Art in the Theatre II: A Shakespearean Revival: *Macbeth*', *The Magazine of Art* (1889), 98–100; *Pall Mall Budget*, 3/1/89.

68 *Theatrical Programme*, 30/9/75; *The Times*, 2/10/75; Shattuck Nos. 92, 97.

69 Scott, *Ellen Terry*, p. 119; in the prompt-book quoted by Manvell she says the same thing: 'By suffering at this point she pays penance and repents – all is forgiven.'

70 Russell, *'Macbeth' at the Lyceum*, p. 3. This was later replaced by another tableau: leaving the hall with his wife, Macbeth stopped and slowly turned to gaze at the spot where the ghost had appeared, wide-eyed with remembered fear. William Winter, *Shakespeare on the Stage*, I (New York, 1911), 485.

71 Shattuck No. 92. The received modern reading, 'in deed', is Theobald's emendation.

72 This could not be the visit promised for the morrow after the Banquet (III.iv.131–2); it must have been one of a long series.

73 *Pall Mall Budget*, 3/1/89; *New York Times*, 3/11/95.

74 *The Times*, 31/12/88; *Saturday Review, Illustrated Sporting and Dramatic News*, 5/1/89; the song is quoted from Irving's text.

75 Shattuck No. 92.

76 Russell, *'Macbeth' at the Lyceum*, p. 4; *Illustrated London News*, 5/1/89; *The Times*, 31/12/88; Spielmann gives eighty witches, but the *Pall Mall Budget* quotes Cattermole and is probably more accurate. The scene change may have been effected by removing gauzes upstage to reveal a distant prospect, without altering the foreground. Mr Paul Rice has suggested to me that there is doubt whether the chorus entered before or after the change.

77 *The Times*, 31/12/88; Archer, 'Scenic Aspects', p. 254. Of 159 lines before Ross enters, 88 are omitted in Shattuck No. 93.

78 Raymond Mander and Joe Mitchenson, *A Picture History of the British Theatre* (1957), plate 336; *Society Herald*, 31/12/88.

79 Shattuck No. 97; Russell, *'Macbeth' at the Lyceum*, p. 4; Archer, 'Scenic Aspects', p. 254; *Spectator*, 5/1/89; *Saturday Review*, 6/7/89; unidentified cutting, Winter letter to Irving, Enthoven Collection; Manvell, *Terry*, p. 362; Drew, *Irving*, p. 70.

80 Spielmann, 'Art in the Theatre', p. 99; *Pall Mall Budget*, 3/1/89.

81 Richard Dickins, *Forty Years of Shakespeare on the English Stage* (n.d.), p. 28; *Saturday Review*, 23/12/76.

82 *Saturday Review*, 5/1/89; Shattuck Nos. 93, 92; *The Times*, 31/12/88.

83 Letter to Irving, 1 December, Enthoven Collection; Russell, *'Macbeth' at the Lyceum*, p. 4.

84 Archer, 'Scenic Aspects', p. 254. In 1875 it took place in the outer court of the castle.

85 *Spectator*, 5/1/89; *The Times*, 31/12/88; Terry, *The Story of My Life* (1908), p. 303.

86 *Theatrical Programme*, 30/9/75; Shattuck No. 97; Russell, *'Macbeth' at the Lyceum*, p. 4; *The Times*, 31/12/88.

87 Thus Diana Rigg: W. Stephen Gilbert, review in *Plays and Players*, January 1973.

88 Irving Ribner, *Patterns in Shakespearian Tragedy* (1969), p. 160.

4 King Lear

1 There were 72 consecutive performances and 4 during the run of *Becket*, which opened 6/2/93. Irving was ill and was replaced for 7 performances, beginning 19/1/93, by W. J. Holloway. Garrick played Lear 83 times in London.

2 Irving, 'Four Favourite Parts', *English Illustrated Magazine*, x (Sept. 1893), 929.

3 *National Observer*, 19/11/92; Joseph Knight, obit., *Athenaeum*, 21/10/05.

4 *Illustrated London News*, 3/1/92; *The Theatre*, xx, 4th ser. (Nov. 1892), 158.

5 H. Chance Newton, *Cues and Curtain Calls* (1927), p. 44.

6 Phelps's total was achieved in 9 short runs; he played *Hamlet* 171 times, *Macbeth* 133, *Othello* 99 and even *King John* 65: Shirley S. Allen, *Samuel Phelps and Sadler's Wells Theatre* (Middletown, Connecticut, 1971), pp. 314–15.

7 Rev. Joseph Parker, 'Church and Stage', *Idler*, III (1893), 92; *Illustrated London News*, *Illustrated Sporting and Dramatic News*, 19/11/92.

8 Kenneth Muir (ed.), *King Lear*, New Arden Shakespeare (1964). All references and quotations are based on this text. Two states of Irving's text survive: a nineteenth-century edition with his MS cuts in the Folger Shakespeare Library, and his study-book, based on his printed acting version but with further MS cuts and notes. The latter is in the Garrick Club, and is taken as authoritative. Phelps cut 750 lines.

9 A. C. Bradley, *Shakespearean Tragedy* (1904), p. 270, finds this effect 'disastrous'.

10 S. T. Coleridge, *Lectures and Notes on Shakespeare and Other English Poets*, ed. T. Ashe (1893), p. 330.

11 G. G. Gervinus, *Shakespeare Commentaries*, trans. F. E. Bunnett (1875), pp. 619, 623.

12 The Introduction to *King Lear* in *The Henry Irving Shakespeare* (1888–90), VI, 335, agreed: commentator was 'R. M. W.'

13 A. W. Schlegel, *Lectures on Dramatic Art and Literature*, trans. John Black (1879), p. 411.

14 E. Dowden, *Shakespere: A Critical Study of His Mind and Art*, 3rd edn (New York and London, 1902), pp. 230–8; Bradley, *Shakespearean Tragedy*, pp. 271, 252.

15 *Illustrated London News*, 12/11/92.

16 Schlegel, *Lectures*, p. 411.

17 *Daily Telegraph*, 11/11/92: all reviews are this date unless otherwise indicated.

18 *Daily Chronicle*; Percy Fitzgerald, *Henry Irving: A Record of Twenty Years at the Lyceum* (1893), p. 313; *The Theatre*, XX, 4th ser. (Dec. 1892), 280; *Daily Telegraph*.

19 *Daily Chronicle*; *Newcastle Journal* in 'King Lear' at the Lyceum ... Extracts from the Press (1893), p. 53, cited below as *Extracts; Nineteenth Century*, XXXIII (Jan. 1893), 47; *Liverpool Post*, 14/11/92; *Morning*.

20 Note in Irving's published acting version.

21 In the courtyard of Gloster's castle, II.i and ii; Albany's castle, I.iii and IV.i in Irving's text.

22 W. Graham Robertson, *Time Was* (1931), p. 168.

23 *Hearth and Home* in *Extracts*, p. 83; *Daily Chronicle*; *The Theatre*, p. 157.

24 See Gervinus, *Commentaries*, p. 637; Bradley, *Shakespearean Tragedy*, pp. 320–1; and Harley Granville-Barker, *Prefaces to Shakespeare* (1958), I, 303; all of whom make Cordelia share the blame. Terry explains her view in *Four Lectures on Shakespeare*, ed. Christopher St John (1932), p. 153; this is based on Mrs Jameson's interpretation in *Characteristics of Women* (1832), II, 100–1. *Nineteenth Century*, p. 48; *Licensed Victuallers' Gazette* in *Extracts*, p. 94.

25 Irving prefers Q, *it may mar ...*' at line 95 rather than F, 'you'.

26 *The Hospital* in *Extracts*, p. 94; *Gentleman's Magazine*, 273 (1892), 628; *Nineteenth Century*, p. 48. The Fool's presence in this scene is not indicated in Q or F.

27 Of the 101 lines after Gloster's entry, 61 were cut.

28 Marvin Rosenberg, *The Masks of King Lear* (Berkeley, California, 1972), p. 121.

29   *Liverpool Daily Post*, 14/11/92; *Funny Folks*, n.d. [1892], 379; *Illustrated Sporting and Dramatic News*, 19/11/92; *Academy*, 19/11/92.

30   Edward Gordon Craig, *Henry Irving* (1930), p. 114. The original 101 lines were cut to 28.

31   Irving follows Q reading at line 223: 'trow' for F 'know', and at line 224, 'it' for F 'it's'.

32   Underlining and annotations from the study-book.

33   This transposition follows a tradition established by Nahum Tate.

34   *Gentlewoman*, 19/11/92; *Nineteenth Century*, p. 49; *The Times*.

35   *Daily Chronicle*.

36   *The Theatre*, p. 280.

37   *The Hospital*; Augustin Filon in *Le Journal des débats*: both in *Extracts*; pp. 94, 114.

38   *Standard* in *Extracts*, p. 25.

39   Study-book, MS note at II.iv.130; Filon and *Society* in *Extracts*, pp. 114, 77.

40   *Saturday Review*, 10/12/92; underlined in study-book.

41   *Daily Chronicle*; W. H. Pollock, *Impressions of Henry Irving* (1908), pp. 109–10 claims the exit business was Booth's, and that Irving said it would 'never do' for him; *Liverpool Post*, 14/11/92.

42   Charles Lamb, 'On Shakespeare's Tragedies' in *The Complete Works in Prose and Verse of Charles Lamb* (1876), I, 261.

43   *Daily Chronicle*.

44   Letter from Irving to Ellen Terry copied into Irving edition of *Lear* at Smallhythe.

45   *Aberdeen Free Press* in *Extracts*, p. 40; *National Observer*, 19/11/92.

46   *Nineteenth Century*, p. 50; *Liverpool Post*, 14/11/92.

47   *Gentleman's Magazine*, p. 631; *Evening News* and *Daily Graphic* in *Extracts*, pp. 39, 35.

48   *National Observer*, 19/11/92; *Punch*, 19/11/92; Robertson, *Time Was*, p. 177.

49   T. Edgar Pemberton, *Ellen Terry and Her Sisters* (1902), p. 292; *Morning*; *The Times*; *Saturday Review*, 10/12/92.

50   Irving letter to Terry, Smallhythe.

51   *Saturday Review*, 19/11/92; *Gentlewoman*, 19/11/92.

52   *Saturday Review*, 19/11/92; *Nineteenth Century*, p. 50; *Sunday Sun* in *Extracts*, p. 66.

53   *Black and White*, 26/11/92, identifies this as Meredith Ball's music; Robertson, *Time Was*, p. 168.

54   *Life*, 19/11/92; *Liverpool Post*, 14/11/92; *Daily Telegraph*.

55   *Brighton Times* in *Extracts*, p. 88; Henry Arthur Jones, *The Shadow of Henry Irving* (1931), p. 55; *Gentleman's Magazine*, p. 631.

56   Robertson, *Time Was*, p. 169; *National Observer*, 19/11/92; *Daily Telegraph*; *The Theatre*, p. 280.

57   Robertson, *Time Was*, p. 170; Rosenberg, *Masks*, p. 311; A. C. Sprague, *Shakespeare and the Actors* (Cambridge, Mass., 1948), p. 296.

58   *Pall Mall Gazette* and *Pall Mall Budget* in *Extracts*, pp. 38, 75; *Gentleman's Magazine*, p. 632; Filon in *Extracts*, p. 116; *Daily Telegraph*.

59   Filon and *Eastern and Western Review* in *Extracts*, pp. 116–17, 101; *The Times*;

Irving's MS note in study-book says he dies in Edgar's arms; *Daily Chronicle* gives Albany; the illustration by Bernard Partridge in the Souvenir shows Kent, and is probably the most authoritative source for actual performance.

60 *Gentleman's Magazine*, p. 629.

61 Wyndham Lewis, *The Lion and the Fox* (1927), p. 180. Critics concerned with demonstrating the redemptive theme, or themes of order disturbed and restored, usually treat the last scene superficially: besides Bradley and Dowden, see D. A. Traversi, *An Approach to Shakespeare* (Garden City, New York, 1969), II, 170, and Irving Ribner, *Patterns in Shakespearean Tragedy* (1969), p. 130. G. Wilson Knight opposes this view: 'In face of the last scene any detailed comment of purgatorial expiation . . . is but a limp and tinkling irrelevance' (*The Wheel of Fire*, 4th edn (1969), p. 204). William Elton, *King Lear and the Gods* (San Marino, California, 1966), concurs.

62 Granville-Barker, *Prefaces*, I, 277–8.

5 Four tragedies

1 Marvin Rosenberg, *The Masks of Othello* (Berkeley, California, 1961), pp. 102–19; A. C. Sprague, *Shakespeare and the Actors* (Cambridge, Mass., 1948), pp. 221–2.

2 William H. Rideing, *Dramatic Notes: 1880–81* (1881), p. 101; *Academy*, 19/2/76; Clement Scott, *From 'The Bells' to 'King Arthur'* (1897), p. 84.

3 *Academy*, 19/2/76. This exact attitude may be seen in an illustration published in the *Graphic*, 18/3/76: see Kenneth Muir and Philip Edwards (eds.), *Aspects of Othello* (Cambridge, 1977), plate VIII.

4 *Saturday Review*, 19/2/76.

5 M. R. Ridley (ed.), *Othello*, New Arden Shakespeare (1965). All references are based on this edition. *Academy*, 19/2/76; Dutton Cook, *Nights at the Play* (1883), p. 308.

6 *Academy*, 19/2/76: the critic thought this odd, when the same accusation had already been made at line 61.

7 *The Hornet*, 23/2/76; Cook, *Nights*, p. 308; Arthur Goddard, *Players of the Period* (1891), p. 50; *Academy*, 19/2/76.

8 *The Times*, 17/2/76.

9 Cook, *Nights*, p. 308; Scott, *From 'The Bells' to 'King Arthur'*, p. 85.

10 *Saturday Review*, 19/2/76; *The Hornet*, 23/2/76; *Westminster Papers*, 1/3/76.

11 *Illustrated London News*, 19/2/76; *The Hornet*, 23/2/76; *The Times*, 17/2/76; *Saturday Review*, 19/2/76; Cook, *Nights*, p. 309.

12 The 1876 *Othello* ran for 49 performances. The reading, at Trinity College, Dublin, was of the drinking scene only: *Academy*, 23/6/77.

13 *Othello* cost £856 1s 6d; *Romeo*, £9,554 9s.

14 *The Theatre*, III, 3rd ser. (June 1881), 359.

15 *The Times*, 5/5/81; *Illustrated London News*, 7/5/81; *The Autobiography of Sir John Martin-Harvey* (n.d. [1933]), p. 42; *Saturday Review*, 7/5/81.

16 Irving's study-book, Shattuck No. 73, is in the Harvard Theatre Collection: at I.iii.301–80, Irving has underlined terms like 'Moor' and 'erring barbarian', and

written 'contempt' in the margin. At II.i.250, 'she would never have lov'd the Moor', he wrote 'Ugh!' See also *Academy*, 7/5/81.

17 Ellen Terry, *The Story of My Life* (1908), p. 205.

18 Percy Fitzgerald, *Henry Irving: A Record of Twenty Years at the Lyceum* (1893), p. 166. Irving's sketch for his Iago costume is reproduced in Bram Stoker, *Personal Reminiscences of Henry Irving* (1906), I, 89.

19 *Athenaeum*, 7/5/81.

20 *The Theatre*, p. 360; *New York Times*, 16/5/81; Terry, *Story*, p. 206.

21 *Punch*, 14/5/81; *Athenaeum*, 7/5/81; *The Times*, 5/5/81; *Saturday Review*, 7/5/81. Lodovico's entry was delayed to line 64; Othello did not appear at all.

22 A. C. Bradley, *Shakespearean Tragedy* (1904), p. 181. Motives are supplied at I.i.22–7, iii.385–6; II.i.286–7, 290–4; V.i.19–20.

23 Walter Herries Pollock, *Impressions of Henry Irving* (1908), pp. 76–8; *Saturday Review*, 7/5/81; *Punch*, 14/5/81; Richard Dickins, *Forty Years of Shakespeare on the English Stage* (n.d.), p. 40. A photograph of Pauncefort in another part may be seen in G. C. D. Odell, *Annals of the New York Stage* (New York, 1927–49), XII, 232.

24 Mowbray Morris, *Essays in Theatrical Criticism* (1882), p. 101; *Academy*, 7/5/81.

25 *Saturday Review*, *Athenaeum*, 14/5/81.

26 Cook, *Nights*, p. 463; Fitzgerald, *Record*, p. 169; *Illustrated London News*, 14/5/81.

27 *Saturday Review*, 14/5/81.

28 Terry, *Story*, pp. 206–7: this must refer to the remainder of the scene, since Desdemona does not enter until line 178 in Irving's text.

29 [Theodore Martin], 'The Meiningen Company and the London Stage', *Blackwood's Magazine*, CXXX (August 1881), 254.

30 George Saintsbury, 'Irving as Iago' in H. A. Saintsbury and Cecil Palmer (eds.), *We Saw Him Act* (1939), p. 201.

31 Fitzgerald, *Record*, p. 165; *Saturday Review*, 14/5/81; Irving's study-book.

32 Study-book; *Illustrated London News*, 14/5/81.

33 Unidentified cutting, Percy Fitzgerald Collection, Garrick Club; *Saturday Review*, 7/5/81; study-book.

34 *Illustrated London News*, 14/5/81; Fitzgerald, *Record*, p. 169; study-book.

35 *Saturday Review*, 14/5/81; Fitzgerald, *Record*, p. 169; study-book.

36 Study-book; Dickins, *Forty Years of Shakespeare*, p. 40.

37 *Saturday Review*, 7/5/81; Saintsbury, 'Irving as Iago', p. 202; Fitzgerald, *Record*, p. 170.

38 Dickins, *Forty Years of Shakespeare*, p. 40.

39 Terry, *Story*, p. 207. On tour, Irving's Othello was J. B. Howard, an Edinburgh actor-manager and Scotland's favourite Rob Roy. The engagement began in Liverpool on 27/9/81 and ended in Edinburgh on 17/11/81: *The Theatre*, IV, 3rd ser. (Sept. 1881), 187; account book, London Museum.

40 Shirley S. Allen, *Samuel Phelps and Sadler's Wells Theatre* (Middletown, Connecticut, 1971), p. 230.

41 *Illustrated Sporting and Dramatic News*, 3/3/77; *Sketch*, 30/12/96.

42 Figures calculated from the text of Mark Eccles (ed.), *Richard III*, Signet

Shakespeare (New York, 1964). All references are based on this text. Irving's
1877 prompt-book is in the London Museum, Shattuck No. 65.

43 Allen, *Samuel Phelps*, p. 230. Bateman: *The Times*, 1/2/77; *Illustrated London
News, Saturday Review*, 3/2/77. Ward: *Academy, Illustrated London News*,
26/12/96; unidentified cutting, Fitzgerald Collection.

44 Similar considerations dictated the omission of II.iv, IV.i and v, and V.i
(Buckingham's execution), and the transposition of portions of II.iii to II.i,
where the Citizens' lines were distributed amongst the major characters, and of
essential information from III.v.72–109 to the end of III.i.

45 V.i and ii were cut. Irving's V.i and iii, the exterior of Richmond's tent in the
first grooves, comprised lines 19–46, 80–118; and 224–72 respectively. V.ii and
iv, a full-stage set representing the interior of Richard's tent, comprised lines
47–79, 132–223; and 277–352 respectively.

46 Cook, *Nights*, p. 328; Dickins, *Forty Years of Shakespeare*, p. 31; Scott, *From
'The Bells' to 'King Arthur'*, p. 106.

47 Olivier's film (1955) is a genuine adaptation. It makes excellent use of Cibber's
other famous point, 'Off with his head: so much for Buckingham.'

48 Scott, *From 'The Bells' to 'King Arthur'*, p. 105.

49 *The People*, 20/12/96; H. Barton Baker, 'Colley Cibber v. Shakespeare', *Gentle-
man's Magazine*, 240 (1877), 349–51; *Graphic*, 3/2/77; Dickins, *Forty Years of
Shakespeare*, p. 32; M. R. Holmes, *Stage Costumes and Accessories in the London
Museum* (1968), items 57, 58, 158, 160 and plate x.

50 Irving, 'Four Favourite Parts', *English Illustrated Magazine*, x (Sept. 1893),
928.

51 *Westminster Budget*, 24/12/96; *Illustrated London News, Academy*, 26/12/96;
Sketch, 30/12/96; unidentified cutting, Fitzgerald Collection.

52 Irving compares Richard to Iago in 'Four Favourite Parts', p. 928. T. H. Hall
Caine, *'Richard III' and 'Macbeth'* (London and Liverpool, 1877), p. 40;
Frederic Daly, *Henry Irving in England and America* (1884), p. 50; *Saturday
Review*, 3/2/77. Irving's 1877 study-book, Harvard Theatre Collection, Shat-
tuck No. 63.

53 *Morning Post*, 30/1/77.

54 In the film the silence was heightened by music. The aside was transposed to
follow Prince Edward's question about the Tower, 'Did Julius Caesar build that
place, my lord?' (line 69). *Morning Post*, 30/1/77; Baker, 'Cibber v. Shakespeare', p. 349; 1877 prompt-book.

55 The 1877 prompt-book identifies the 'reverend fathers' as Dr Shaw and Friar P.
Daly, *Irving in England and America*, p. 50; unidentified Belfast paper, Birmingham Public Library; Austin Brereton, *The Lyceum and Henry Irving* (1903), p.
204.

56 Irving, 'Four Favourite Parts', p. 928; *Weekly Dispatch*, 2/2/77; Cook, *Nights*, p.
328; *Athenaeum*, 3/2/77.

57 *Saturday Review*, 17/3/77; Dickins, *Forty Years of Shakespeare*, p. 32; Baker,
'Cibber v. Shakespeare', p. 350.

58 H. M. Walbrook, 'Henry Irving: His Personality and Art', *'The Stage' Year
Book* (1928), pp. 100–1; *Saturday Review*, 3/2/77; E. R. Russell, 'Sir Henry
Irving's *Richard III*', *The Theatre*, XXIX, 4th ser. (May 1897), 251.

59 Prince Edward, Henry VI, Rivers, Grey and, of course, Vaughan.
60 Hall Caine, '*Richard III' and 'Macbeth'*, p. 44; *Illustrated Sporting and Dramatic News*, 3/2/77.
61 G. B. Shaw, *Dramatic Opinions and Essays* (New York, 1906), II, 131; Baker, 'Cibber v. Shakespeare', p. 350.
62 *Saturday Review*, 3/2/77; Charles Hiatt, *Henry Irving: A Record and Review* (1899), p. 152; J. T. Grein, *Dramatic Criticism* (1899), p. 187.
63 1877 prompt-book; the set was used with fireplace in I.iii and II.ii, and without, in III.i.
64 Shaw, *Dramatic Opinions*, II, 139; *Athenaeum*, 26/12/96; *Daily Graphic, Daily Mail*, 21/12/96; unidentified cutting, Fitzgerald Collection.
65 *Illustrated London News, Academy*, 26/12/96.
66 *Athenaeum*, 26/12/96; Henry James, *The Scenic Art* (1949), p. 288.
67 Grein, *Dramatic Criticism*, p. 186; unidentified cutting, Fitzgerald Collection.
68 Russell, 'Irving's *Richard III*', p. 251; Irving, 'Four Favourite Parts', p. 928; William Winter, *Shakespeare on the Stage* (New York, 1911), I, 116.
69 *The Queen*, 26/12/96; *Sketch*, 30/12/96.
70 Terry, *Story*, p. 214; *The Merchant of Venice* cost only £2,163 10s 9d.
71 Introduction to Irving's printed acting version.
72 William Cuthbert painted two sets and William Telbin four.
73 Fitzgerald, *Record*, pp. 185–6; William Telbin, 'Art in the Theatre: Act Drops', *The Magazine of Art* (1895), 339; *Illustrated London News*, 28/10/82; programme, 18/3/82; Clement Scott, *The Theatre*, V, 2nd ser. (April 1882), 234–6; E. R. Russell, '*Romeo and Juliet* at the Lyceum', *Macmillan's Magazine*, XLVI (1882), 328; *The Times*, 9/3/82.
74 *Academy, Illustrated London News*, 18/3/82; Hiatt, *Henry Irving*, p. 193; Morris, *Essays in Theatrical Criticism*, p. 10; A. B. Walkley, *Playhouse Impressions* (1892), p. 259; William Archer, *Henry Irving, Actor and Manager*, 2nd edn (n.d. [1883]), p. 49.
75 The Chorus wore mediaeval Italian costume, and Scott wrongly identified him as Dante, who is unconnected with *Romeo and Juliet*.
76 Terry, *Story*, p. 124; Fitzgerald, *Record*, p. 186; Russell, '*Romeo and Juliet* at the Lyceum', p. 327. I have used Russell and Scott extensively: references are given only when they are quoted directly.
77 Terry, *Four Lectures on Shakespeare*, ed. Christopher St John (1932), pp. 138–40; J. A. Bryant, Jr (ed.), *Romeo and Juliet*, Signet Shakespeare (New York, 1964). All references are based on this edition.
78 Michael Williams, *Some London Theatres, Past and Present* (1883), p. 213; Bram Stoker, *Personal Reminiscences of Henry Irving* (1906), I, 99; Henry R. Pettit, 'Irving as Romeo' in Saintsbury and Palmer, *We Saw Him Act*, pp. 224–6.
79 Fitzgerald, *Record*, p. 186.
80 Stoker, *Personal Reminiscences*, I, 96; advertisement, *The Times*, 8/3/82; *Illustrated London News*, 13/3/82; Scott, *The Theatre*, V, 235; I.i and ii were combined.
81 Scott, *The Theatre*, V, 235; *Saturday Review*, 11/3/82; Terry, *Story*, p. 214.
82 W. H. Pollock, 'Henry Irving's Stage Management', *Century Magazine*, XXVI (1883), 954.

83 Fitzgerald, *Record*, p. 187; *The Times*, 9/3/82.

84 *All the Year Round*, 1/4/82; Scott, *The Theatre*, v, 239.

85 Altogether, 104 of her 283 lines were cut; Percy Allen, *The Stage Life of Mrs Stirling* (1922), pp. 204–6; Fitzgerald, *Record*, pp. 188–9; Terry, *Story*, p. 211; *Academy*, 18/3/82.

86 Terry, *Story*, p. 211; *Saturday Review*, 11/3/82.

87 Pettitt, 'Irving as Romeo', p. 226; *The Times*, 9/3/82.

88 Russell, '*Romeo and Juliet* at the Lyceum', p. 332.

89 Scott, *The Theatre*, v, 236, 240; spectator's annotated text, Seymour Collection, Princeton University, Shattuck No. 45; *Saturday Review*, 11/3/82.

90 *Academy*, 18/3/82. An engraving in the *Illustrated London News*, 18/3/82, shows enough of W. Cuthbert's set to suggest that it was much like the L-shaped room Craven designed for Forbes-Robertson and Mrs Patrick Campbell at the Lyceum in 1895. The latter, in the Enthoven Collection, may be examined in Robert Speaight, *Shakespeare on the Stage* (1973), p. 63.

91 *Illustrated London News*, 18/3/82; Terry, *Story*, p. 211.

92 Terry, *Lectures*, pp. 139–40.

93 Terry, *Story*, p. 173; *Graphic*, 18/3/82; Edward Gordon Craig, *Henry Irving* (1930), p. 128; *The History of Don Quixote by Cervantes*, ed. J. W. Clark, illus. Gustave Doré (n.d. [1870]), p. 416.

94 Harley Granville-Barker, *Prefaces to Shakespeare* (1958), ii, 341; Terry, *Story*, p. 215.

95 *Illustrated London News*, 18/3/82.

96 Terry, *Story*, p. 215.

97 *Punch*, 18/3/82; an interior view of the tomb has been widely published, and can be consulted in Richard Southern, *The Victorian Theatre: A Pictorial Survey* (Newton Abbot, 1970), p. 99.

98 Annotated text, Princeton.

99 Last produced by Phelps, at Sadler's Wells, 15/9/60, except for a production by Benson at the Comedy, 13/2/01. Irving had never seen the play.

100 *Ally Sloper's Half-Holiday*, 10/5/01; letter to Irving, 26/4/01, Enthoven Collection. The season ended with a 37th performance on 20/7/01; it toured the provinces in autumn, but did not go on the American tour.

101 Illustrations in *The Stage*, 16/4/01 and *The Queen*, 20/4/01; Dickins, *Forty Years of Shakespeare*, p. 100; *Madame*, 20/10/01; Frederick Harker, 'Irving as Coriolanus' in Saintsbury and Palmer, *We Saw Him Act*, p. 383.

102 Dickins, *Forty Years of Shakespeare*, p. 100; *Athenaeum*, 20/4/01; unidentified cuttings, Irving scrapbooks, Garrick Club; Austin Brereton, *The Life of Henry Irving* (1908), ii, 288; Harker, 'Irving as Coriolanus', p. 384.

103 Arthur Symons, *Plays, Acting and Music* (1903), p. 52.

104 Philip Brockbank (ed.), *Coriolanus*, New Arden Shakespeare (1976). All references are based on this edition. Irving's study-book is in the Folger Shakespeare Library, Shattuck No. 24: it is based on his published acting version. Apart from its three-act structure, it much resembles Kemble's text.

105 Marginalia at, respectively, II.iii. 51, 140, 145, 82 and 67, in Ellen Terry's study-books in the Ellen Terry Memorial Museum, Smallhythe, Shattuck Nos. 25 and 26.

106 *Punch*, 1/5/01; *Daily Graphic*, 16/4/01; Irving's study-book; unidentified cutting, Garrick Club; *Athenaeum*, 20/4/01; *The Times*, 16/4/01.
107 Unidentified cutting, Garrick Club.
108 Terry, *Story*, p. 371.
109 *Daily Graphic*, 16/4/01.
110 Bram Stoker, 'The Art of Ellen Terry', *The Playgoer*, 1 (Oct. 1901), 47.
111 II.i.161–202, in Act I of Irving's text; III.ii and V.iii.
112 R. Phené Spiers, 'The Architecture of *Coriolanus* at the Lyceum Theatre', *Architectural Review* (July 1901), 6–10; Sybil Rosenfeld, 'Alma-Tadema's Designs for Henry Irving's *Coriolanus*', *Shakespeare Jahrbuch* (1974), 87–8; *Madame*, 20/4/01; unidentified cutting, Garrick Club; *Daily Graphic*, 16/4/01; *Era*, 20/4/01; *Graphic*, 22/4/01; Terry's study-book, Shattuck No. 25; *Black and White*, 27/4/01.
113 Terry's study-books; Irving's emphases are from his study-book.
114 Irving's and Terry's study-books; Harker, 'Irving as Coriolanus', p. 383; *The Times*, 16/4/01.
115 Spiers, 'Architecture of *Coriolanus*', p. 14; Terry, *Story*, pp. 178 and 214.
116 These walls were probably those originally intended by Alma-Tadema for Antium: Spiers, 'Architecture of *Coriolanus*', pp. 20–1; illustrations, *Illustrated London News* and *Graphic*, 20/4/01.
117 Harker, 'Irving as Coriolanus', p. 384; *The Times*, 16/4/01.
118 Terry's study-book, Shattuck No. 25; illustrations, *Illustrated London News* and *Graphic*, 20/4/01.
119 Unidentified cutting, Garrick Club.
120 Study-books; unidentified cutting, Garrick Club; *Graphic*, 22/4/01; Rosenfeld, 'Alma-Tadema's designs', p. 92.
121 Spiers, 'Architecture of *Coriolanus*', pp. 9–12; Irving's study-book; Harker, 'Irving as Coriolanus', p. 385; *Illustrated London News*, 20/4/01.
122 Harker, 'Irving as Coriolanus', p. 385; *Illustrated London News*, 20/4/01; *Punch*, 1/5/01; Irving's study-book.

6 Much Ado about Nothing

1 *The Times*, 12/10/82; *New York Times*, 1/4/84.
2 By 1895 there had been 306 performances at the Lyceum. Its first season there yielded the largest profit realized during Irving's management, nearly £16,000.
3 Helena Faucit, *On Some of Shakespeare's Female Characters*, 6th edn (Edinburgh, 1899), pp. 302–3.
4 David L. Stevenson (ed.), *Much Ado about Nothing*, Signet Shakespeare (New York, 1964), I.i.139. All references and figures are based on this edition.
5 Irving sometimes, if not always, played the first scene 'Before Leonato's House'.
6 See Appendix 1.
7 Bram Stoker, *Personal Reminiscences of Henry Irving* (1906), II, 198.
8 The gag was printed in many editions of the play: for example, in the Modern Standard Drama text (1848) in which George Becks made numerous notes on Irving's production: it is in the New York Public Library, Shattuck No. 47.

Irving wrote all but one line of his abbreviated gag in a copy of his printed acting version, Shattuck No. 45, in the Folger Shakespeare Library. The line he omits – the second last – is drawn from standard texts and Ellen Terry, *The Story of My Life* (1908), p. 163. She misquotes the last line. Traditional stage texts ended with a gag: Don Pedro says he has toothache; Benedick recommends marriage as a cure, and rhymes:

> Your gibes and mockeries I laugh to scorn;
> No staff more rev'rend than one tipt with horn.

Irving did not use it.

9   *The Theatre*, VI, 3rd ser. (Nov. 1882), 294.
10 A. W. Schlegel, *Lectures on Dramatic Art and Literature*, trans. John Black (1879), p. 386; G. G. Gervinus, *Shakespeare Commentaries*, trans. F. E. Bunnett (1875), p. 417; Faucit, *Shakespeare's Female Characters*, pp. 291, 301.
11 Gervinus, *Commentaries*, pp. 414–19; Faucit, *Shakespeare's Female Characters*, pp. 302–6.
12 Mrs Jameson, *Characteristics of Women* (1832), I, 65; Gervinus, *Commentaries*, p. 421.
13 George Fletcher, *Studies of Shakespeare*, quoted in H. H. Furness (ed.), New Variorum *Much Ado about Nothing*, 4th edn (1899), p. 386. Faucit and her husband, Sir Theodore Martin, saw a good deal of Irving at this time. Irving played Benedick to her Beatrice in a private reading at her home on 29/7/82: Austin Brereton, *The Life of Henry Irving* (1908), I, 363.
14 Ellen Terry, *Four Lectures on Shakespeare*, ed. Christopher St John (1932), pp. 85–6.
15 *Ibid.*, pp. 83–4; *Graphic*, 21/10/82.
16 W. H. Pollock, *Impressions of Henry Irving* (1908), p. 85; MS note in a preparation copy in the Folger Shakespeare Library, Shattuck No. 46.
17 Played by her son, Edward Gordon Craig, in 1891: his study-book, in the Craig Collection at the University of California, Los Angeles, Shattuck No. 50, gives disappointingly little information.
18 Ellen Terry study-book, based on Cassel's National Library edn (1901), at Smallhythe, not in Shattuck; Montreal *Star*, 3/10/84; *Saturday Review*, 10/1/91.
19 Harcourt Williams, 'Irving as Benedick' in H. A. Saintsbury and Cecil Palmer (eds.), *We Saw Him Act* (1939), p. 235; Anon., *Letters of an Unsuccessful Actor* (n.d.), p. 301; *Illustrated London News*, 10/1/91.
20 Terry, *Story*, p. 162; *Saturday Review*, 10/1/91.
21 Irving's study-book.
22 Here Irving has noted '*glove*' beside Benedick's speech in his study-book.
23 *Boston Daily Advertiser*, 28/2/84; Gareth Lloyd Evans, *Shakespeare*, III (1971), 21.
24 J. G. Robertson, b. 1849, played Ralph Rackstraw, Frederic in *Pirates of Penzance* and Nanki-Poo in 1887–8.
25 Boston *Daily Evening Traveller*, 28/2/84; Irving's study-book.
26 *Standard*, n.d., Percy Fitzgerald Collection, Garrick Club; Chicago *Tribune*, quoted in Brereton, *Life of Henry Irving*, II, 41; *Saturday Review*, 18/6/87.

27 Unidentified Glasgow paper, Fitzgerald Collection; *Standard*, n.d.
28 *Ariel*, 17/1/91; *The Theatre*, VI, 300; William Winter, *Henry Irving* (New York, 1885), p. 65.
29 Forbes-Robertson, 1882; Alexander, 1887; Terriss, 1891; *Academy*, 17/3/83; *The Theatre*, XVII, 4th ser. (Feb. 1891), 95, and VI, 3rd ser. (Nov. 1882), 303; *Academy*, 21/10/82; Terry, *Story*, p. 225.
30 John in 1882, Pedro in 1887.
31 *Saturday Review*, 21/10/82; *The Theatre*, VI, 3rd ser. (Nov. 1882), 301; *Punch*, 21/10/82; *Illustrated London News*, 28/10/82.
32 Terriss: *The Theatre*, XVII, 4th ser. (Jan. 1891), 6; *Saturday Review*, 10/1/91.
33 *Standard*, n.d.; Austin Brereton (ed.), *Dramatic Notes, 1882-83* (1883), p. 50.
34 *The Theatre*, VI, 3rd ser. (Nov. 1882), 297; *Boston Daily Advertiser*, 28/2/84; Terry, *Story*, p. 224; Laurence Irving, *Henry Irving: The Actor and His World* (1951), p. 401; Johnston Forbes-Robertson's oil painting in The Players Club, New York.
35 Graham Storey, 'The Success of *Much Ado about Nothing*' in John Garrett (ed.), *More Talking of Shakespeare* (New York, 1959), pp. 140-1, believes that Shakespeare intends a distancing effect.
36 *Graphic*, 21/10/84.
37 *Philadelphia Inquirer*, 19/3/84. Irving cut most of John's lines (94-8, 110-11).
38 *Saturday Review*, 18/6/87 and 21/10/81; *Illustrated London News*, 21/10/82.
39 *Saturday Review*, 18/6/87; Ellen Terry study-book, Smallhythe, Shattuck No. 48.
40 *Saturday Review*, 18/6/87; *Boston Daily Advertiser*, 28/2/84; Terry, *Lectures*, p. 90; *Standard*, n.d.; *Playgoer*, I (Oct. 1882), 44.
41 *The Theatre*, VI, 3rd ser. (Nov. 1882), 300; *Saturday Review*, 21/10/82.
42 *Montreal Star*, 3/10/84; Betty Bandel, 'Ellen Terry's Foul Papers', *Theatre Survey*, X, I (May 1969), 51.
43 Storey, 'Success of *Much Ado*', p. 137.
44 J. C. Trewin, '*Much Ado about Nothing* in the Theatre' in Laurence Lerner (ed.), *Shakespeare's Comedies* (Harmondsworth, 1967), p. 220.
45 *Philadelphia Inquirer*, 19/3/84; unidentified cutting, Enthoven Collection; Winter, *Henry Irving*, p. 61; *Athenaeum*, 7/6/84.
46 *Punch*, 28/10/82.
47 *Montreal Star*, 3/10/84; Irving's study-book; *The Theatre*, VI, 3rd ser. (Nov. 1882), 299.
48 Terry, *Story*, p. 230.
49 *Saturday Review*, 10/1/91.
50 See for example Ralph Berry, *Shakespeare's Comedies: Explorations in Form* (Princeton, N.J., 1972), pp. 164-6, 172-3.
51 The prison scene (IV.iii) and 16 of Dogberry's lines in III.iii were cut after opening. *Saturday Review*, 18/6/87, says cuts were extensive, and *Graphic*, 29/1/91, notes numerous restorations.
52 *Standard*, n.d.; see also *The Times*, 6/1/91; *Academy*, 10/1/91.
53 *Illustrated London News*, 21/10/82; *The Times*, 12/10/82 and 6/1/91. Internal evidence suggests that the treaty just concluded at the beginning of the play is the Peace of Cambrai, signed in 1529 after the victory of Charles V over

François I. Several earlier productions took the same interpretation: *The Times*, 9/10/82; Winter, *Henry Irving*, p. 66.

54 E. C. Pettet, *Shakespeare and the Romance Tradition* (1949), p. 86; Ralph Berry, *Shakespeare's Comedies*, p. 18; Alexander Leggatt, *Shakespeare's Comedy of Love* (1974), pp. 152–5. See for example T. W. Craik, '*Much Ado about Nothing*', *Scrutiny*, XIX, 4 (Oct. 1953), 297–316.

7 Twelfth Night

1 *Illustrated London News*, 5/7/84 and 23/8/84; Alan Hughes, 'Henry Irving's Finances: The Lyceum Accounts, 1878–1899', *Nineteenth Century Theatre Research*, I, 2 (Autumn 1973), 84.

2 An announcement in *The Times*, 28/7/84, shows that she was unable to play on Saturday, July 26. The New York revival opened at the Star on 18/11/84.

3 *The Autobiography of Sir John Martin-Harvey* (n.d. [1933]), pp. 79–80; *Daily Telegraph*, 12/7/84; *The Theatre*, IV, 4th ser. (Aug. 1884), 87. Leclercq played Portia to Phelps's Shylock at the Gaiety on 15/1/76.

4 *Academy*, 26/7/84; *Daily Telegraph*, 12/7/84; William Archer, '*Twelfth Night* at the Lyceum', *Macmillan's Magazine*, L (Oct. 1884), 268; *Punch*, 19/7/84; Clement Scott, *From 'The Bells' to 'King Arthur'* (1897), p. 272.

5 T. Edgar Pemberton, *Ellen Terry and Her Sisters* (1902), p. 253; *The Theatre*, IV, 4th ser. (Aug. and Sept. 1884), carried extensive comment on this disturbance, by Joseph Knight, Frank Marshall, J. Palgrave Simpson and correspondents.

6 Austin Brereton, *The Life of Henry Irving* (1908), II, 337–45. Adelaide Neilson played the Haymarket, 2/2/78–2/3/78; her Malvolio was Henry Howe, Antonio in Irving's production. Kate Terry starred at the Olympic, 7/6/65. Edward Compton and Virginia Bateman played matinees at the Strand on 5 and 12/1/84, while Irving was in North America, and Tree appeared in an amateur matinée on 26/5/83. Phelps played Malvolio on 4 and 11/3/76: Irving probably never saw him in it at Sadler's Wells.

7 Shirley S. Allen, *Samuel Phelps and Sadler's Wells Theatre* (Middletown, Connecticut, 1971), pp. 182–3; W. May Phelps and John Forbes-Robertson, *The Life and Life-Work of Samuel Phelps* (1886), pp. 158–63 and 326–7; Westland Marston, *Our Recent Actors* (1883), II, 24; *Athenaeum*, 29/1/48.

8 Note from Johnson's edition of *The Works of William Shakespeare*, in D. J. Palmer (ed.), *Shakespeare, 'Twelfth Night': A Casebook* (1972), p. 29.

9 Charles Knight (ed.), *The Pictorial Edition of the Works of Shakespere* (New York, 1843), II, 132.

10 A. W. Schlegel, *Lectures on Dramatic Art and Literature*, trans. John Black (1879), p. 392. Shakespeare's immediate source is Barnabe Riche, *Riche His Farewell to Militarie Profession* (1581); see J. M. Lothian and T. W. Craik (eds.), *Twelfth Night*, New Arden Shakespeare (1975), p. 157. All references and figures are based on this edition.

11 William Hazlitt, *Characters of Shakespeare's Plays* in *Works*, ed. P. P. Howe

(1930), IV, 314; E. Montégut, *Oeuvres Complètes de Shakespeare* (1867) in H. H. Furness (ed.), New Variorum *Twelfth Night* (Philadelphia, 1901), pp. 383–4.

12 Archer, '*Twelfth Night* at the Lyceum', p. 277.

13 Unidentified cutting, Fitzgerald Collection; *Daily Telegraph*, 12/7/84.

14 537 of 2,550 lines: see Appendix 1. No prompt-book is known.

15 *The Theatre*, IV, 4th ser. (Aug. 1884), 102.

16 *Academy*, 26/7/84. Gervinus thought Orsino inactive and cold: Irving disagreed.

17 Archer, '*Twelfth Night* at the Lyceum', p. 274; Martin-Harvey, *Autobiography*, p. 87; Scott, *From 'The Bells' to 'King Arthur'*, p. 270; *Athenaeum*, 12/7/84.

18 Northrop Frye, *A Natural Perspective* (New York, 1965), pp. 91–117.

19 Bertrand Evans, *Shakespeare's Comedies* (Oxford, 1960), pp. 122–3.

20 Ellen Terry, *Four Lectures on Shakespeare*, ed. Christopher St John (1932), p. 128; *The Theatre*, IV, 90, 103; *The Times*, 9/7/84.

21 Archer, '*Twelfth Night* at the Lyceum', pp. 277–8.

22 W. Graham Robertson, *Time Was* (1931), p. 273; Terry, *The Story of My Life* (1908), p. 232.

23 *The Era*, 12/7/84; *The Theatre*, IV, 103.

24 E. R. Russell, 'Mr. Irving's Work', *Fortnightly Review*, XXXVI, N.S. (Sept. 1884), 405.

25 *The Era*, 12/7/84; *Punch*, 19/7/84.

26 *Saturday Review*, 12/7/84 and 19/7/84; Terry, *Story*, p. 232.

27 Charles Lamb, 'On Some of the Old Actors', *Elia* (1827), p. 308.

28 M. R. Holmes, *Stage Costumes and Accessories in the London Museum* (1968), items 105–7, plate XIV, note, p. 85; William Winter, *Shakespeare on the Stage*, II (1915), 33; *New York Herald*, 19/11/84.

29 *Morning Post*, quoted *The Times*, 14/7/84; *Illustrated London News*, 12/7/84 and 16/8/84; Russell, 'Mr. Irving's Work', pp. 402–3.

30 Russell, 'Mr. Irving's Work', p. 404; Scott, *From 'The Bells' to 'King Arthur'*, p. 270; *Pall Mall Gazette*, quoted *The Times*, 14/7/84.

31 Archer, '*Twelfth Night* at the Lyceum', p. 276.

32 A study-book belonging to Irving, Shattuck No. 28, in the Folger Shakespeare Library, is lightly marked, almost exclusively for this scene. Russell, 'Mr. Irving's Work', pp. 404–5; *Academy*, 26/7/84; *Morning Advertiser* and *Globe*, quoted *The Times*, 14/7/84.

33 *Saturday Review*, 12/7/84.

34 Archer, '*Twelfth Night* at the Lyceum', p. 279; *Daily Telegraph*, 12/7/84; W. H. Pollock, *Impressions of Henry Irving* (1908), p. 91; Russell, 'Mr. Irving's Work', p. 403.

35 Russell, 'Mr. Irving's Work', p. 403.

36 Scott, *From 'The Bells' to 'King Arthur'*, p. 270; *Saturday Review*, 12/7/84; *Illustrated London News*, 12/7/84; *World*, n.d., and cuttings, Fitzgerald Collection.

37 *Saturday Review*, 19/7/84; W. H. Pollock, letter to Irving, 24/7/84, Enthoven Collection.

38 See e.g. Archer, '*Twelfth Night* at the Lyceum', pp. 272–3.

8 Cymbeline

1 See for example Northrop Frye, *A Natural Perspective* (New York, 1965), pp. 61–70; Derek Traversi, *Shakespeare: The Last Phase* (1954), pp. 43–104; F. R. Leavis, *The Common Pursuit* (1952), pp. 176–8; E. M. W. Tillyard, *Shakespeare's Last Plays* (1958), pp. 26–40, 68–76; Bertrand Evans, *Shakespeare's Comedies* (Oxford, 1960), pp. 247–8.

2 Tillyard, *Last Plays*, p. 74.

3 Charles Mayne Young played Iachimo in 1823 and Macready played him twenty years later, but neither made much impression. Faucit last played Imogen at Drury Lane, 6 and 10/5/65. Henrietta Hodson had a brief run at the Queen's, Long Acre, in 1872.

4 First published in *Blackwood's Magazine*, CXXXIII (Jan. 1883), 1–41, then in *On Some of Shakespeare's Female Characters* (1885), which had reached five editions by 1896.

5 It closed after 72 performances despite Irving's prediction that it would run for 100 performances: Christopher St John (ed.), *Ellen Terry and Bernard Shaw: A Correspondence* (New York and London, 1931), p. 74. Irving's injury after the first night of *Richard III* forced him to revive *Cymbeline* with Julia Arthur and Cooper Cliffe for 10 performances, 26/12/96 to 2/1/97. Without either star it lost money: Terry was obliged by illness to proceed with a planned vacation in Monte Carlo. On her return it reopened for 6 performances, 25–29/1/97, Arthur playing on the 27th. It was never revived again. The sets were destroyed in the fire of 1898. The next West End production was in 1923, with Sybil Thorndike.

6 Algernon Charles Swinburne, *Shakespeare* (1909), p. 54; G. G. Gervinus, *Shakespeare Commentaries*, trans. F. E. Bunnett (1875), p. 657.

7 G. B. Shaw, *Geneva, Cymbeline Refinished, and Good King Charles* (1946), p. 149.

8 St John, *Correspondence*, p. 40.

9 J. M. Nosworthy (ed.), *Cymbeline*, New Arden Shakespeare (1969), I.vii.113; III.iv.125. All references and figures are based on this edition.

10 *Ibid.*, pp. lviii and lxi.

11 Walter Raleigh (ed.), *Johnson on Shakespeare* (1925), p. 183.

12 III.iii.79ff; IV.ii.24ff, 169ff; IV.iv.53–4. Ellen Terry's study-book, Shattuck No. 26, Smallhythe.

13 Iachimo, II.ii.15–23; Pisanio, III.ii.7–9; Belarius, III.vii.13–15; brothers, IV.ii.16ff; these are only examples.

14 Evans, *Shakespeare's Comedies*, pp. 286–7.

15 A rough count yielded more than eighty.

16 Arnold Edinburgh, 'A Gallic Romp through Shakespeare', *Shakespeare Quarterly*, XXI, 4 (Autumn 1970), 458.

17 See the discussion in John Russell Brown, *Shakespeare's Plays in Performance* (Harmondsworth, 1969), p. 122.

18 In this discussion I am principally indebted to F. D. Hoeniger, 'Irony and Romance in *Cymbeline*,' *Studies in English Literature 1500–1900*, II, 2 (Spring 1962), 219–28, and Anne Righter, *Shakespeare and the Idea of the Play* (1962), pp. 172–82.

NOTES TO PP. 209–11

19 G. B. Shaw, 'Blaming the Bard', *Dramatic Opinions and Essays* (1906), II, 54–5.
20 *Ibid.*, p. 54.
21 Brown, *Shakespeare's Plays in Performance*, p. 121; St John, *Correspondence*, p. 43.
22 St John, *Correspondence*, p. 69.
23 See below, p. 221.
24 Shattuck lists three scripts belonging to Ellen Terry at Smallhythe. No. 25 has disappeared. No. 26 is a proof copy with preliminary MS notes, some of them modified by comments attributed to 'B. S.' – presumably Bernard Shaw. No. 27 is a shorter proof edition, substantially nearer the printed acting version. In it Terry's MS notes refer to the playing of other actors, indicating that it was used in rehearsal. The page references in Shaw's letter (St John, *Correspondence*, pp. 46–9) refer to this text. I am indebted to Russell Jackson, '*Cymbeline* in the Nineteenth Century', unpublished thesis, University of Birmingham, 1971.
25 St John, *Correspondence*, pp. 46–9. Shaw's influence was strongest in I.vii and IV.ii. *Correspondence*, pp. 49–50, and Irving's text show that she followed Shaw's advice in restoring IV.ii.303b–5 to her own part, and persuaded Irving to restore II.ii.21–3 to his. She did not cut III.iv.35b–6 or 'to pieces with me', III.iv.54, for example, nor persuade Irving to let Arviragus (Gordon Craig) restore the 'clouted brogues' (IV.ii.214).
26 See Winter, *Shakespeare on the Stage*, III (New York, 1916), 90; and Laurence Irving, *Henry Irving: The Actor and His World* (1951), pp. 586–8. A script which belonged to Irving in the Folger (Shattuck No. 24) may have been sent him by Winter; it cuts II.i, and also III.iii.12–21a, which Irving retains, but retains 21b–6, which Irving cuts.
27 See Appendix 1.
28 I.iv is printed in Shattuck No. 26, and Ellen Terry has written, 'This scene must be Kept – but *bother!* – unless first sc. were a front sc!' This does not make much sense: in the first text, the big garden scene (I.i/ii) was followed immediately by the spectacular Roman set of the wager scene (I.v).
29 For example, when the troglodyte brothers report 'Fidele's' death to Morgan, the following cuts were made (IV.ii):

Irving	Garrick	Kemble	Phelps
		196–7a	
201b–14a	202–9	202–3a	204–6a
		206b–8	
		214–15a	
	215b		
224b–31a	220b–42a	216–42	224a–7
232b–4			230–3
235b–6a			235b–6a
237–8			241–2a
246b–9a	246b–9a	246b–9a	246b–9a
27.5 lines	33.5 lines	37 lines	15.5 lines

All three of the others cut V.v.158–63a and 186b–91a, which Irving played.

30 *Punch*, 3/10/96; *Sketch*, 30/9/96; Terry, *The Story of My Life* (1908), p. 350. William Archer, *The Theatrical 'World' of 1896* (1897), p. 276.

31 Illustration, *Illustrated Sporting and Dramatic News*, 26/9/96; *Penny Illustrated Paper*, 26/9/96.

32 *Athenaeum*, 26/9/96; Edward Gordon Craig, *Henry Irving* (1930), p. 115; *Westminster Gazette*, 20/11/96.

33 Henry James, *The Scenic Art* (1949), p. 283; *Westminster Gazette*, 20/11/96; Warwick Bond, '*Cymbeline* at the Lyceum', *Fortnightly Review*, LX, N.S. (1896), 644.

34 *The Queen*, 3/10/96; *The Times*, 23/9/96; *Pick-Me-Up*, 24/10/96.

35 James, *Scenic Art*, p. 283; Bond, '*Cymbeline* at the Lyceum', pp. 641–2; *Pall Mall Gazette*, 23/9/96.

36 Augustin Filon, quoted T. E. Pemberton, *Ellen Terry and Her Sisters* (1902), pp. 286–7.

37 Archer, *Theatrical 'World'*, p. 272; Richard Dickins, *Forty Years of Shakespeare on the English Stage* (n.d.), p. 82.

38 Robinson had played juvenile leads with Phelps; he was now 65. St John, *Correspondence*, p. 55; *The Daily Telegraph*, 23/9/96; *Westminster Gazette*, 23/9/96; *Sketch*, 30/9/96.

39 James, *Scenic Art*, p. 284; *Pall Mall Gazette*, 23/9/96.

40 *Telegraph*, 23/9/96. The painting, bequeathed to the National Gallery by Samuel Rogers in 1855, is now thought to be an imitation. It lacks the attributes of either a Man of Sorrows or, strictly speaking, of an *Ecce Homo*; in Scott's time, however, it was known by the latter title, and considered 'the most popular and at the same time the most characteristic' of the works attributed to Reni in the National: Paul G. Konody, Maurice W. Brockwell and F. W. Lippmann, *The National Gallery* (1909), I, 95.

41 *The Queen*, 3/10/96; see Clarence Cook, *Art and the Artists of Our Time* (New York, 1888), II, 90, and compare plate 32. Munkacsy was a rather vulgar commercial painter.

42 Faucit, *On Some of Shakespeare's Female Characters*, 6th edn (1899), pp. 169, 190, 222.

43 W. Graham Robertson, *Time Was* (1931), 287; Terry was not so confident as to let Belarius call her 'divineness no older than a boy' (III.vii.16–17): the line was cut. *Telegraph*, 23/9/96; Terry, *Four Lectures on Shakespeare*, ed. Christopher St John (1932), pp. 159–60; Shattuck Nos. 26, 27.

44 *Athenaeum*, 26/9/96; *Daily Graphic*, 23/9/96; *Pall Mall Gazette*, 23/9/96; *Sketch*, 30/9/96; *Westminster Gazette*, 20/11/96; Bond, '*Cymbeline* at the Lyceum', p. 645; Shattuck No. 27.

45 Shattuck Nos. 26, 27; Terry, *Lectures*, p. 160; Bond, '*Cymbeline* at the Lyceum', pp. 645–6; Archer, *Theatrical 'World'*, pp. 274–5.

46 Archer, *Theatrical 'World'*, p. 275; James, *Scenic Art*, pp. 283–4; Robert Farquharson, 'Irving as Iachimo' in H. A. Saintsbury and Cecil Palmer, *We Saw Him Act* (1939), pp. 346–7; *The Queen*, 3/10/96.

47 *Punch*, 3/10/96; Shattuck Nos. 26, 27; Bond, '*Cymbeline* at the Lyceum', p. 645; James, *Scenic Art*, p. 284. Pinero suggested the shadow in a letter to Irving, J. P.

Wearing (ed.), *The Collected Letters of Sir Arthur Pinero* (Minneapolis, 1974), p. 174. Irving thanked him for the idea, 'which I have put into practice greatly' (Austin Brereton, *The Life of Henry Irving* (1908), II, 252).

48 *Telegraph*, 23/9/96; *The Times*, 23/9/96; *Illustrated Sporting and Dramatic News*, 23/10/96; *Globe*, 23/9/96.

49 *Telegraph*, 23/9/96; Shattuck No. 27.

50 *Athenaeum*, 26/9/96; Shattuck No. 27.

51 *The Theatre*, XXVIII, 4th ser. (Oct. 1896), 213; *Telegraph*, 23/9/96; Shaw, 'Blaming the Bard', p. 59.

52 Shaw, 'Blaming the Bard', p. 56; Dickins, *Forty Years of Shakespeare*, p. 82; *The Theatre*, p. 214; *Telegraph*, 23/9/96; *The Queen*, 3/10/96; *Daily Graphic*, 23/9/96; *Punch*, 3/10/96.

53 *Sunday Times*, 27/9/96.

9   The Merchant of Venice

1 Ralph Berry, *Shakespeare's Comedies: Explorations in Form* (Princeton, N.J., 1972), p. 113.

2 Harley Granville-Barker, *Prefaces to Shakespeare* (1958), I, 335.

3 A. W. Schlegel, *Lectures on Dramatic Art and Literature*, trans. J. Black (1879), p. 379; G. G. Gervinus, *Shakespeare Commentaries*, trans. F. E. Bunnett (1875), pp. 235–9.

4 William Hazlitt, *Characters of Shakespeare's Plays* in *Works*, ed. P. P. Howe (1930), IV, 320–1; H. N. Hudson, *Shakespeare: His Life, Art and Characters* (1872), I, 291. See also Rev. John Hunter (ed.), *The Merchant of Venice* (1861), XV.

5 The first article was Frederick Hawkins, 'Shylock and Other Stage Jews', *The Theatre*, III, 2nd ser. (Nov. 1879), 191–8. The next number contained a 'Round Table' with pieces by Theodore Martin, F. J. Furnivall, Frank Marshall, James Spedding, Israel Davis, David Anderson, Frederick Hawkins and 'An Actor' (Irving): (Dec. 1879), 253–61. Other relevant papers are S. L. Lee, 'The Original of Shylock', *Gentleman's Magazine*, CCXLVI (Feb. 1880), 185–200 (on Roderigo Lopez), and Moncure D. Conway, 'The Pound of Flesh', *Nineteenth Century*, VII (May 1880), 828–39. Irving's article inclines towards Hazlitt's position.

6 H. B. Charlton, *Shakespearian Comedy* (New York, 1938), pp. 123–60; John Russell Brown, *Shakespeare and His Comedies* (1962), pp. 61–75: he has considerably modified his position in *Free Shakespeare* (1974), p. 15; Northrop Frye, *A Natural Perspective* (New York, 1965), p. 91.

7 Amongst these are the historical school, who argue that Elizabethans would see Shylock as a villain: E. E. Stoll, *Shakespeare Studies* (New York, 1942), pp. 255–75, 302–36. M. C. Bradbrook, *Shakespeare and Elizabethan Poetry* (1961), pp. 170–9 and Nevill Coghill, 'The Basis of Shakespearian Comedy', *Essays and Studies*, III (1950), 18–23, make a good case for the theme of Justice and Mercy, the Old Law and the New. Leslie Fiedler, *The Stranger in Shakespeare* (1973), 85–136, is concerned with archetypes.

8 John Russell Brown, 'The Realization of Shylock' in Brown and Bernard Harris (eds.), *Early Shakespeare* (1961), p. 206, says that Antonio's silence at the end 'looks like an author's mistake'. Graham Midgely, '*The Merchant of Venice*: a Reconsideration', *Essays in Criticism*, x, 2 (April 1960), 119–33, assumes that this effect is intentional, and comes up with a unifying theme based on the 'kinship of loneliness' between Shylock and Antonio.

9 Alexander Leggatt, *Shakespeare's Comedies of Love* (1973), p. 121.

10 Brown, 'The Realization of Shylock', gives an excellent summary of the Macklin and Kean readings.

11 Phelps, Sadler's Wells 1844–62, played the part 81 times: only *Hamlet*, *Macbeth*, *The Winter's Tale* and *Othello* were more popular. Faucit produced the play at Covent Garden in 1836. See Booth's own account of his reading in H. H. Furness (ed.), New Variorum *Merchant* (Philadelphia, 1888), pp. 383–4.

12 Advertisement, *The Times*, 16/2/76; Terry's Shylock was Charles Coghlan: see *The Times*, 19/4/75.

13 See Appendix 1 for details of Irving's text. All references and figures are based on John Russell Brown (ed.), *The Merchant of Venice*, New Arden Shakespeare (1967).

14 Joseph Hatton, *Henry Irving's Impressions of America* (Boston, 1884), I, 269: Hatton quotes Irving *verbatim*.

15 *The Times*, 3/11/79; *Saturday Review*, 21/5/87; J. Ranken Towse, *Century Magazine*, XXVII (March 1884), 664.

16 Irving's prompt-book, British Theatre Museum, Shattuck No. 56a (supplement). There is a similar book, based on the 1887 edition of Irving's text, in the Akademie der Künste, Berlin (not in Shattuck). The prompt-book in the Folger Shakespeare Library, Shattuck No. 55, appears to be genuine, but sketches do not relate to the production. An annotated spectator's copy in the same Library, dated 1888, Shattuck No. 59, gives some useful details. Of the numerous Ellen Terry study-books at Smallhythe, only Shattuck Nos. 61, 62, 64 and 65 give much information.

17 *Academy*, 20/3/80. George Rowell, 'A Lyceum Sketchbook', *Nineteenth Century Theatre Research*, 6 (Spring 1978), 12, identifies the two small figures as 'umpires', but they are evidently the Pages.

18 Irving adopted Charles Kean's version of the traditional stage solution to the muddle over the names of the characters called Solanio and Salerio in modern texts. In Irving's time the William Jaggard text of 1619 (Q2) was accepted as copy-text; this gave three characters, who were amalgamated by the actors. Elwood and Pinero played Guildenstern and Rosencrantz in the previous season.

19 *The Times*, 3/11/79; [Theodore Martin], 'Theatrical Reform: *The Merchant of Venice* at the Lyceum', *Blackwood's Magazine*, CXXVI (Dec. 1879), 653; *Saturday Review*, 8/11/79. Forrester was 53, but some later exponents were in their late thirties; Ellen Terry, *The Story of My Life* (1908), p. 191; *Referee*, 2/11/79.

20 *Boston Herald*, 13/12/83.

21 Set changes were effected without using a curtain: see above, p. 17. *Seattle Post-Intelligencer*, 21/9/93; *Saturday Review*, 21/5/87; E. R. Russell, '*The Mer-*

chant of Venice' (Liverpool, 1888), p. 16; unidentified Manchester paper, 1887, Stoker Collection.

22 Terry, *Story*, p. 187; Arthur Goddard, *Players of the Period* (1891), p. 61 (compare Hudson, *Shakespeare*, I, 293); emphasis from *The Dial* (Chicago), 16/10/93.

23 Hatton, *Impressions of America*, pp. 267–8.

24 San Francisco *Daily Report*, 6/9/93; *The Theatre*, III, 2nd ser. (Dec. 1879), 293; *Pictorial World*, 8/11/79; Irving in Hatton, *Impressions of America*, p. 267; Russell, *'Merchant of Venice'*, p. 17; Percy Fitzgerald, *Henry Irving: A Record of Twenty Years at the Lyceum* (1893), p. 131; Clement Scott, *From 'The Bells' to 'King Arthur'* (1897), p. 166.

25 A. C. Sprague, *Shakespeare and the Actors* (Cambridge, Mass., 1948), pp. 22–3.

26 Prompt-books, 1879 and 1887; Terry, *Story*, p. 188.

27 Terry, *Story*, pp. 186–7; Russell, *'Merchant of Venice'*, p. 18; Philadelphia *Times* and *Evening News*, 29/11/83; Chicago *Tribune*, 13/1/84; *Spectator*, 8/11/79.

28 *Referee*, 2/11/79; *The Times*, 3/11/79; Edinburgh *Scottish Leader*, 3/9/87.

29 William Winter, *Shakespeare on the Stage*, I (New York, 1911), 139, claims that he did, but it is impossible that none of the hundreds of descriptions I have studied should have mentioned it if Winter were right.

30 Hatton, *Impressions of America*, pp. 269–70; Russell, *'Merchant of Venice'*, p. 18; unidentified Manchester paper, 1887; *To-Day*, 26/2/98; emphasis from *The Dial* (Chicago), 16/10/93.

31 Glasgow *North British Daily Mail*, 8/9/83; *Liverpool Post*, 3/10/83; Boston *Daily Evening Traveller*, 13/12/83; Edinburgh *Scottish Leader*, 3/9/87; New York *Daily Tribune*, 7/11/83.

32 Chicago *Tribune*, 13/1/84; Scott, *From 'The Bells' to 'King Arthur'*, p. 273; *Seattle Post-Intelligencer*, 21/9/93; Russell, *'Merchant of Venice'*, p. 21; A. B. Walkley, *Playhouse Impressions* (1902), pp. 259–60.

33 Betty Bandel, 'Ellen Terry's Foul Papers', *Theatre Survey*, 10 (May 1969), 48. Terry subsequently altered the 'loafer' phrase to read 'something of an idler', and Prof. Bandel explains the role of the actress's editor in establishing published texts which sometimes soften or alter her ideas.

34 Boston *Herald*, 13/12/83; San Francisco *Morning Call*, 6/9/93: I have given details of costume etc. in 'Henry Irving's Tragedy of Shylock', *Educational Theatre Journal*, 24 (Oct. 1972), 258–9.

35 [Martin], 'Theatrical Reform', p. 653; Terry, *Story*, pp. 183–4; *Referee*, 2/11/79; *The Times*, 3/11/79; Edinburgh *Courant*, 24/9/83; *San Francisco Chronicle*, 6/9/93.

36 Boston *Herald*, 13/12/83; Fitzgerald, *Record*, p. 130; Scott, *From 'The Bells' to 'King Arthur'*, p. 167; *Referee*, 2/11/79. In 1976 the Curator of the Ellen Terry Memorial Museum at Smallhythe showed me a remarkable photograph of stage-hands on the trial scene set: unfortunately, this picture cannot now be found. It proved that Richard Foulkes is mistaken in thinking that Irving used a diagonal set here (see Foulkes, 'The Staging of the Trial Scene in Irving's *The Merchant of Venice*', *Educational Theatre Journal* 28 (Oct. 1976), 315). I do not think the plan in the 1879 prompt-book suggests it, either. I was wrong, in

'Henry Irving's Tragedy of Shylock', when I said that real tapestries were used.

37 Shattuck No. 59; *Athenaeum*, 8/11/79; Scott, *From 'The Bells' to 'King Arthur'*, p. 274; Boston *Herald*, 13/12/83.

38 Terry, *Story*, p. 163; *Referee*, 2/11/79; [Martin], 'Theatrical Reform', p. 655; Hatton, *Impressions of America*, p. 273; Philadelphia *Times*, 23/11/79; *Saturday Review*, 21/5/87.

39 *The Dial* (Chicago), 16/10/93; *Brooklyn Times* in *Mr. Henry Irving and Miss Ellen Terry in America: Opinions of the Press* (1884), p. 21; William Winter, *Henry Irving* (New York, 1885), pp. 36, 76; *Birmingham Daily Post*, 3/9/91; Edinburgh *Evening News*, 3/9/87; *Saturday Review*, 8/11/79; *Baltimore Herald* in *Opinions*, p. 17.

40 Boston *Daily Evening Traveller*, *Herald*, 13/12/83; Toronto *Mail*, 23/2/84; Philadelphia *Times*, 4/6/80; [Martin], 'Theatrical Reform', p. 653. Emphasis in Terry study-book, Shattuck No. 62.

41 Ellen Terry, *Four Lectures on Shakespeare*, ed. Christopher St John (1932), p. 121; Fitzgerald, *Record*, pp. 133–5; *Baltimore Herald* in *Opinions*, p. 17; New York *Daily Tribune*, 7/11/83.

42 Fitzgerald, *Record*, p. 135; Shattuck No. 65.

43 *Spectator*, 8/11/79; Hatton, *Impressions of America*, p. 274; *Chicago Inter Ocean* in *Opinions*, p. 25; Fitzgerald, *Record*, p. 135.

44 Scott, *From 'The Bells' to 'King Arthur'*, p. 274; [Martin], 'Theatrical Reform', p. 655; Dutton Cook, *Nights at the Play* (1883), p. 392; Chicago *Times*, 10/1/85; *Punch*, 15/11/79.

45 Prompt-book 1879; *Athenaeum*, 8/11/79.

46 Philadelphia *Times*, 4/6/80; 'An Actor' [Irving], *The Theatre*, III, 2nd ser. (Nov. 1879), 255.

47 Cook, *Nights*, p. 392; *Punch*, 15/11/79; *Saturday Review*, 21/5/87; *Spectator*, 8/11/79; Charles Hiatt, *Henry Irving: A Record and Review* (1899), p. 172.

48 Bandel, 'Foul Papers', p. 48.

49 Toronto *Globe*, 23/2/84; *West-End Review* (July 1898), p. 32.

50 Charles Kean also omitted Thisbe.

51 Study-books; Shattuck No. 59; Brooklyn *Daily Eagle*, 3/1/84.

52 'An Actor', *The Theatre*, III, 254–5; my italics.

53 *San Francisco Chronicle*, 6/9/93; *Spectator*, 8/11/79.

10 Conclusion

1 Edward Gordon Craig, *Henry Irving* (1930), p. 87.

2 H. Chance Newton, *Cues and Curtain Calls* (1927), pp. 9–10.

3 Craig, *Henry Irving*, p. 131.

4 A. C. Bradley, *Shakespearean Tragedy* (1904), p. 12; Irving, *The Drama: Addresses* (1893), p. 20.

5 Bradley, *Shakespearean Tragedy*, p. 21.

6 W. J. Lawrence, *Speeding up Shakespeare* (1937), pp. 210–14, says that this tradition may go no further back than 1779, but this is quite far enough for deadliness to set in.

7 See above, pp. 123–4 and 139.

Index

The names of CHARACTERS, and the titles of PLAYS, are listed respectively under those headings.

299

Imogen 205–6, 217–22; as Juliet 160–5;
as Lady Macbeth 88, 91, 93–4, 97–109,
112; as Ophelia 37, 46–7, 57–60, 68–9;
as Portia 229, 232–3, 235–41; as Viola
193, 194–9, 203; as Volumnia 168–72
Terry, Fred, as Sebastian 194
Terry, Marion, as Viola 190
texts *see* Irving, texts
Tillyard, E.M.W. 86
Traill, H.D. 21
Traversi, D.A. 5
Tree, Ellen, as Lady Macbeth 88
Tree, Herbert Beerbohm 25, 242

Vancouver Playhouse 203

Ward, Genevieve: as Queen Margaret 152; as
Cymbeline's Queen 215
Warner, Mrs: as Lady Macbeth 88; as Queen
Margaret 152
Weitz, Morris 82
Wilde, Oscar 98
Wills, William Gorman 8, 21
Wilson, J. Dover 30, 60, 66, 74, 82
Winter, William 112, 210
Wyatt, Frank, as Sir Andrew Aguecheek 190